SCHOOL SYSTEM REFORM

How and Why Is a Price-less Tale

John Merrifield

ISBN 978-1-64559-961-6 (Paperback)
ISBN 978-1-64559-962-3 (Hardcover)
ISBN 978-1-64559-963-0 (Digital)

The information in this book has been updated in <u>2022</u>

Covenant Books
11661 Hwy 707
Murrells Inlet, SC 29576
www.covenantbooks.com

To my school system reform mentor, Mike Lieberman,
and to all the people determined to create a
school system that can engage every child.

Driven by multiple authoritative non-partisan and bipartisan Nation at Risk declarations, the federal government and all fifty states have been pursuing school reform; trying to productively change schools without tackling controversial school system reform… Each attempt at change, without fundamental change, is a desperate attempt to deny/pretend that the system isn't the problem; hope triumphing over experience, again or still. That's why we're stuck at Nation at Risk performance levels despite frenzied activity and massive funding growth. We keep adding gold to a gold-plated disaster!

Lays out the big picture issue the best I have seen

Hon. Rep. Kent Grusendorf
Texas Legislator, 1987–2006
Education Committee Chair, 2003–2006

*****

Merrifield's thorough but accessible analysis of both what's wrong and what can be done is a must read for economists and non-economists alike. Although the USA is his main focus of analysis, Merrifield's insights and recommendations for action are applicable and relevant for education policy thinkers across the world.

Deani Van Pelt
Former Director
Fraser Institute's Barbara Mitchell
Center for Improvement in Education

Merrifield talks about critical issues that other education academics are unaware of.

Dr. Corey DeAngelis
School Choice Director, Reason Foundation

*****

This is a thorough and deep analysis of school reform. Moreover, it injects a breadth of fresh air into the discussion with its careful attention to economic fundamentals—e.g., incentives, competition, and specialization—that is sorely lacking in many other treatments of school reform. An excellent and informative read.

John Garen
Economics Professor, University of Kentucky

*****

Comprehensive, rigorous, principled, and spot-on analysis. You really cut through so much garbage to get at the essential points. I will be quoting from it extensively.

Lance Izumi,
Koret Senior Fellow and
Senior Director of Education Studies at the
Pacific Research Institute for Public Policy

*****

Provides fresh insight that will challenge your core assumptions about how US education systems should operate.

Aaron Garth Smith
Education Policy Analyst, Reason Foundation

CONTENTS

FOREWORD

The future and the shape of societies are contingent on the education of youth. Moms and dads around the country struggle with the question: how can they secure the best education for their children? Realtors consistently say schools are a key consideration for property sales and property values.

Education is one of the most important things we do as a society. Yet as a nation, and as individual states, we have done a poor job in this vital arena.

Business leaders and academics have known for decades that the current education system is failing to achieve its potential. This is evidenced by the number of high school graduates who require remediation at college, by numerous reports of "crisis" or "nation at risk" findings, by businesses who find remediation of employees necessary, by the low number of high school graduates today who can pass an eighth-grade exam administered to students at the end of the nineteenth century, by our rankings in international standards, and by teachers who fear that their students are becoming the "lost generation."

Over the past four decades, many attempts at school reform have been implemented, yet the disappointing results speak for themselves. Dr. Merrifield calls to our attention the fact that school reform alone has not and will not work. He calls instead for school <u>system</u> reform—systemic reform.

Dr. Merrifield examines the problem, the causes, and explores the transformational changes necessary to assure the needs of children are adequately met. Those interested in designing a system that will meet the real needs of society and its children should seriously consider Dr. Merrifield's work.

Policymakers in particular should read this book. Will they look back in four or five decades and point to their wisdom and determination? Or, will they again look to Band-Aid school reforms as attempted in the past and then realize after their retirement from public service that they wasted the chance to implement the systemic changes necessary to achieve true success?

The future of society depends on such decisions.

Kent Grusendorf
Texas Legislator, 1987–2006
Education Committee Chair, 2003–2006

PREFACE

There have been a lot of books written about school reform, focusing on details such as the pupil-teacher ratio, teacher training, and use of technology in school. Fewer have been written about *school system* reform, meaning changes in who has decision-making power over school funding, and the specifics of the "business plan." Many authors don't know the difference. Confusion about the difference between school reform and school system reform is a huge part of the explanation for why seemingly frenzied effort to foster better schooling outcomes continues to produce little more than growing disappointment with a higher price tag.

The other school system reform books lament the terrible symptoms of the fifty-one US school systems, and then wish for changed behavior by policymakers and educators. They imagine that unchanged decision-making processes will suddenly yield much-changed results. The other school system reform books hope that enlightenment of policymakers and citizens is enough to cause a central planning process—a process that never yields a high-performing economy or industry—to suddenly begin yielding high-performing and relentlessly improving school systems. It is hope triumphing over mountains of experience, including extensive experience with K-12 schooling.

Even the world's top-ranked school systems are widely seen by their own citizens and policymakers as low performing. Central plan optimization, with an inherently low upside, has been the only reform approach. That has to change. We need real school *system* reform. We need productive change in the governance and funding policies that directly and indirectly impact all schools, public and private.

Experience and enlightened common sense tells us that we must foster the development of alternatives to the traditional public school and the central planning inherent in the traditional public school system. The pandemic enhanced the enlightenment. Decentralized planning results from parental freedom of choice, free enterprise, and competition orchestrated by the information and incentives that arise from market-based prices that reflect the cost of actual and potential different ways to deliver different kinds of instruction.

It's been nearly one hundred years since economists across the ideological spectrum agreed that the incentives and information provided by correct, dynamic price signals are the ***only*** route to efficient industry outcomes. The formal schooling industry is not an exception to the priceless, widely shared insight that pricelessness is unacceptable.

This book identifies root causes of persistently disappointing classroom outcomes, identifies the policy root causes of the classroom causes of Nation at Risk, persistently low school system performance, and then lays out a strategy for identifying the key elements of a high-performing school system, and then achieving their implementation.

There is a discussion forum for each of my chapters at https://objectivepolicyassessment.org/K-12

John Merrifield

Acknowledgments

These people provided extensive comments on an early draft of this book:

Dr. Corey DeAngelis, Dr. John Garen, Hon. Rep. Kent Grusendorf, and Mr. Lance Izumi.
I am most grateful!

———•———

CHAPTER ONE

A School System Reform Focus

Driven by multiple authoritative non-partisan and bipartisan Nation at Risk declarations, the federal government and all fifty states have been pursuing ***school reform***, trying to productively change schools without tackling controversial ***school system reform***. John Merrow (2017) called it *Addicted to Reform*. Blair Lybbert noted that all of the major efforts and proposals—including the latest, Merrow (2017) and Osborne (2017)—at all levels, "seek to implement reforms that will introduce positive change to the system without fundamentally redesigning it." Stanford's Terry Moe was more specific about the untouchables. "Change" is fine, "as long as it doesn't affect anyone's job, reallocate resources, or otherwise threaten the occupational interests of the adults running the system." *Education Week* founder Ronald Wolk noted, "We want to reinvent our schools without making fundamental changes. We prefer 'tinkering our way to Utopia'" (Tyack 1974)…tinkering won't get us there."[1] Each attempt at change, without fundamental change, is a desperate attempt to deny/pretend that the system isn't the problem, hope triumphing over experience, again or still. That's why we're stuck at Nation at Risk performance levels despite frenzied activity and massive funding growth. We keep adding gold to a gold-plated disaster![2]

"HANG ON! HERE WE GO AGAIN!"

My definition of "school system" is all of the formal schooling options, ***public and private***. Geographically, the world's school systems are the political jurisdictions that make the key schooling governance and funding policies. In the United States, the states and the Federal Government for the District of Columbia have the primary responsibility for school system governance, and for specifying how we fund K-12 schooling. So, the US has fifty-one school systems, with considerable diversity within many of them. Since the fifty-one sets of governance and funding policies are very similar—all substantially price-less—I often implicitly lump them together with references to "our current system." Likewise, each Canadian province is a separate school system. Countries have a single school system when the central government makes schooling policies and specifies how formal schooling is paid for.

The governance plus funding policy basis for defining a school system's area recognizes that many school systems regulate all schools, public and private. And even when there is not much direct regulation of private schools, public school system rules often greatly impact all schools. Since authors and speakers widely use "school system" as a synonym for "public school system," I am apologizing in advance for periodically reasserting the proper "public + private" definition of "school system." "Public education," properly used to mean our commitment to quality schooling for all children, subsidized for equity and because of potential for positive spillovers, is synonymous with "school system" (not "public school system") policy. But "public education" is so widely misused as a synonym for "public school system" that I avoid the term.

Widespread Confusion

There is too little discussion of actual, substantial school system reform, and the widespread tendency to confuse school system reform with school reform hinders progress on both fronts. A good example is this announcement from the Walton Family Foundation. The title asserted "Three School Reform Lessons," yet none of the specific lessons could be learned from experience derived from changing particular schools. For example, the "school reform" non-sequitur of Lesson 1 is "we still must do a better job of ensuring variety in high-quality educational options," which is a correct assertion that US school systems need a more diverse menu of schooling options. Lesson 2, likewise, is not about school reform. It asserts that we need more favorable policy environments for school choice expansion—again, for more and better instructional approach choices. Lesson 3 is that we need to do a lot more to supply talent to public schools and support teaching, which again doesn't have anything to do with school-level changes, except perhaps that some possible school-level changes might attract more of the existing talent and increase retention rates.

Let's also be clear about the difference between school system reform and school reform. It is up to school operators and school-based educators to relentlessly improve their schools, to work within the constraints of their school system to competitively provide always-improving, high-value instruction. School improvement is their job. Because humans have strengths and weaknesses, and because children have diverse interests and engagement factors, high-value instruction, in a high-performing school system, very likely means mostly specialized instruction. In contrast, right now, given the highly diverse classroom composition (engagement factor-diverse and learning style-diverse) of the public school system, high-value instruction means "offer as much differentiated instruction as each teacher can manage."

It is up to policymakers and researchers to find and implement the funding and governance policies that optimize the conditions in which school-based educators plan and deliver instruction. As our decades of frustration with attempts at productive school reform have shown, there has not been nearly enough useful school system reform. Systemic changes have been rare, which has been good and bad, depending upon the nature of the proposed systemic changes. Policy inertia precluded quickly abandoning bad ideas. And half-baked versions of good ideas can poison the well; that is, jeopardize the political feasibility of the good ideas done right. It is too early to tell for sure, and policy perception varies by place, *but* it seems that is exactly what has happened in a lot of places for school choice expansion. And half-baked versions are causing some people to dismiss it as an old idea.

As I argue in chapter 2, the world's best school systems are still pretty bad. It is seen in the relatively small differences between the world's top-ranked systems and the average outcomes of the fifty-one Nation at Risk-level, low-performing US primary and secondary (K-12) systems. And some of the small measured international differences are due to socioeconomic factors and culture rather than more effective schooling strategies and practices. Indeed, because so many of the efforts to discover key policy and practice determinants of effective schooling from US data found that only the socioeconomic control variables were statistically significant determinants, there is a widespread perception that schools don't matter. *If* the average level of student performance was high, "schools don't matter" or "the schools are mostly quite good" could be a proper interpretation of the statistical insignificance of the available school descriptors. But those studies explain the variation in schooling outcomes around the very low Nation at Risk average effectiveness of schools. So, the correct interpretation of the statistical insignificance of the school descriptors is that the system matters a lot—that what is driving the findings are the governance and funding policies that directly affect all traditional public schools (TPS) and indirectly affect the other schools. The system is very likely the reason the vast majority of schools are approximately equally ineffective.[3] It should not be a surprise. The vast majority of schools, and school systems worldwide, suffer the same debilitating attributes, including especially the heroic assumptions, discussed in chapter 2. ***Better funding, for example, doesn't make one size fit all, or make central planning work.***[4] Because of that, and that even the top-ranked schools and countries see much room for improvement and an urgent need for it,[5] it would be a terrible mistake to just imitate better schools or better school systems (more on this below).

Finding the Key Elements of High-Performing School Systems

The policy differences between the world's school systems are probably still large enough that comparisons will reveal at least some key elements of higher-performing systems. We may also learn what to avoid from the similarities. The data may not contain examples of every key element of a high-performing system. But as much as possible, we need to ground the case for transformational school system change in genuine direct evidence, findings derived by correctly processing numbers that qualify as data. Pushing for major change *just* through theoretical arguments has already been shown to be politically infeasible once and, even supplemented just by indirect (from other industries) evidence, is likely to continue to be politically infeasible.

Methodology

So, what are our options for achieving the significant performance gains we need? (A) A supposed no-brainer I've heard suggested many times is to find a model system and replicate it here. There are many key reasons to not do that, including the just-noted, widespread systemic handicaps and thus the relatively small gains to be had by copying one of the slightly better, but still low-performing systems. (1) Given the Herculean political task of school system transformation, we should aim higher than the approximately 10 percent improvement achieved by vaulting to near the top, worldwide. Amazingly, while a 10 percent improvement would yield a non-trivial trillion dollars per year in higher GDP (Hanushek and Woessman 2008), much more is possible. We could see a copycat approach as part of a two-track strategy *if* the first step of replicating a slightly better system would not foreclose much larger gains from the implementation of a much-higher-performing, different system.

I believe that imitation of an existing system would foreclose implementation of a different, possibly much better system. My favorite analogy for this issue is a multi-peaked mountain. If you climb one of the lower sub-peaks (a better system, but not the best possible system), the energy and time it takes can prevent you from reaching the summit, the best system. Also, there is a huge inertia issue. Overcoming the inertia of the status quo will be very difficult, a heavy lift the political system will not wish to quickly revisit to replace the new, better system with a higher performing system. Elected officials evade tough votes. (2) A process can yield good results in some places and still disappoint elsewhere, and (3) the likely gains don't justify or require the means employed by some of the higher-performing systems. So, there may be some trade-offs in deciding which foreign school systems to copy. School systems yielding slightly smaller academic gains may lack the egregious means we see in two of today's top performers, South Korea (2012) and Japan (2012 and 2015), top-ranked countries in math and reading,[6] respectively. Children there are under extreme pressure to excel academically, so much so that South Korea and Japan have the world's most unhappy children. Or better yet, a more effective system may avoid the egregious means, which means achieve more than the best existing systems, after some transition bumps (see chapter 14), but without major longer-term negative side effects such as legions of unhappy children.

My position is that we can improve much more than the roughly 6 to 15 percent gap between the US., Canada, Japan, and South Korea without the pressure that yields so many stressed and unhappy children. A key reason for my contention that a high-performing school system would make the US number 1, by far, is the Hanushek (2010) global finding that the US would join the top-ranked school systems of the world if we replaced the 5–8 percent of teachers least able to perform in the typical, unnecessarily difficult classroom circumstances of the US public school system with teachers with an average ability to cope with those adverse circumstances.[7] The Hanushek (2010) finding means the US can leap to the top without any noteworthy change in funding or governance policies, just with slightly better people staffing a very low-performing system. What if we were to successfully address the classroom roots of the low-performance problem (see chapter 3) by creating a school system grounded on realistic assumptions (see chapter 4)? We should!

(B) To discover much-higher-performing alternatives to the best-performing existing school systems, I recommend rigorous school system comparison to identify key reasons for performance differences. Given the limits of existing national and international data, many of the school system comparisons may have to involve only a tiny subset of all of the world's school systems, often as few as two countries. For example, a key issue to gain recognition of, research, and address empirically is the significance of ongoing, long-standing price control, something that is rare outside school systems, but the norm globally, among at least the OECD K-12 school systems.

To help further explain what I mean by price control, I'll note that Sweden-Chile is a much-needed school system comparison.[8] Both countries somewhat level the playing field between public and private schools. Both countries extensively regulate public and private schooling content and personnel characteristics. Sweden has de facto price control because subsidized private schools cannot charge fees. Sweden does not allow co-payment for compulsory schooling, which creates a virtual price ceiling at the per pupil subsidy amount. Chile avoids price ceiling effects by allowing co-payment.[9] So, for example, a $4,000 voucher plus a $1,000 private add-on can secure admission to a private school with a tuition level of $5,000.[10] A co-payment that can vary by private school and dynamically over time means that market forces set Chile's private school tuition levels. Schools with instructional approaches that cost more than the voucher amount can exist competitively in Chile if they can persuade enough families that the school's approach is worth the requested co-payment, i.e., that for some children the school's approach is worth more than a less expensive (smaller co-payment) private school or a zero-tuition public school. Swedish private schools with instructional approaches that cost more than the voucher amount are wholly donor dependent, which means they are likely to be rare and often wait-listed (shortage of seats).

A well-constructed Sweden-Chile school system comparison may provide some valuable insight on the importance of price decontrol, but with caveats that must arise from both countries' restrictions on schooling personnel and content. For example, all Swedish schools must teach the national curriculum, which takes ~95 percent of the schooling time. School choice in Sweden substantially means just pedagogical choice, how the national curriculum is taught. Chile also intensively regulates public and private schooling (Gauri 1998).

(C) In addition to discovery of key elements of high-performing systems through empirical analysis of school system differences, I recommend extensive exploitation of indirect evidence pertaining to theory-based, likely key elements of high-performing school systems. Indirect evidence is relevant experience with industries other than schooling for children. The price control issue provides an example[11] of what that means. Outside some insights from comparisons such as the Sweden-Chile differences noted above, it will be difficult to use school system experience to confidently predict the likely effects of price decontrol for school systems. Overwhelmingly, price control is the school system norm. But we have forty centuries of abundant indirect evidence[12] of the consequences of price control. Except temporarily in wartime, price control has always been a disaster. Nation at Risk means that the price-less US system is a disaster. Economic theory is a solid basis for a hypothesis that price control is a major basis for that widely acknowledged gold-plated disaster, perhaps enough of a basis for a credible simulation model.

Schooling has the classic symptoms of price control, including low quality and sinking productivity. The indirect evidence says that many terrible, persistent schooling circumstances will quickly disappear with price decontrol as they have whenever price decontrol occurred in other industries. Even without direct evidence from school systems that price decontrol alleviated many terrible outcomes, we can confidently surmise from the indirect evidence that schooling could benefit greatly from the price decontrol that would result from the potential for public-private shared financing of schooling alternatives according to market forces. Indirect evidence can and, I believe, must show the way forward for much of the policy entrepreneurship needed for significant school system improvement. Failure to willingly rely, where necessary, on indirect evidence, means that other places must try everything first. Only places willing to rely, at least partially, on indirect evidence can be the first to implement a new policy-based reform. Requiring direct evidence takes a lot off the table and puts a lot more on hold for a long time. In the meantime, we will under-educate and miseducate additional K-12 cohorts.

Keep in mind that while pricelessness is the key defect of the fifty-one US school systems, the price control issue is one of many possibly helpful school system redesign possibilities that school system similarities might prevent us from properly vetting with direct evidence. Reliance on indirect evidence is not ideal, but it can be sufficient to favor specific ways to implement general approaches that empirical evidence from other industries, and other indirect evidence, favors. For example, school choice expansion is a possibly useful general strategy. There are many specific ways to expand choice. The overwhelming indirect evidence that price control is something to avoid should push policy design in the direction of specific implementation strategies in which price control cannot easily arise. For example, tuition tax credits and education savings accounts (see chapter 8) are school choice expansion strategies that are much less vulnerable to price-control-creating provisions than are direct payment to private schools and tuition voucher strategies.

Best Practices Confusion

There are two kinds. One is obsessed with discovery of the magic pedagogical bullet and then applying it everywhere (expanding to scale). There is no such magic bullet. For example, Eric Hanushek and Berner (2017) argue that there are probably no universal best practices.[13] Hanushek's former Stanford colleague, Larry Cuban, agrees: "Since children differ in their motivations, interests, and backgrounds, and learn at different speeds in different subjects, there is no single best way for teachers to teach and for children to learn that can fit all situations… No particular teaching approach, no matter how successful its champions say it is, yields the desired outcomes with all students, all of the time." And there's the Fordham Institute's mantra, "no school can be everything to every student." The second kind of best practices confusion is that the best schools and systems necessarily contain only (or mostly) best policy practices, and those systems are the only places to find them.

A big downside to the first is that beyond the repeatedly relearned fact that no one size fits all is that the pedagogies that are, or could develop into, best fit practices for many children end up in the dustbin of history because they didn't work acceptably for everyone. Open education, or informal education, is a good example. Peddled as one of many in a succession of silver bullet answers to disappointment with US school systems, it became a faddish imperative in the early 1970s and then quickly faded into disrepute because it was not compatible with the current system. That means it wasn't the best fit for all of the students to have them in open classroom settings, or for all of the educators hired to apply it, probably a combination of the two. Open education still exists in a few of the current systems' schools of choice, but because of the 1970s experience, open education purveyors have to keep their heads low to avoid incoming fire. In a more entrepreneurial initiative-friendly system, several, more refined versions of open education might be the best fit for millions of schoolchildren.

The second kind of best practices confusion arises if we examine only the best systems, and don't allow for the fact that even the best systems could be better, perhaps including even some counterproductive policies. That's especially likely to be true in an assessment of existing school systems where we know that even the best are not that much better than the low-performing norm (next chapter), and thus are still pretty bad. Also, lower-performing systems may contain some key elements of high-performing systems that are not found elsewhere.

Potential for Misleading Evidence

Assessing and possibly copying school system policies will suffer from political spin, the often limited nature of available numbers (masquerading as data), and it may suffer from the non-uniformity of the existing examples of the various policy options. The similar names of many, still diverse existing policies cause excessive attention to lousy experiments.

Assessments of tuition voucher policies provide a good example of the struggle (Hess 2002, Merrifield 2008, Epple 2017) to ignore lousy experiments.[14] Existing US programs are small and very diverse. The studies of the existing tuition voucher programs yielded some important insights, but they cannot directly address questions about the transformational potential, for better or for worse, of large, universal, unrestrictive tuition voucher policies (or ESAs or tuition tax credits). Milton Friedman called the latter *education vouchers*. Friedman thought we needed such vouchers to achieve the bulldozer effects (Hess, 2002; much change in the menu of schooling options) as a first huge step towards a much-improved school system. But such a program simply does not exist to study. There are some universal, reasonably large foreign voucher programs, but all contain extensive regulation of private schooling content, and except in a few countries such as Chile, price control (pricelessness), which among other bad things is a huge market entry barrier.[15]

Most voucher programs, including nearly every US case,[16] are what Milton Friedman called *charity vouchers*. There are several telling synonyms for "charity voucher": escape hatch, narrowly targeted, and my favorite, restriction-laden. Each synonym conveys that the voucher is a relatively small dollar sum, with only a small fraction of the students eligible for a tuition payment that is less than what many private schools charge and significantly smaller than the per-pupil funding of traditional public schools. They may also contain other noteworthy restrictions such as price control (no third party supplementation of the government funding), special education mandates, and curriculum mandates. Since charity vouchers are too small and restriction-laden to be transformational, they mostly just move a few children among the existing options. Charity vouchers have had only a minimal impact on the schooling options and student outcomes, maybe pickaxe effects, certainly not bulldozer effects (Hess 2002). Studies of non-transformational programs' outcomes amount to comparisons of the private and public school choices that exist in the current low-performing system, which means the choices that exist as a result of the current governance and funding policies, especially the high market entry barriers.

Given those very limiting features of the tuition voucher programs available to study, we cannot be surprised that assessments have yielded this political spin: the school choice opposition half-truth talking point that "they [voucher programs] don't make much difference" (Obama 2014), liberally translated from the genuine, limited truth that the limited programs available to study haven't made much difference. So, the talking point is a half-truth because we haven't tested the education voucher programs that might make a big difference, for better or for worse. We know that the escape hatches created by charity vouchers yielded high levels of parental satisfaction among the eligible few, probably from benefits not captured by the small differences between the test scores of voucher program participants and the unsuccessful voucher applicants. Predictably, charity vouchers have not notably budged the needle on measured school system performance. Unfortunately, for informed debate, many analysts expected a lot of measured impact from charity vouchers, good and bad.

The Flip Side of School System and School Comparisons

Comparisons can identify the key reasons for performance differences. They can also suggest, alongside theory and indirect evidence, the reasons for similar outcomes. So, using the 2015 PISA results, why is the U.S. Nation at Risk system, ranked #20 in reading and #36 in math, still within 6 and 13 percent of number 1?[17] Answer: the PISA test participant school systems have much in common. Those common elements are why Hanushek found that the US system would be top-ranked if the US just replaced the 5–8 percent of teachers that are least effective in the unnecessarily, exceptionally challenging nature of existing public school classroom circumstances with teachers with average effectiveness in those unnecessarily, exceptionally challenging settings.

The world's well-documented school systems are similarly low-performing because the central planning process, driven by the political process, predictably yields very similar outcomes. Decentralized planning—aggregated individual behavior driven by the information and incentives contained in market-determined prices—has always massively outperformed every attempt to use politically correct experts to decide what is produced, how and where it is produced, and who consumes what is produced. Central planning's overwhelming missing information and perverse incentive issues are well documented in print (among many: Ludwig von Mises' *Socialism*), and well documented by its massive failures to perform in practice.

My use of the term "decentralized planning" must *not* be confused with the existing, widespread use of "decentralization" to mean pushing decision-making and budgetary authority closer to the campus level, which can be a useful central plan improvement, but unlikely to yield much school system improvement. For example, when William Ouchi said, "Urban school districts are dysfunctionally centralized," he was right, but he was not talking about creating schooling options through free enterprise and choice orchestrated by market-driven price change. I am. Decentralized planning means addressing the what, where, how, and for whom of formal instruction with enterprise-created, mostly independent private schools of choice, mostly orchestrated by a price system, probably market-based, but administered price changes need more exploration. Likewise, choice is most likely to be parental choice, but perhaps constrained or informed by collective choice considerations. Chartered public schools (CPS) and school district-run magnet schools may supplement the private schools of choice.

Chapter 2 explains the many symptoms of school system failure and why it is of critical importance to pursue transformational school system change. The direct threat—the key reason why our fifty-one low-performing systems yield Nation at Risk status—is not among the most widely cited reasons why a low-performing school system endangers us. Before I use chapter 2 to define transformational change and explain why, for example, that international competitiveness is not what should motivate us to create a high-performing school system, I want to establish this book's key definitions and practices. A noteworthy practice is a focus on beliefs and ideas, not their source. That matters a lot when intense criticism is in order. So, I avoid naming authors when especially strong criticism of their assertions is in order.[18]

Since a school system's final product is what matters, the PISA exam is my basis for rare international test score comparisons. PISA[19] tests fifteen-year-olds. For US trends, the most useful assessment basis is the NAEP test for seventeen-year-olds. I use them even though the scores reflect only cognitive skills, but rarely, with hesitation, in part because the no-stakes-for-students may fail to adequately motivate the student test-takers (Sawchuk 2018). Despite the low stakes, the scores correlate with other indicators, many of them anecdotal, such as high rates of high school graduate remediation and employer complaints about entry-level skills. That test scores of children are often not strongly correlated with later attainments such as graduation, higher education proficiency, and income is another reason to use test scores rarely, with hesitation.

I avoid use of graduation rates because of the high potential for, and occurrence of, fraud defining graduation. Results for younger children matter for diagnosing where academic gains falter or accelerate. For example, the United States' fifty-one (see below) school systems seem comparatively better for younger children. "Engagement," as defined by Gallup, falls from 75 percent in fifth grade to ~33 percent by the end of high school.[20]

Finally, in this initial rendition of key definitions, "school system" is not synonymous with "education system," which is a broader term that includes informal and formal education options. Much intellectual growth and skill attainment occurs outside formal school settings. From the well-known correlation between student test scores and socioeconomic status, we know that informal education yields a head start plus greater home reinforcement of formal schooling content. And increasingly, US families choose the informal home school option.

---

[1] Ronald Wolkin Ed Week: https://www.edweek.org/ew/articles/2012/12/05/13wolk_ep.h32.html

[2] California governor Gray Davis (D).

[3] Best Is Still Pretty Bad: Hess (2010b) quote (*Greenfield*) p 7; Top of the Cellar Stairs (Finn 1991); "Not as Good as You Think" (Izumi 2007, 2014, 2015)

[4] Not just logical, but empirically supported: http://journals.sagepub.com/doi/abs/10.3102/01623737019002141

[5] Plank, David N. and Gary Sykes, eds. 2003. *Choosing Choice: School Choice in International Perspective*. New York: Teachers College Press.

[6] Canada managed number 1 in reading in 2015 without the pressure present in South Korea and Japan.

[7] The rate of academic improvement with improved teaching would have to be constant at the rate measured by Hanushek—in economics lingo, constant marginal benefits.

[8] The US choice expansion programs have too many restrictions, including narrow targeting of eligibility to provide a reliable test of the effects of price decontrol.

[9] The small dollar amount, and nearly universal co-payment in Chile—mostly small—argues against the presence of price floor effects.

[10] Because Chile taxes co-payment, it takes slightly more than a $1000 co-payment to make up the difference between a $4,000 tuition voucher and a $5,000 tuition.

[11] https://objectivepolicyassessment.org/K-12/pricesystemexample.pdf

[12] See Schuettinger and Butler.

13 See also https://educationnext.org/best-practices-are-the-worst/

14 Find in *Journal of Economic Perspectives*.

15 I am still holding out hope that with further study or policy change, I will discover additional price decontrol countries.

16 The sole US exception was the now-expired, privately funded Edgewood voucher program, whose effects were tarnished by its temporary nature.

17 I didn't include city states such as Singapore and Hong Kong in the rankings.

18 I am interested in demolishing wrong beliefs and bad ideas without alienating their authors. Names may be in the footnotes or hyperlinks in the electronic editions of the book. We should engage in a civil, public online conversation on the issues at https://www.schoolsystemreformstudies.net/opinion-forum-clusters/

19 PISA: Program for International Student Assessment. NAEP: National Assessment of Educational Progress.

20 http://www.edweek.org/ew/articles/2016/03/23/gallup-student-poll-finds-engagement-in-school.html?qs=Student+Engagement+Drops

Chapter Two

The School System Transformation Imperative

There is much room for improvement, virtually everywhere, because the world's major school systems have at least one critical, debilitating element in common. They are largely or totally price-less. Price-lessness means that a central planning process must determine what will be taught, where, how, and to whom, a process that has **never** worked well for **any** economy or industry. Even the core government functions of defense and justice suffer mightily from their inability to benefit significantly from decentralized planning through price change to signal the highest and best use of resources, and to motivate producers and consumers to heed those signals.[1]

The most frequently given reasons are not the key reasons why the failure to confront and productively transform school systems is of critical importance. For example, productivity gains and international economic competitiveness are important, but they're not the most compelling reasons to urgently seek transformational change in the schooling of children (K-12 in the US). That's true everywhere but in the world's absolute worst school systems.

"Comparatively" is a critical but sometimes misleading perspective at several levels. While some schools and school systems are better than others, few perform acceptably, either in terms of economic efficiency or few children left behind. Most prominently, Standard

& Poor's[2] and Lance Izumi repeatedly documented that the best US schools are not as good as you think. Comments like this one from John Merrow's call to arms are common: It is "within our power to build a system of schools that allows dedicated educators to be successful" instead of "setting up most teachers to fail" (Merrow 2017, xiv). I agree with the well-traveled Merrow (journalist and former teacher) that the current US systems make it very difficult for even dedicated educators to be widely and consistently successful (next chapter and others). Former school district superintendent and long-time educator Marc Bernstein sums it up this way:

> Our students are not improving. This [2016] spring, the "nation's report card," the National Assessment of Educational Progress, showed a drop in 12th graders' math scores and no improvement in reading—results unfortunately consistent with those previously released for 4th and 8th graders. Other recent news, such as New York state's easing of graduation requirements for special-needs students, highlights how state requirements for earning a high school diploma are being dumbed down, while self-satisfied educators and politicians praise higher graduation rates. All too many graduating high school students enter college requiring remedial courses.

Anthony Roselli, author of *Dos and Don'ts of Education Reform*, says we have a "grotesque level of failure. The past two decades of failed reforms have left us with children and young adults who cannot read with understanding and worse yet, are morally illiterate" (Roselli 2005, 138).

So, in the US, systemic change is needed everywhere, but most critically at, and near, the secondary level. That is not nearly a new finding. For example, E. D. Hirsch Jr., author of the *Core Knowledge Sequence*, said, "High school has become a place where students are offered a smorgasbord of watered-down subjects, because watered-down subjects are all that our ill-educated students are now prepared to understand." Charles Silberman, after first condemning the entire public school system—"profound disappointment with the public schools as an institution" (Silberman 1971, 69)—and US high schools, says this of US junior high schools (~age 12–14):

> The junior high school, by almost unanimous agreement, is the wasteland—one is tempted to say cesspool—of American education (Silberman 1971, 324)

The persistence of the system's declining effectiveness with student age signifies systemic inability to address alarming outcomes or resistance to much-needed genuine solutions, perhaps both.

Silberman's (1971) observations were made at the same time (1960s) that David Osborne (2017, 2) said a now "obsolete," once great system was at its peak, before there was much federal or state intervention. In the 1960s, accountability and change occurred through local political forums. It must have been a comparatively low peak. Admiral Hyman Rickover's 1957 book and the Sputnik-catalyzed education call to arms *Why Johnny Can't Read* occurred near that Osborne-alleged peak that must been the basis of the first Nation at Risk report (1983). Also, then, Tyack (1974)[3] described major systemic problems. Indeed, that may have been the system's peak, but as Diane Ravitch points out in *Left Back: A Century of Failed School Reforms* (2000), there has never been a golden age. David Kirkpatrick asked, "What good old days?" Best does even not assure good, much less great. Merrow (2017) also argued that the current system has become obsolete. It must have been a comparatively low peak since Merrow argues that only now, with the Internet and advanced computing technology, is a high-performing school system possible. Certainly it has been better in terms of cost per unit of academic achievement, but never good.

*****

Low average academic gains are not a major ***direct*** threat to individual earning power or US (and many other places') international economic competitiveness because

1. In the 2015 PISA exam, the USA average PISA score was in the middle of the pack, but only 6 percent behind in reading and 13 percent behind math top scorers Canada and Japan respectively. In 2012, the USA average PISA score was 11–15 percent behind top scorers Japan and South Korea. Among the top twenty or so (depending upon subject) countries, the USA's similar fifty-one school systems are not being outperformed by much, but this is, at best, very mixed news.
2. The answer to "if we're so dumb, why are we so rich?" is that the US has some significant institutional advantages: low corruption, secure property rights, etc. And individuals can earn a great living without great schooling by being quite good at just one thing. As Oliver DeMille noted, many people—most Americans—are well trained (at something), but poorly educated. Effective specialization in a highly valued skill is possible without good formal schooling or a good education; and
3. Countries such as the US can substantially offset the negative competitiveness effects of domestic skills' deficiencies by attracting skilled immigrants. US attractiveness to skilled immigrants carries with it the secondary benefit of slowing some of our competitors while it helps elevate us.

Regarding the small gap between top-ranked countries and countries such as the US, in the middle of the PISA pack,[4] laggards such as the US can take some comfort in being close to the best. But for the US failure to respond productively to the compelling language of the first (1983) Nation at Risk report, we could be well ahead. And even with that failure, the gap would be smaller but for the extreme performance pressure placed on Japanese and South Korean children. Japan and South Korea (2012) achieved number 1, but they have the world's most unhappy children.[5] That is too high a price to pay, especially for such a small increment of gain and especially when less costly ways may yield larger gains. Canada's school systems (the provinces) have more school choice than the USA, but its results only top our Nation at Risk results by 6 percent.

Proximity to #1 is nice, but that tight clustering of national PISA scores is mostly bad news.[6] We know from the specifics in *Nation at Risk I–VI*[7] and from high school graduates' and dropouts' poor skills that the US school systems don't adequately exploit their advantages of cultural diversity, freedom of thought, and $13,000/child/year;[8] triple the inflation-adjusted per-pupil cost of the mid-1960s, eight times higher since WW2. With the world's top-ranked countries barely ahead of us, we know they must also be pretty bad. And indeed, many, maybe all, of the world's major, developed countries are unhappy with the performance of their school systems. For example, former South Korean Education Minister Byong-man Ahn said (2012), "within Korea, that same [world number 1 in 2009 and 2012, close in 2015] education system has been called the nation's biggest problem."[9] Carnoy, Garcia, and Khavenson (2016) provided evidence that all school systems produce disappointing results; that score clustering would be even tighter if the scores just reflected formal schooling: "There is no causal evidence that students in some Asian countries, for example, score higher on international tests mainly because of better schooling" (Carnoy et al., 2016).

The world's major school systems have very similar, disappointing aggregate academic performance outcomes because they share many predictable sources of low performance. One key factor is that incentive systems are typically weak and not well aligned with the public interest. For example, genuine differences in teacher skill, skill scarcity, and classroom effectiveness may be poorly reflected in salary differences. It's not a conspiracy. Price-less schooling is politically correct, by definition, which means a central planning process[10] decides what is taught, how, where, and to whom. That places a high premium on uniformity, often a subject of harsh criticism.[11] At other times, greater uniformity—for example, through a Common Core curriculum—is openly, widely asserted as a key objective. The fifty-one US school systems demonstrate that an electoral political process can produce very consistent school system policies and relatively, consistently low academic performance outcomes. The policy differences between the whole-country school systems are larger, but there are still remarkable key similarities.

School systems that aim to serve a diverse clientele with too little diversity in the widely accessible instructional approaches are a global norm. Through a combination of direct provision of schooling by the government, high direct and indirect barriers to independent provision of schooling options, and/or prescriptive regulation of all schooling options, the international norm is funding and governance policy that implicitly aims for one best general schooling approach for everyone.

Direct provision of schooling through a public school system with a monopoly on taxpayer funding marginalizes private schooling. It does so by forcing private schools to levy tuition when schooling is widely available for no additional charge ("free") beyond taxes that all households must pay whether or not they have children in public schools. The enormous challenge to sell something with one or more popular, free substitutes (assigned public schools and sometimes chartered public schools) is the reason for the rare, mostly nonprofit, church-run nature of the current US systems' private schooling options. Another common route to insufficient diversity in the menu of instructional approaches is through regulation.[12] It often occurs through rules such as a national curriculum and detailed teacher credentialing that apply equally to government-owned/run public schools and privately owned schools.

A huge problem is that central planning is price-less. It is likely the biggest problem with most school systems, ***as well as the least recognized***. With political processes deciding what is taught, where, how, and to whom, we get distorted (misleading) implicit prices, random outcomes, and chaos. The school systems of developed countries are largely price-less. Central planning—bureaucratic resolution of what is taught, where, how, and to whom—has not worked well for schooling. It is very rare when a price-less (price-controlled) industry doesn't quickly become a total mess, which has always been the eventual result. In his massive tome, *Capitalism*, economist George Reisman (1998) argues that "a government that imposes price controls on schooling is in the process of destroying the education system of its own country."[13] Price caps eliminate the basis for knowing or incentivizing the best use of resources; for example, the best mix of instructional approaches and content becomes unknowable, which leads to complacency and chaotic outcomes. Competitive market-produced prices provide producers the information and incentives necessary to know and meet consumers' highest priorities. In the context of "price controls and shortages…the seller's motives work in the direction of reducing the quality of his product."[14] Shortages sharply reduce seller accountability to customers. Sellers can trim costs/quality without losing sales or revenue. Unhappy customers are readily replaced from the wait list.

Even John K. Galbraith, a WWII price control practitioner and a rare economist that saw some limited potential value in temporary uses of price controls, noted that "the [price control policy] record appears to be one of unrelieved botchery and failure" (Galbraith 1952, 3). And he was describing experience with prices fixed at a market-set level. For most schooling options, there have never been explicit market-set prices. Low and falling school system efficiency (Hoxby 2003, Hoxby 2004, Coulson 2009) has been the predictable outcome and well-established result of long-term absence of dynamic (change quickly, as necessary, to reflect genuine scarcity) price signals.

So, it is not an overstatement to generalize that central planning approaches haven't worked well, if at all, for very long, under *any* circumstances, for *anything*. When attempted on a national scale, central planning yields riches-to-rags stories, sadly still seen in abundance during the last 100 years, most recently in Venezuela, North Korea, Cuba, and the former Soviet Union.

Central planning, by default because of pricelessness, mostly with the best of intentions, yielded our Nation at Risk conditions, which is predictable especially for complex endeavors such as the schooling of diverse schoolchildren. Even the industries that are obvious government duties—justice and defense—are in obvious need (the Pentagon's infamous $7,600 coffeemaker and $640 special toilet seat) of as much creative infusion of market-driven price change as a team of clever mechanism-design[15] economists can discover. During recorded history,[16] a process best described as decentralized planning (independent action coordinated by market-driven price change) has proven to be the ***only*** way to efficiently orchestrate complex economic decision-making within industries (such as schooling) and between industries (economy-wide). It may also be the best way to optimize employee behavior within large business firms (Koch 2007),[17] or school districts.

The Direct Threat

The proper key rationale for unrelenting pursuit of massive school system improvement is not widely recognized. Diane Ravitch, despite having documented the terrible outcomes of formal schooling in the US, still did not specify the key threat posed by poor schooling. And despite her awareness of persistent, widespread poor school system performance, Ravitch now actively opposes transformational change in school system funding or governance. Before her attitude reversal, she noted that half of all twelfth graders were still below basic and then opined, "The consequences of this [history] knowledge vacuum are severe. We can't have thoughtful public discussions of issues when the public is so woefully uninformed about the past." And many citizens are not just woefully ignorant of who did what when. They are also woefully unable to discern from history why good or bad effects typically follow specific causes. The social science literacy rate is terribly low, especially its economic element. Poor grasp of history and low social science literacy have had severe consequences and are likely to continue to do so. Jacques Barzun (2001, quoted by Roselli 2005, 68) correctly sensed *the threat*: "we need to return to teaching [critical] knowledge or risk a return to barbarism." According to Thomas Jefferson, "if a nation expects to be ignorant and free, in a state of civilization, it expects what *never* was, and *never* will be." He wrote in 1789, "Wherever the people are well informed, they can be trusted with their own government." Don Willett noted that Jefferson's "prognosis underscored what the

Constitution presupposes: An enlightened citizenry is indispensable to American self-government."

The growing, widespread inability of citizens to discern good public policies from bad will lead to gradual political strangulation of the economic system[18] through bad policy, probably gradually including tyranny. Failure to learn from past policy mistakes—through facts and economic literacy—raises the probability that those mistakes will occur again. Low-performing school systems represent a menacing, ominous direct threat to liberties and thus a huge indirect threat to economic prosperity everywhere. Dr. T. Robinson Ahlstrom, chairman of the George Washington Scholars Endowment, believes that the conduct and reporting of 2016's political campaigns demonstrate that we are far down that likely riches-to-rags road:

> The 2016 presidential race may prove to be the first in more than half a century in which education emerges as a key national issue, but *not* because the candidates demonstrate any particular concern over or passion for the quality of America's schools. This is the election that fully vindicates that ominous prophecy—the day when, for all the world to see, we are, in Postman's phrase: "amusing ourselves to death." Neither the Jerry Springer quality of our national discourse nor the money-hued jousting of the media to provide a megaphone for the madness is the real problem. They are but surreal symptoms of a society reduced to a semiliterate state, addicted to titillation and estranged from the higher uses of the mind.[19]

And Jonathan Jacobs notes that as education declines, so does civic culture: "A generation of college graduates unable to write or reason bodes ill for liberal democracy."[20]

Earlier, Robert M. Hutchins, former chancellor, University of Chicago, had similar thoughts: "When we listen to the radio, look at television, and read the newspapers, we wonder whether universal education has been the great boon that its supporters have always claimed it would be."[21]

Note also that universal access through public funding did not quickly increase enrollment rates.

Such a process can only accidentally produce great leaders. Whether or not any president produces mostly growth- and liberty-promoting policies, there is also ample precedent for concern that the political process, under the current policy semi-literacy circumstances, will eventually yield some terrible leadership with tyranny and self-destruction.[22] There is also ample evidence that the US is on that road, from Baumol et al.'s (2009) comparisons of good and bad (crony) capitalism, to chapter 12 in Hubbard and Kane (2013), to James Bovard's (2000) *Freedom in Chains*. The latter was written before this millennium's further major encroachments on individual initiative and economic liberty that pushed the US from number 1 in the Fraser Institute Economic Freedom of the World Index (EFWI) in 2003, among major countries (city-states Hong Kong and Singapore ranked ahead of the US), to number 6 in 2019. Modern empirical studies have told us that there is a high correlation between national prosperity and economic freedom as defined by the EFWI. *Less and better government, a high minimum level of opportunity, much-enhanced individual liberty, and global prosperity are the reasons to pursue school system improvement and urge other countries to do the same.*

Clear Signs That We Need Massive School System Improvement

Whatever the roots of the US problem of persistently low performance are[23]—Nation at Risk low—we know from a series of authoritative, nonpartisan school system assessments before and after the 1983 national commission report that created the Nation at Risk label, and most recently from former Secretary of Education Rod Paige (2015) and prominent former teachers, that those roots remain intact:

> Despite massive new education policies from previous legislative sessions, and after decades of effort, tons of money, and volumes of educational punditry and political debate, we are left with relatively little to show for considerable effort.[24]

Education entrepreneur and former teacher Peter McAllister (2018) said,

> Despite these [considerable post-'Nation at Risk'] efforts, the performance of our schools is still unsatisfactory. We have one of the world's highest levels of per-pupil spending, but our performance in international comparisons of educational quality is consistently mediocre.

That persistent failure to successfully address the roots includes Dr. Paige's 2001–2004 term as Education Secretary under a supportive president in a "do something" environment. In the 2000 election campaign, both major party presidential candidates, Dr. Paige's boss, George W. Bush and his Democrat opponent, Al Gore, declared school system improvement their top priority. Secretary Paige's accurate assessment of reform efforts, to date, demonstrate that the core reasons for the US system's persistently low performance survived that promise of a full-court press.

Secretary Paige argued for better integration of education practice and education policymaking, i.e., better central planning everywhere. Sure, let's try that. Even though all central plans suffer serious deficiencies, some plans are still significantly better than others (see chapter 7). But the history of central planning and the solid consensus on central planning's inherent flaws tell us that Secretary Paige's suggestion for improving the central planning process has a low upside. It will mostly amount to another case of hope likely not triumphing over experience.

The practice-to-policymaking disconnect is one of the failure symptoms that arise when policymakers, with incentives not well aligned with the public interest, confront the complexity, inadequate information, and perverse incentives of the central planning process. Inability to push policy changes into classrooms and failure to notably involve education practitioners in the policymaking process are among the many noteworthy signs that the current system needs transformational change. Transformational change is much more than new programs. Fundamental governance and funding changes are in order.

There are many other signs of school system dysfunction and thus need for transformational change. The implied business plan of the fifty-one US systems has many implicit heroic assumptions. Another Bush cabinet secretary, two-time Defense Secretary Donald Rumsfeld said, "A successful leader must develop reasonable assumptions and base a plan of action on them."[25] A common-sense corollary to Secretary Rumsfeld's sensible point is that you cannot build a good plan of action on unreasonable assumptions. So, another sign of a compelling need for school system transformation is that several of the US K-12 school system's implicit central tenets are heroic (highly unreasonable) assumptions. A key indicator of the heroic nature of the US school system's key implicit assumptions is huge need for public school turnaround, or replacement, and the very high failure rate for public school turnaround efforts (Smarick, 2012).

US School Systems' Heroic Assumptions

The least recognized implicit heroic assumption by transformational change advocates and their opponents alike, but likely the most important, is that **(A)** we can have great school systems without the market-driven price change process[26] that orchestrates participation and production in nearly all industries. I've already noted that persistent pricelessness (including formal price control) is a key reason for central planning failure. There are no examples of high-performing price-less or price-controlled industries. K-12 schooling is an example of a persistently low-performing, almost totally price-less industry. We have forty centuries worth of evidence[27] that pricelessness is a reliable recipe for disaster, but price-less school systems are still overwhelmingly the international norm.

In case this needs a bit more clarification before I get into other examples, and paths to price decontrol, later in the book, here are two prominent examples of school system price controls and some key outcomes. (1) Nearly everywhere, a single salary schedule[28] sets teacher salaries within districts, and often statewide, without regard to differences in teacher training (except BA vs. MA) or site placement. At the prescribed single price, there are often shortages of some types of teachers and too much supply of other types. Math, science, and special needs training are in short supply especially often. That has led to much out-of-field teaching,[29] with likely frequent low-ability and low-enthusiasm teaching in a lot of classrooms. Enthusiasm is a prerequisite for student-teacher engagement, what economists call the coproduction of knowledge and skills.

The widespread failure to allow pay to vary by school often leads to difficulty placing and keeping teachers at the least desirable schools. Districts assign teachers to schools, but with them leaving the least desirable schools as fast as possible (transfers, exiting the district or profession), students most in need of experienced teachers often have the least experienced teachers.[30] (2) There are two price controls for public schools, zero tuition for parent-customers, and a politically set per-pupil payment to school districts for traditional public schools (TPS) and to chartered public school (CPS) operators. Because of the absence of market-driven price adjustment, public schools have persistent space shortages and surpluses. Districts often do not readily correct imbalances by changing TPS attendance zone boundaries because of the unpopularity of attendance zone changes.

Because CPS lack attendance zones to adjust, the impact of that double price control is most readily evident for them. Many parents want a better fit (Rose 2016) for a child than the assigned TPS, so the demand for a CPS slot at the tuition price of zero is often much greater than the supply available for the state-set per-pupil payment plus whatever the CPS can rustle up from donors. Many CPS are donor dependent, which means they cannot finance the delivery of the instructional approach they offer for just the government's per-pupil payment. That there's not enough donor funding available to avoid large shortages is evident in the long waiting lists of many CPS.[31] Probably the persistence of the wait lists, apart from failure to decontrol the tuition price, results from donors' preference for new schools over increased capacity in existing CPS with long wait lists. Donors and activists (often one and the same), by failing to grasp the huge economic and education costs and high political risks created by the wait lists (described below), may leave wait lists intact while creating new schools that will likely also have wait lists. They also appreciate wait lists as convenient, easily understood indicators that CPS funding is too low and start-up barriers are too high.

The large shortages virtually close many CPS to most families, especially the CPS that have existed for a while. A wait list often develops before an announced CPS opens its doors. Because of the ubiquitous shortages, CPS often represent **school chance** (admission by lottery), not school choice. And the random lottery process mandated to assure fairness prevents the allocation of scarce slots to the best fits for the CPS mission. Also, shortages are known to erode quality,[32] which can yield devastatingly embarrassing scandals,[33] which is a huge liability and threat to the political feasibility of charter law[34] and school choice expansion. So, because of price control, we have too few CPS slots, the system rewards the bad behavior of some CPS operators, and we fail to get the most alternative schooling benefit out of those limited offerings of alternatives to the TPS.

Unmet demand and quality erosion are not the main drawbacks of price-setting by the authorities. The key drawback of price control is the lack of price-change-based information, combined with incentive, to orchestrate a dynamic mix of specialized schooling options to match the diverse learning needs and content engagement factors of each school system's schoolchildren.

(B) Another of the US systems' breathtakingly heroic implicit assumptions—what has to be true for the system to be high-performing—is that having a virtual monopoly enhances efficiency; breathtakingly heroic! In nearly all of the US, the public school system has a total monopoly on public funding, and each traditional public school (TPS) has an exclusive franchise within its designated attendance zone. This is another pricelessness issue. Having to pay twice to opt for a better fit through a private school does not signal the true cost of either TPS or private schools.

We've enshrined into federal antitrust law that much less market dominance (market share) than any public school system possesses is severely detrimental to the functioning of industries and public welfare. But we foolishly exempt K-12 schooling from that well-grounded logic. We all understand instinctively that except in industries that are natural monopolies (city water, for example), robust competition is the desirable state of affairs. Except in very small towns, K-12 schooling has never been a natural monopoly, and improving Internet-based software technology is increasing potential market contestability everywhere, including small towns and rural areas.

(**C**) A bizarre implied heroic assumption closely related to the heroic "monopoly is best" assumption is that public funding earmarked for schooling should belong to a particular service provider (the public schools), not the service customers from whom the money was taken through taxation. The incredible upshot of that brazen public school system claim is that the families that want to opt out of the assigned TPS must leave behind the subsidy funding financed by their taxes. Even in the rare cases where public funding follows children to an alternative to the assigned public school, much of the subsidy funding stays behind. For example, in Milwaukee, with the oldest private school choice program and the largest per-pupil portable subsidy amount, the public funds paid to private schools are ~65 percent of the per-pupil funding of Milwaukee's traditional public schools. That policy of strongly favoring public school users is contrary to the reality that taxpayers pay school taxes to provide schooling to all children, not just the children for whom the mainstream pedagogy is a good fit, and to pay the school system personnel that serve all the schoolchildren.

(**D**) There are very few places that adjust pay to reflect public school educators' measured effectiveness. That genuine merit pay is rare implies the incredibly heroic assumption or hope that incentives don't matter—again, hope triumphing over mountains of experience. This is another pricelessness issue. System governance assigned a price of zero to effectiveness.

Some of the resistance to genuine merit pay arises, appropriately, from the difficulty of gauging teacher effectiveness in the unnecessarily challenging circumstances of our current system's public school teachers, including lack of a direct client role, via choice, in signaling merit. Resistance to merit-based pay also arises from our school system's failure to provide public school teachers the professional status to decide how to accomplish their mission. Indeed, public school teachers are typically assigned a curriculum and textbooks ("teacher-proof" is a growing trend), and quite often, the lessons are on a strict schedule. Teachers hate micromanagement, but it is common. That basis for resistance to merit pay argues that it is unfair to hold teachers responsible for conditions they have little control over. Every place needs a school system where teachers have enough autonomy to be held responsible for the outcomes of their circumstances.

Indeed, under the circumstances of the US public school system, it may be improper and unfair to hold teachers responsible for their effectiveness in such an unprofessional environment. That's a key sign we need transformational change. ***We should not tolerate a school system that makes it especially hard to be successful, makes it especially hard to measure effectiveness (need more than test scores), and makes it especially hard to finance merit raises.*** Unlike the private sector where merit increases revenue, public sector merit barely increases the district's revenues. Indeed, the opposite may be more likely, where failure attracts increased funding.

(E) A key implicit underlying assumption of the public school system's growing propensity to rely on large, shopping mall-like "comprehensively uniform" schools (Powell et al. 1985)[35] is that specialization within large, uniform conglomerate organizations is better than specialization by organizations. That implicit assumption is another example of hope triumphing over experience, including but definitely not limited to our school system experiences. Also, student choice within large schools can be counterproductive. It creates hard-to-manage complex schools (Segal 2004), and makes it hard for parents to monitor and motivate student progress.

(**F**) Another implicit heroic assumption is that there is one set of best practices for the vast majority of schoolchildren[36] and the political process will discover them, adopt them, and optimally deploy them, something the US systems have yet to manage. A closely related, implied huge assumption is one-dimensional student ability and educator talent. Generic policy debates do not see teachers or students as having strengths and weaknesses. Student ability is either great, good, mediocre, or poor, not a mixture that depends on pedagogy or varies with subject matter. Even within declared, credentialed subject fields, teachers have strengths and weaknesses. And definitely between subject fields, that will be the case, but reform debates do not recognize that.

But whether a teacher is teaching out of field or not, a competent teacher is often great for some students, but less helpful for others. A different competent teacher would be more effective with a different subset of the students than those assigned to their classrooms and less effective with others. For example, my wife's traditional public school (TPS) classroom was especially helpful to discipline-challenged children. Some of her colleagues struggled with discipline but were quite effective for children where such challenges were not a major factor. Student ability and teaching talent is multidimensional. Most of us know, from just looking in the mirror, that human talent is only rarely one-dimensional. We recognize our own strengths and weaknesses, but our K-12 governance and funding policies don't recognize that students and teachers have them. Except for utterly dysfunctional schools, schools are also typically multidimensional. Even officially unspecialized schools—all TPS, some CPS, and some private schools—sometimes work better, often by accident, for some types of multidimensional children than others.

In a school system that recognizes that schools, student ability, and teacher talent are multidimensional, schools with a pedagogical specialization or thematic content packaging would be widespread, rather than unusual (i.e. magnet schools). For example, packaging academic content around, say, a sports theme or arts theme would greatly improve the engagement of *some* children. Because specialized packaging would improve the engagement of some children but do the opposite for others, you can't assign children to such schools. Specialized schools often, perhaps mostly, have to be chosen by parents, or administrators (magnet schools) must decide who to enroll (who is the best fit). Subsidy funding policy that does not favor public school users would foster specialized schools of choice offered by entrepreneurs as alternatives to TPS and public magnet schools. Thematically or pedagogically specialized schools attract teachers with a strength, likely including passion, related to each school's professed mission, while also attracting students for whom those teachers' greatest abilities would be of greatest value.

And finally, an emerging heroic assumption (**G**) that the newly recognized need for "customization"—no doubt uniformly delivered—"is to be achieved by [further] centralization,"[37] for example, despite Common Core standards that many reformers advocate. Centralizing oversight and standards, despite a disconnect between mandated and actual outcomes that Jay Greene points out will drive assessment, which will make curriculum and textbook content more uniform.

Those heroic assumptions, and others that are less prominent, amount to a still evolving-from-the-political-process, dysfunctional business plan. It is a multicenter (Washington, DC; state capital; and school district central office), central plan that condenses to: Sort children, only by age, into classrooms with teachers told what to teach (politically correct books and curricula) and how (micromanaged), and not paid more when they are more effective. Sort children, only by neighborhood, into price-less, centrally planned schools with a monopoly on public funding, aiming, by political necessity, to have every schooling option available to anyone available to everyone. Does it seem like a schooling strategy that can produce better than Nation at Risk results?

Possible School System Transformation Catalysts

Ted Kolderie's (2014) mostly outstanding *The Split-Screen Strategy* dismisses school system transformation as politically infeasible because of its complexity. Ravitch (2010), Tyack and Cuban

(1995), and others make the same point. But school system transformation does not require what they assume, namely the rewriting of the schooling industry central plan (chapter 7 discusses central plan optimization), and such a rewrite likely has a low upside. Appropriate transformation can probably proceed without much public school system rule change. Nobel laureate Friedrich von Hayek called for transformational "gardening" (change the underlying conditions), carefully differentiating it from the "engineering" approaches assumed by Cuban, Paul Hill, David Osborne, Ted Kolderie, John Merrow, Ravitch, Tyack, and others.

Ending the Public School System Monopoly on Public Funding

Indeed, because of the likely impossibility of delivering transformational change through an overhaul of the school system central plan, the likely catalyst for school system transformation—publicly provided and privately provided schooling options—is an opening of the system to new schooling options, public (some CPS) and private. Eliminating the public school system's monopoly on public funding is the first step toward a financially level playing field between TPS, CPS,[38] and private alternatives vetted by the decentralized planning process driven by price change.

There is also the futility issue. Some central plans are better than others, but none are very good ways to dynamically address the "What will be produced, how, where, when, and for whom"—questions all industries and every economy must address. So, because the current, supposed one best system (Tyack 1974) yields a poor fit for a lot of children, a more open system would cause some replacement of existing public schools and/or public schools that would otherwise be built. That yields growth in the independent school market share so that the rest of the system does well what the public school system does especially badly. It may turn out that new private schools can do better what TPS do best. If so, independent schools will gradually displace the vast majority of TPS. My crystal ball is not clear on which of those—partial or total TPS replacement—is the more likely long-run outcome of much-reduced barriers to new, independent schools, for-profit or non-profit, private or semi-public through chartered public schools (CPS).

What we know from the US experience with school choice programs is that even in the larger programs (Milwaukee and Edgewood), the change in the public-private enrollment share is gradual. A lot of families love their assigned TPS, and for many of them, not even an arguably better way of delivering well-known instructional approaches would quickly overcome the inertia of long-standing ways of doing things. A close, free TPS is very attractive to some families just for that. It can provide an okay fit for mainstream kids and likely work even better for those children after the students for whom the mainstream-focused approaches are a bad fit have gone elsewhere. That, for example, is what happened in Edgewood. Privately funded tuition vouchers did not yield a competitive response from the Edgewood public schools. But the exit of the Edgewood TPS outliers (poorest fits) improved the test scores of the students that stayed in their assigned TPS.

So, what exactly is a much more open school system? In the current US environment, it is very difficult to start or sustain a private school. Private school operators must persuade parents to pay tuition when generously financed, zero-tuition public schools are available. It is very difficult to sell something with a free substitute. So, as noted above, it will take elimination of the public school monopoly on public funding to truly open the school system to private alternatives to public schools. The opening is meaningful to the extent that the private alternatives are truly independent, not forced by regulation to deliver instruction just like, or nearly like, the traditional public school. Public funding for independent school users can come in the form of direct payment (for legal reasons, not in the US, but elsewhere), education savings accounts, tuition tax credits, or tuition vouchers. The difference between the per-pupil public funding of TPS users and independent school users, and limits on public-private shared financing, determines the degree of opening.

Limited to tinkering with the current system, we have often made things even worse. Nationally, the USA is no less at risk than when the original Nation at Risk report (1983) triggered a reform frenzy that still left the roots of the problem intact. The US result of that frenzy, so far, is fifty-one more costly, still persistently low-performing school systems. Per-pupil funding of schooling hasn't mattered much,[39] by itself a powerful symptom of systemic dysfunction. In a high-performing system, funding would matter.

I'm hopeful that COVID19-triggered increased interest in school system reform,[40] especially West Virginia's universal Hope Scholarship, or the 2017 Arizona legislation upgrading its ESA to universal will yield empirical evidence for a productively transformational approach. But even if empirical analysis gradually demonstrates that I'm right, there are other ways to drive productive school system change. We can explore those while we wait until new laws yield enough evidence (or fails to)[41] to become the ignition point of the Milton Friedman wildfire; the rapid spread of a policy after it yields noteworthy academic gains or other benefits such as economic growth through migration to states or metro areas that significantly enhance private school choice.

More Open—Plan B

Another promising approach, where universal access to private school choice is not yet politically feasible, is private school choice targeted to low-income **places** within metro areas.[42] Limiting eligibility to **all** residents of low-income places, rather than to just low-income people (traditional means-testing) can create some local markets large enough to drive the entrepreneurial initiative we need to develop dynamic menus of schooling options as diverse as the learning styles and engagement factors of our schoolchildren. The reason for the possibly greater political feasibility of this approach is that it has the potential to stem middle-upper income flight from inner cities. Maybe it can even slightly reverse the flow, while still focusing on places with high concentrations of poverty and avoiding opposition from suburban and rural voters that believe that private school choice will undermine what they too often believe are high-quality assigned TPS.

Transformation Must Improve Equity Outlook

Later discussion will include detailed explanations, but it is well worth noting here in this early chapter that the perceived success of any market-mechanism-based approach to school system transformation (such as West Virginia's or Arizona's ESA) will depend heavily on whether donor initiative significantly lessens the disadvantages of lower-income families in school systems where the choices no longer—as is the current US reality—have either identical zero tuition or price tags that are prohibitive for most families. I said donor initiative, not generosity, because it is foolish to anchor expectations for progress on finding a lot more money for something. Also, practically speaking, perceived equity will depend much more on whether donors effectively re-allocate existing education-related charity than on any increase in their spending on education they are willing to muster. Any market-mechanism-based approach to school system transformation needs donor-funded subsidies for low-income family consumers of non-TPS schooling. Much current philanthropic support for low-income family access to TPS alternatives is indirect because much of the immediate problem is having not nearly enough CPS seats available, not affordability (CPS charge no tuition). At least the philanthropic funds now being given directly to schooling providers should be re-allocated to tuition co-payment subsidies for low-income families; that is, to finance some of the difference between government per-pupil funding and market-determined, higher tuition levels of *some* private schools and *some* price-decontrolled CPS (see below).

A Short Route to Productive Transformation, But Maybe Impassable

Chartered public schools (CPS) face daunting start-up and expansion barriers such as the donor dependence described earlier, rare or inadequate facilities funding, barriers to use of surplus TPS campuses, and lower per-pupil operating funding than TPS. Furthermore, CPS struggle to legally practice the school mission-based selectivity that would greatly improve CPS ability to specialize (~1/2 of CPS, nationally). A major cost uncertainty arises from CPS legal obligation to at least indirectly serve special-needs applicants. The zero-tuition price control limits CPS instruction to approaches that are comfortably cheaper than the publicly funded per-pupil payment, and to quantities of more expensive instructional approaches based on availability of long-term philanthropic support. Even where deep-pocket donors such as the Walton Family Fund (Wal-Mart) are willing to make long-term commitments to CPS operators, the space made available through that donor support is predictably, typically far below the amount sought by applicants. Given state government fiscal constraints and the co-pay ban, school expansion to meet existing unmet demand, much less likely demand growth, can be met only through increased donor support.

Price decontrol—allowing CPS to charge a market-based tuition co-payment—is a reform that addresses those issues. That one well-defined step would yield productive transformation. Price decontrol would end the persistent shortages and curb the debilitating, corrupting side effects (including especially often scandalous quality erosion) of frustrated customers in waiting. But so far, zero tuition **only** for schools getting public funds is so politically correct and entrenched that there is not even discussion of creative price decontrol.

"Only" is the essence of the problem. Setting the public funding level so that competition will yield many nearly free alternatives to TPS does not compromise the benefits of price decontrol. But demanding that every option charge no tuition creates major problems. Price decontrol would eliminate shortages/wait lists, end CPS donor dependence, and creatively deal with equity concerns (see chapter 9). ***Without price decontrol, especially in states that allow profit-seeking, the charter movement, while just barely short of the much-needed transformational catalyst, is a serious threat to the political feasibility of choice-based school system reform.***

Supply limits may be the most obvious drawback of donor dependence, but not necessarily the worst drawback. Public or private subsidy of service producers always creates risks that are readily avoided, usually by following Milton Friedman's advice to subsidize rarely and then only subsidize consumers of subsidy-worthy services. Never subsidize specific service providers. The problematic nature of zero-tuition-*only*—its contribution to the presence and persistence of low-performing systems—and pros and cons of creative alternatives will receive much more attention throughout this book.

Having made a case for transformational school system change and some key drivers of productive transformational change (increased openness to new privately conceived schools and/or charter law reform that includes price decontrol and mission-based specialization), the next chapter explains how inattention to genuine school system reform has left in place many systemic factors that undermine classroom effectiveness, the roots of the persistent low-performance problem.

---

[1] https://objectivepolicyassessment.org/K-12/pricesystemexample.pdf

[2] Standard & Poor's. 2005. "Standard & Poor's Separates Fact from Fiction in Analysis of Urban School Districts." New York: SchoolsMatter.com, May 26, 2005.

[3] Tyack, David. 1974. *The One Best System: A History of American Urban Education*. Cambridge, MA: Harvard University Press.

[4] The latest report issued by the Program for International Student Assessment ranks US 15-year-olds 14th in the world in reading skills, 17th in science, and 25th in math.

[5] http://qz.com/153380/korea-is-the-worlds-top-producer-of-unhappy-school-children/#153380/korea-is-the-worlds-top-producer-of-unhappy-school-children/

[6] Hanushek measured the benefit of catching up: roughly $1 trillion per year, nothing to sneeze at. But it doesn't change my point that we can and must (explained shortly) do much more than catch up to a low ceiling.

[7] http://www.schoolsystemreformstudies.net/wp-content/uploads/2016/10/Nation-at-Risk-Declarations.pdf, see also Hersh, Richard H. 2009. "Our 21st Century Risk," *Education Week* 4/22/09, p 28–29

[8] That figure is for the public school system. Adding private school users' expenditures to the numerator and private school users to the denominator would not change it much.

[9] "Education in the Republic of Korea: National Treasure or National Headache" http://www.edweek.org/go/qc12

[10] An example: see the pending 792-page Every Child Achieves Act that aims to revise the spelling out of the federal government's secondary role in school system policy. States have the primary role that they have partially delegated to the local level through

public school districts. http://townhall.com/columnists/janerobbins/2015/06/30/alexander-murray-bill-tightens-the-screws-of-mandated-assessments-n2018919

[11] Example: Bednar, Christian M. 2009. "Education as Ritual." *Education Week* 4/8/09; p 24.

[12] See Chapter 9 of *School Choice Myths* (2020)

[13] Reisman, George. 1998. Capitalism. (Ottawa, IL: Jameson Books; p 221). I substituted "education" for "economic" in Reisman's original.

[14] Reisman (1998, 239), see note #14.

[15] https://en.wikipedia.org/wiki/Mechanism_design

[16] Hubbard, Glenn, and Tim Kane. *Balance.* New York: Simon and Schuster, 2013

[17] Koch, Charles. 2007. *The Science of Success.* Hoboken, NJ: John Wiley and Sons.

[18] See Hubbard, Glenn, and Tim Kane. Balance. NY: Simon and Schuster, 2013, especially the Rome chapter. Also, see Baumol et al.'s *Good Capitalism, Bad Capitalism* (2009).

[19] http://www.edweek.org/ew/articles/2016/03/09/education-is-absent-from-the-2016-presidential.html?qs=Amusing+Ourselves+to+Death

[20] https://www.wsj.com/articles/as-education-declines-so-does-civic-culture-1379373249

[21] Kirkpatrick, David W. 2006. "School Criticism: Older than the System." *School Report* 695, 3/9/06.

[22] See, for example, the discussion of the rise and fall (sometimes more than once) of Rome, China, Spain, the Ottoman Empire, Japan, Britain, Europa, and California in Hubbard and Kane's (2013) *Balance: The Economics of Great Powers from Ancient Rome to Modern America.*

[23] Chapter 3 has my diagnosis of the low-performance problem at the public and private school classroom level.

[24] http://edexcellence.net/articles/why-has-education-policy-produced-such-little-improvement

[25] http://www.edweek.org/ew/articles/2013/02/20/21kimmelman_ep.h32.html

[26] https://objectivepolicyassessment.org/K-12/pricesystemexample.pdf

[27] https://mises.org/library/forty-centuries-wage-and-price-controls-how-not-fight-inflation

[28] Dale Ballou and Michael Podgursky. 1997. Teacher Pay and Teacher Quality. Kalamazoo, MI: The Upjohn Institute. p. 55: The single salary "schedule is essentially a grid specifying salary as a function of experience and education (degrees or credits). All teachers employed in a district, regardless of grade level or subject matter, are paid on this basis, hence the term, 'single salary schedule'."

[29] Ronald Wolk in *EdWeek*: https://www.edweek.org/ew/articles/2012/12/05/13wolk_ep.h32.html

[30] As noted in more detail later, teacher experience is valuable early in a typical teacher's career, but not so much later.

[31] It may be most CPS, but there are no data to confirm that.

32 DiLorenzo, Thomas J. 2005. "The Price Control Calamity." *The Free Market* 23:12, p 1–3; Hirsch, Julius. 1943. *Price Control in the War Economy* (New York: Harper). Murphy, Michael M. 1980. "Price Controls and the Behavior of the Firm." International Economic Review 21:2, pp 285–291; Rockoff (2008—see below), Rockoff (1984), Note #52; Ross, Ernest G. 1983. "The Price of Education." *The Freeman* 33:2. http://www.libertyhaven.com/politicsandcurrentevents/education-homeschoolingorchildren/priceeducation.shtml; Rothbard (1993), see note #1; Shuettinger, R. L. and E. F. Butler. 1979. *Forty centuries of wage and price controls* (Thornwood, NY: Caroline House Publishers, Inc.); and Sowell, Thomas. 2004. *Basic Economics: A Citizens Guide to the Economy* (NY: Basic Books).

33 Google: "charter schools, scandals" yielded over 900,000 hits (2/16/18), including a website dedicated to documenting them (charterschoolscandals.blogspot.com) but not rigorously explaining them, just there to tarnish the charter and school choice concepts.

34 Forty-four states, plus DC, have a charter law, but many of those in name only. So, there is plenty of room for charter law spread and reform, even without adding price decontrol to the reform list. Currently, all 45 charter laws are price-less: https://www.edreform.com/wp-content/uploads/2018/03/CER_National-Charter-School-Law-Rankings-and-Scorecard-2018_screen_3-21-18.pdf

35 Powell, A.G., E. Farrar, and D. Cohen. 1985. *The Shopping Mall High School.* Boston: Houghton-Mifflin.

36 All but the most severe special needs children are thrust into regular classrooms, "mainstreamed."

37 Petersen, Paul E. 2011. *Savings Schools.* Cambridge, MA: Harvard University Press, p 18.

38 In most of the forty-four states that allow CPS, some TPS-CPS leveling is also needed to create a more open system.

39 "Pouring more money into our K-12 schools won't help our students" is a central theme of Eric Hanushek and Alfred Lindseth. 2009. *Schoolhouses, Courthouses, and Statehouses.* Princeton, NJ: Princeton University Press.

40 Stalled by a court finding that the ESAs need a different funding source.

41 Changes in Phoenix, Tucson, and the Las Vegas area may be sufficient to demonstrate noteworthy positive effects. But states with more people, especially more and larger urban areas have greater potential to foster the specialization and competition that will maximize school system improvement (discussed in more detail in chapter 14).

42 Danielsen, Bartley. 2017. "CPR Scholarships: Using Private School Choice to Attack Concentrated Poverty, Crime and Unemployment." American Enterprise Institute.

CHAPTER THREE

Roots of Low-Performance Persistence

A lot of very complex things are very simple if you think things through.

—Ronald Reagan

Chapter 1 asserted that we need a new system much different from any existing system. We can learn a lot—and must—by comparing the world's school systems, but we should not copy an existing system. Chapter 2 made the case for transformational school system change. This chapter describes what I believe are the classroom dysfunction roots of the persistent overall low performance in US public school system and private school classrooms. Later chapters will describe the key political challenges and how to address the most pressing research issues.

The Roots of a Public School System Persistent Low-Performance Norm

Although it is intuitive to believe that the best at anything is great, we have many good reasons to expect low performance from top-performing global and US school systems, locally and statewide.

Despite a widespread consensus that centrally planned industries and economic systems will be awful, a lot of people around the world still believe that the decentralized planning through markets alternatives amounts to chaos driven by greed—that the decentralized planning process of free enterprise and consumer choice orchestrated by market-driven price change should not orchestrate schooling for children. Inertia plus that distrust of markets has kept K-12 extensively government-run and funded, with schooling for children mostly produced through government-owned schools and typically regulated extensively and intensively worldwide.

A more sophisticated (but largely wrong) basis for preferring centralized to decentralized planning of school systems is the alleged pervasiveness of "market failure," an unfortunate term because failure to achieve economic efficiency is very much a matter of degree. Equity concerns argue only for a large public funding role, but not for government-run schools or extensive regulation of non-public schools. The assertion that a fatal flaw arises from market failures in the production of schooling arises mostly from an overreaction to the correct beliefs that delivering proper instruction to children yields some positive spillovers to the rest of society and that market-driven schooling might suffer some information availability challenges.

Failure to achieve maximum efficiency occurs throughout the economy, in different forms for market vs. political control. **When** some degree of market failure exists, the issue is whether such failure will yield better/worse outcomes than ubiquitous political failure (i.e., central-planning failure, coalition building, special interest influence) to achieve maximum efficiency. Interventions such as contract enforcement are essential, and subsidies for buyers, information provision, and research can complement decentralized planning approaches. And since there are no known modern extensively market-driven school systems, we cannot be certain that market-driven systems would not produce even worse outcomes than the centrally planned systems we now have. But evidence from past market-driven school systems (Coulson 1999, West 1994) and evidence from other industries indicates that central planning at its best will very likely produce much worse school system outcomes than imperfect but genuine predominantly market-driven outcomes. That should be enough to at least warrant widespread experimentation with genuine, extensively market-driven determinations of what will be taught, how, where, and to whom.

Also, alongside some confusion and legitimate controversy about likely sources and degrees of market failure, some folks probably reject broad-brush condemnation of central planning because of the big political differences between the oppressive poster-child central planning regimes of Soviet Russia, Red China, Cuba, and North Korea and the election-driven political systems of the PISA test nations. But more open political systems and the opportunity to peacefully change the central planners' bosses through elections does not much improve the efficiency of the central planning process, whose major shortcomings arise mostly from huge inherent information and incentive problems. For example, the central planning process motivates producer understatement of what they have the capability to do, and it fails to punish ineffectiveness.

The ultimately futile struggle against the overwhelming incentive and information challenges of a political, price-less process for deciding which instructional approaches to produce how, where, and for whom is evident in studies such as *Why Johnny Can't Read*, the Coleman Report (1966), in books such as Diane Ravitch's *Left Back*, and in the five authoritative Nation at Risk declarations despite the frenzied efforts[1] that followed the original 1983 Nation at Risk[2] declaration. Because those efforts did not produce noteworthy, large-scale academic gains, they must have failed to address the roots of the problem. The latest edition of the Nation's Report Card (National Assessment of Education Progress) shows that ***despite tripling inflation-adjusted per pupil spending over the last fifty years, test scores have barely budged***, and still only 38 percent of seventeen-year-olds are proficient in reading, with 27 percent lacking even basic skills.

So, the likely core reasons for insufficient student engagement in high-value academics survived the frenzied activity after the original 1983 Nation at Risk declaration. Again, I say "likely" because common sense supported by established theory is only enough for a credible hypothesis that things would be much different and better with a decentralized planning approach. Empirical confirmation is mostly missing and will be until there is a basis for comparison to a market-driven system, or a well-constructed experiment that lacks the alleged reasons for persistent low performance. The reasons may be hard to test empirically, but they are not that hard to grasp. They've all been noted in a piecemeal fashion, some widely noted.

1. Weak, often poorly targeted incentives, including difficulty defining and rewarding merit; much talk of accountability; little actual, meaningful accountability
2. Low levels of parental involvement arising in part from powerlessness to influence many of the things that could help their children
3. Classroom composition policy that maximizes learning issue diversity, minimizes engagement, makes the public school teaching task as difficult as it can be made without increasing that difficulty as a formal goal. That makes one size fit all especially badly, probably worst for the least advantaged students.
4. High rates of out-of-subject-field teaching, for example, coaches "teaching" math
5. Frustration with persistent low performance led to educator micromanagement
6. Teacher tenure, combined with high rates of teacher burnout
7. Misleading, boring, politically correct curricula and textbooks
8. Difficulty maintaining discipline; regulation and lawsuit fear
9. Compliance-driven behavior.

They've remained intact because we've lacked leaders with the wisdom and will to propose and successfully fight for the systemic change needed to greatly improve our educators' effectiveness. As noted in chapter 1, the focus was on change that left the fundamentals of the system intact. Now, for a closer look at each of the points listed above:

(1) Eric Hanushek and Ludger Woessman (2008) argue that "the largest problem in current school policy is the lack of incentives for improved student performance." Except in private schools and some chartered public schools (CPS), US teachers see few, if any, tangible consequences for effectiveness or ineffectiveness, even for widespread burnout (Dworkin 1987 and 2003,[3] see number 6 below). Reward for individual educator merit, or punishment for lack thereof, is rare, though effective. Genuine individual merit-based pay raises are rare because rewarding individual merit is widely politically incorrect. What is rewarded in many of the rare instances of something called merit pay may not result from a very robust definition of individual merit. Even the intangibles are often misaligned. For example, it is common for educators to face negative peer pressure for entrepreneurial and innovative initiatives.

The widespread disconnect between pay and performance results from more than the political challenges of implementing genuine merit pay. It includes the challenges of top-down-only merit assessment, unprofessional circumstances, and the difficulty financing merit in the public sector. In the public school system, school merit does not readily yield new revenue for the best schools. The system puts teachers in tough circumstances (see number 3 below) and then micromanages them (see number 5 below), so it is difficult to reasonably hold teachers accountable for poor results. Merit measurement by observation, and a test score basis is misleading, incomplete, and fraught with perverse incentives that have narrowed the curriculum to specific tested items and test-taking skills. Despite the widespread failure to impose sanctions for low performance, some educators responded to assertive exhortations to improve test scores by correcting student mistakes with hints or by correcting answers on the answer sheets.[4] The fraction caught, so far, may be quite small.

Teacher merit assessments lack the choice and client consent that pervades merit assessment by businesses. In businesses, choice and client consent links merit and revenue. Because of the measurement and financing challenges, Milton Friedman doubted whether public sector merit pay policies could reliably identify and finance genuine employee merit. And so we see that in TPS, those factors and the difficult circumstances of TPS teachers combine to make merit pay rare and ineffective. The current system's rare efforts to assess and reward individual merit yield statistically significant student gains of about 1 to 2 percentage points.

(2) Insufficient readily accessible information about genuine academic progress and potential for greater progress and parents' inability to influence many of the things that concern them curb parental involvement. Children are widely passed through the system regardless of their actual academic progress. Lacking well-established grounds for comparison, misinformed and underinformed parents and disengaged children may not quickly recognize the effects of poor choices or the absence of choices, failure to pay attention, and circumstances that were not working for them.

(3) The nature of primary accountability to political authority means that the appearance of fairness and political correctness will be paramount, and it means reliance on inherently incomplete, objective, top-down accountability measures, or none at all.[5] So, for example, it seems to make political sense to offer the same schooling package to everyone. According to Anthony Roselli (2005),[6] the political process can cause school systems to forget and abandon sound ideas, which seems like a particularly damning indictment of democratic (political) control in practice.

The political process created attendance zones to assure every child a slot in a neighborhood public school and to assure a substantial enrollment for every traditional public school (TPS). As it became increasingly apparent that one size did not fit all children, the assigned campuses became larger—despite considerable evidence that schools were mostly too big—so that TPS could be "comprehensive";[7] that is, contain enough instructional diversity to appear to accommodate nearly every politically recognized, noteworthy difference in schoolchildren. Typically, only the most severe special needs children are sent to specialized campuses or even sent to separate classrooms.

So, despite widespread agreement that TPS are often too big, the political consensus has still been to strive for uniformly comprehensive TPS, or "comprehensive uniformity" (Brown 1992). But we've learned that uniformly comprehensive schooling under-addresses student diversity and that it creates new problems on the large, shopping mall-like, comprehensive mega-campuses (Powell et al. 1985), huge problems such as student alienation, complex management issues, parental struggle to monitor their child's choices and progress, and outright fraud (Segal 2004) abetted by the complexity of such huge, multifaceted schools.

In large part, because school system authorities had mistakenly assumed that overall student ability is one-dimensional, formal tracking by demonstrated student ability became increasingly politically incorrect. That, and increased school size, led to sorting children by age into grades, an objective, non-stigmatizing, non-judgmental rough indicator of average ability. That greatly increased the how-students-learn diversity and engagement factor diversity of TPS classrooms.

One-dimensional formal tracking is not just stigmatizing; it is foolish and inefficient. So is the total rejection of sorting by ability. As noted earlier, humans typically have strengths and weaknesses. Ability is mostly not one-dimensional. That means there's a non-deterministic and mostly non-stigmatizing approach to the ability sorting needed to greatly increase teacher effectiveness. It is fluid sorting by ability, *by subject*, something that used to be even more common, if not widespread, depending upon how it was defined.

A typical modern TPS classroom draws a ~22–30 student same-age random sample from the school's attendance zone. Because the ability diversity, how-students-learn diversity, and subject-interest diversity of such a random sample creates a huge "differentiated instruction" challenge, teachers sometimes attempt sorting by ability within their classrooms with different, changing groups for each subject. Even though it works, such ability grouping by subject is no longer common. It suffers some of the stigma of one-dimensional tracking, and with the TPS classroom starting point, sorting by ability can significantly increase teachers' workload. It can yield multiple sets of lesson plans and student assessments, and it requires possession *and use* of differentiated instruction skills that are quite rare, especially when expected alongside the US school systems' widespread out-of-field teaching. Sadly, alongside the rising importance of differentiated instruction talent, teacher aptitude has fallen (Hoxby and Leigh

2004). The system has made the job more difficult, while retaining fewer high-ability teachers.

Stanford emeritus professor Larry Cuban urges the schools of the current US systems to address student diversity—so, the nonexistence of near-universal best practices[8]—by including "traditional and progressive ways of teaching and learning. Smart teachers and principals have carefully constructed hybrid classrooms and schools that reflect the diversities of children." But it is difficult for every school, much less every classroom, to have everything for everyone. Despite that difficulty, many educators believe it must be attempted, perhaps out of resignation that we need to do the best we can within the political-correctness constraints of the current system. Multidimensional sorting between classrooms and/or between specialized schools would avoid the workload expansion, most of the potential for stigma, and the greater differentiated instruction struggle that exists when sorting by ability, by subject occurs, or doesn't, within an assigned TPS classroom group.

The unintended but devastating result of sorting children only by age and attendance zone is TPS classroom composition that makes teaching as tough as unintentionally possible. Teachers are being saddled with absurdly high expectations.[9] "What is unworkable and undesirable are…the daunting challenges that face teachers who must deal with non-engaged, non-responsive, and often rebellious students." Indeed, the pursuit of political correctness inherent in state ownership "systematically undermines the authority of the teacher in the classroom."[10]

"Non-engaged" in the system's attempt at one size fits all yields "nonresponsive" and contributes to "rebellious." In our system, "the greatest challenge facing America's [traditional public] schools is the enormous variation in the academic level of students coming into any given classroom" (Petrilli 2011), a problem former US education secretary Arne Duncan says is getting worse. The student population is considerably more diverse than in the past.

Even with growing student diversity, it's an avoidable challenge created by the current system. Indeed, we do not have a "system of schools that allows dedicated educators to [typically] be successful"

(Merrow 2017, xiv). Sorting children just by age and where they live maximizes learning-style diversity and diversity in students' subject theme interests. For example, consider the possibilities with, say, a high-quality science or sports (not athletics) subject theme, and a key critical limitation of such subject theme-based approaches. Specialization by well-crafted subject themes would likely achieve much-increased engagement of some children, but total tune-out of others, perhaps the vast majority. Such specialized schools cannot have attendance zones, which is why we only have them rarely, as magnet schools; not widely available, centrally planned, and there is virtually no room for entrepreneurial entry. To achieve the appropriate sorting among specialized schooling options, enrollment must be by choice or by a very information-intensive, enlightened administrative sorting algorithm.

On the learning style side, some children learn more in front of a computer loaded with great instructional software. Others do better in a traditional face-to-face classroom setting. For others, a high-tech and low-tech mix is best. The public school system achieves very little of the much-needed sorting of children or educators by learning style or subject theme interest. And the public school system's monopoly on public funding severely limits the availability of private sector options for families willing to find the money for private school tuition; that is, to pay for schooling twice.

Insufficient, well-conceived sorting multiplies student-teacher mismatch problems. When the children in a TPS classroom have only their approximate age and neighborhood in common, you need a superhero-level teacher/communicator to avoid getting lots of overwhelmed, distracted, and bored students. Indeed, "boredom plagues many highly capable students who are forced to follow the curriculum for their age-peers," or in cooperative learning settings where the high-ability students for a given subject are held back by having to help lower-performing peers rather than receiving instruction that would accelerate their own progress. ***Not leaving behind the least able is a moral imperative. Achieving the potential of the most capable is a survival imperative.***

Incredibly, there seem to be some teachers that can achieve high levels of engagement from a very diverse set of children, but so far, that ability has not been teachable. Efforts to improve teacher training have not greatly improved teaching effectiveness in the typical TPS classroom setting that includes overwhelming learning issue diversity challenges even within the mainstream population. The federal Individuals with Disabilities Education Act further raised that challenge by forcing the mainstreaming of special needs children. It is very difficult to address diverse needs with a uniform product. Education reform scholar Dr. Herbert Walberg makes this salient point:

> Compared with privately provided goods and services, perhaps the most fundamental market problem with publicly funded schools is to provide a uniform education that is satisfying to all families. How difficult would it be for automobile manufacturers, restaurants, hairdressers, and barbers to satisfy the majority, let alone all, of their clients with a single, uniform product or service?

The resulting difficulty feeling successful and maintaining good relations with parents and administrators is a key reason why many teachers quickly abandon teaching careers and why many teachers burn out but stay on the job through tenure and union protections (insufficient pressure to improve or exit) and for lack of viable income-yielding alternatives.

That overwhelming challenge—the diversity of learning challenges that arises from sorting children into complex, uniformly comprehensive TPS by attendance zone—partly explains why school district superintendents struggle to dent districts' abysmal performance and why they suffer high turnover rates, especially in large urban districts. They struggle because they inherit a dysfunctional business plan—the public school system—and because they serve at the pleasure of often poorly trained, weakly accountable school boards. Longtime education scholar Paul Hill noted that "many superintendents have concluded that, in the words of one, the job is undoable. Most agree that a successful superintendent now is usually one who has avoided a financial crisis or survived a tense labor negotiation, not one who has transformed a district's schools." Note that implied in the Professor Hill quote is that the typical district desperately needs transformation. The high turnover rate of urban superintendents is likely an average of the very short stays by superintendents that attempt transformation and the copers that avoid seriously rocking the boat.

Trying to make politically correct schooling fit all also takes its toll on public school principals that also "just" cope or risk pursuing transformation. Robert Evans, who works with current and former principals around the world, argued in a brutal critique of the public school principalship that "to attract, retain, and support the best and brightest principals, we need to focus on making their jobs more doable." Like Hill's comment about superintendents, Evans' preference for principals that are transformers demonstrates that transformation is typically needed.

(4) A key information and incentive problem noted in the previous chapters is the absence of market-generated price change to inform educator and parent/student decision-making and to create strong incentives to appropriately take account of cost differences. For example, price control effects are painfully evident in the single salary schedule that applies to the vast majority of US teachers and many more throughout the world. In nearly every jurisdiction, teacher pay reflects only formal credentials and years of classroom experience. Jacob Vigdor's plea that we "scrap the sacrosanct salary schedule" did not even include the policy's failure to take account of differences in the market value of different subject field competencies. One of Vigdor's key points is that experience, typically rewarded by contracts at a constant rate, doesn't increase teacher effectiveness much after the first few years.

The alleged rationale of a single schedule is that math and history teachers, for example, are doing the same work with the same children, so it would be unfair to pay one more than the other. But is it fair to not compensate math and science teachers for foregoing lucrative alternatives to teaching? And to avoid shortages, surpluses, and out-of-field teaching, it is more efficient to vary pay by subject field expertise and effectiveness in the system's teaching conditions. It is unfair to schoolchildren and teachers alike to have, for example, history and English majors teaching math and science. When such misallocated teachers are great in their fields, the out-of-field teaching yields a double whammy, making educators do something they are not good at. The single salary schedule deliberately ignores effectiveness, except increased effectiveness assumed to arise from graduate degrees and increased job experience. The same single salary also creates shortages of teachers in some of the least desirable places. Without a financial incentive to endure less desirable places, experienced teachers transfer out as quickly as they can.

Out-of-field teaching is not rare.[11] The math instructors of 69 percent of fifth to eighth graders lack a mathematics degree or certificate, and 93 percent of those same students are being taught physical sciences by teachers with no physical science degree or certificate. With so many math and science courses staffed by coaches, English and history (etc.) teachers, it's no wonder that so few American children become engaged in math and science courses, and then it's also obvious why the US government, universities, and American businesses must hire so many of their scientists and engineers from outside our US-schooled population?

(5) Partly compounding the lack of appropriate strong incentives to relentlessly improve performance and partly as an attempt to offset the current school system's weak incentives, our current system allows little teacher autonomy. There is extensive teacher micromanagement to force the teacher behavior seen as appropriate in the unnecessarily challenging, diverse settings of typical public school classrooms. Widespread micromanagement may include highly scripted curricula often insultingly characterized as "teacher-proof." The term arises from efforts by learning-material producers to get districts to adopt materials that will allegedly work regardless of teacher talent deficiencies (out of field is a price-control-created deficiency) and thus avoid training costs.

(6) The weak tangible incentives and burnout described above **_plus teacher tenure_** are, by themselves, a predictable recipe for the persistent Nation at Risk low performance seen in the US, and nearly so, more or less, throughout the world. Yes, we put public school teachers in very challenging circumstances (unnecessarily challenging) and provide no tangible reward for succeeding against the odds, or penalty for being less effective, even by reasonable standards that could exist for those demanding circumstances. For many teachers, there are few, if any, well-paying alternate uses of their teacher training, so even if they have become one of the many burnout victims (Dworkin 1987, 2003), they may lean on the tenure promise of lifetime employment and decide to keep their teaching positions.

(7) All of that exists alongside boring, politically correct textbooks and curricula sanitized of informative, exciting controversy.[12] American poet John Saxe asserted (widely misattributed to German statesman Otto von Bismarck[13]) a more arcane version of "The making of laws, like the making of sausages, is not a pretty sight." The same thing is true for textbook selection;[14] you wouldn't respect the outcome if you saw the process in action. And unlike many laws and some sausages, the textbook outcome is as ugly as the selection process. Bernard Fryshman, a physics professor and periodic *Education Week* contributor, believes the "traditional high school curriculum… has little relevance to anyone."

Diane Ravitch's *Language Police* (2003), Peter McAllister's "A Teacher's Perspective on What's Wrong with our Schools" (2018), and many others describe the devastating consequences of politically correct curricula. McAllister argues that the widespread result of political correctness in curricula is students that (a) substitute memorization for comprehension; (b) rarely rely on their own informed judgment, relying on emotional reactions or uncritically adopting the opinions of others; and (c) recognize few, if any, moral or ethical absolutes. As a result, "we have produced students who do not think, who do not question, and who do not care about what is right or wrong."

(8) Each of the above need further thought and empirical modeling. The same thing is true of the politicization of student disciplinary policies, something entirely predictable once you need a policy appropriate for everyone assigned to a school, for students compelled to attend. The Thomas P. Fordham Institute notes that 85 percent of teachers and 73 percent of parents felt (2004 poll) the school experience of most students suffers at the expense of a few chronic offenders. And, "more than 1/3 of teachers in 2012 reported that student behavior problems and tardiness interfered with their teaching."[15] That was *before* the recent push to reduce suspensions. A February 2018 high-level discussion of school discipline policies found its way to the central cause: How do we move past deep disagreements on policy to find common ground? Deep disagreement arises from the difference between imposing public policies through a political process and creating school policies that families can buy into or not. Another significant aspect of the appearance of discipline problems, as opposed to how such problems are dealt with, is that forcing children into schools because opting out of the assigned school is too costly creates disengagement because of content/ability/interest mismatches that the presence of choice may avoid. Mismatch-induced boredom/disengagement leads to absence or misbehavior that prevents the engagement of others.

What is agreed to, including what is left out, can be devastating. The following mind-boggling example also yields some insight into how political control makes it harder to be an effective educator. The Obama administration's DOE Office of Civil Rights (OCR) was so certain that "disparate impact" signaled discrimination[16] and was so determined to purge it—intelligent, educated people thought this was wise policy—that they said unlawful discrimination existed even when "a policy is neutral on its face—meaning that the policy itself does not mention race—and is administered in an evenhanded manner but has an alleged disparate impact (i.e., a disproportionate effect on specific student categories)." To avoid a citation, school administrators must go beyond the already difficult job of maintaining discipline and pursuing justice and make sure the numbers come out so that it doesn't look bad (more on federal intervention in chapter 5).

This is another example of how the appearance of fairness imperative of political control can increase actual unfairness, while also causing headaches and inefficiency. Can you imagine the eye-rolling and discipline headaches that result when a school or district administrator says we can't discipline any more (blank) children or we'll be in violation of federal law? We'll be branded racists for having (blank) children overrepresented in our discipline records. The result: softer discipline policies are having a negative impact on student test scores, which empower students to distract and disrupt, which the current system's low engagement rates make more likely. The legal risks can be seen to be so significant that students threaten legal action, and educators may become unwilling to even restrain children having tantrums. In one instance, teachers and administrators stood by while a child tore up her surroundings,[17] afraid of the consequences of touching her.

Avoiding disparate impact adds to the chaos already caused by the politically correct practice of sorting children into public school classrooms only by where they live and how old they are, and then including all but the most severe special needs cases because it would be unfair to have them stigmatized by placing them in anything less than the least restrictive environment. The unfairness to the rest of the class of being slowed academically by attention to a special-needs child is not as obvious and not enshrined in law. Indeed, if anything, the opposite: "In making the mainstreaming decision, schools cannot—at least not officially—consider the well-being of the other students at the school."[18] We're not just talking about disabled children. The special-needs child inappropriately included in a regular classroom could be a high-ability child that acts out when subjected to a pedagogy and/or slow pace that utterly bores them.

The alleged wrongful overrepresentation of black students, especially boys, in special education is another great example of how making something political—need for-broad-based agreement, obsession with appearance of fairness to all—undermines academic achievement. Black students' apparent disproportionate need for special needs attention magnifies the tragic effects of assuming that disparate impact proves racism. A Brookings study found that while "black students are *more* [emphasis in the original] likely to be in special education than whites," blacks are not "*too* likely to be in special education"; indeed, it is "not likely enough." Academic research shows that racial bias is not the cause of disproportionate representation of black pupils in special ed. Higher incidence of premature birth, some environmental factors, and lower average socioeconomic status means that black students should be overrepresented. Disparate-impact concern would not only keep some students from gaining access to needed services, it would undermine the instruction of other students. Michael Petrilli (2018) gets it right, but his common sense, evidence-based discipline policy guidelines are likely politically incorrect, or else why the need to assert them?

Combine the sufficient challenges of maximized learning issue diversity with the aforementioned weak, misaligned educator incentives, politically correct curricula and textbooks, widespread poor subject mastery and out-of-field teaching, decreasing teacher control of their classrooms, and you begin to understand why objective data show some TPS to be better than others, but few are adequate, much less good for all, or even nearly all, of the children sent to them. And even for the children for whom the pedagogy is a good fit, you can argue that TPS don't offer all the high-quality properly deployed instruction you should get for over $13,000/child/year.

(9) There are so many laws and rules that educators must maintain a compliance-driven focus. Phillip Howard argues that "our institutions and their leaders are paralyzed by tangles of legal rules and diverted from doing what they or we think is right by being unfairly hauled into court." With three levels of government and union contracts creating laws and rules, it is no surprise that the Thomas B. Fordham Institute's "Red Tape or Red Herring" (Stuit and Doan, 2013) makes similar points. The political process' frequent response to problems with rules is more rules, to avoid upsetting the special interests that guard the problematic rules. Indeed, because every rule has assertive friends, President Wilson said, "if you want to make enemies, try to change something," which is why President Truman told policymakers seeking friendships to "get a dog," and longtime House of Representatives majority and minority leader Richard Gephardt correctly observed, "Politics is a substitute for violence."

The Roots of the Perceived *Private* School Low-Performance Norm

Depending upon a study's control variables, the private schools *of the current system* are deemed somewhat more effective, no more effective, or slightly less effective than the TPS *of the current system*. There are often too many control variables. A frequent bizarre comparison is current public schools vs. current private schools if private schools had the same obligations as public schools; that is, if we shackle their educators equally. Maybe a key reason for poor public school system performance is that we expect individual public schools to do too many things.

One of the things that arises under "What if we shackle them equally?" is attempts to statistically control for private schools' mission-based selective admissions. Studies that control for selective admissions tell us how much the current system's public and private schools differ if each private school had to admit everyone. Typical finding: if the private schools in our current system didn't specialize in particular subgroups of students, including special needs, they'd be no more effective, perhaps slightly less effective. Private schools are also typically smaller and more readily dismiss ineffective teachers. So, if we take away key virtues of schools of choice, even within the very limited means of the current system's typical private schools, there is no advantage. It's a circular point. Without their key advantages, private schools seem no better, maybe not as good since most private schools have lower levels of per-pupil funding. Indeed!

What should be controlled for is a discussion for another time, or perhaps left undone. Parents with the means to have choices must compare the current system's public and private schools, but policymakers and academics should probably limit formal comparisons to TPS. The intended uniformity of TPS is compatible with a one-dimensional scale such as an A–F grade. Note, however, that an A grade signifies that a TPS is among the best at what the political process compels it to attempt, but not that one size fits all. A colleague of mine that works in the public school system trenches senses that a 60 percent good fit rate is about as good as it gets.

A key reason for policymakers and academics to mostly avoid public-private comparisons is that it is very likely the case that we can't learn much of significance by comparing one part of a dysfunctional whole to another part of the dysfunctional whole. Furthermore, specialized schools are not compatible with a one-dimensional scale. Policymakers should publish descriptive data from specialized schools. Another key reason is that a transformational school system change that addressed the pricelessness and political correctness issues would cause the new system's private schools, and perhaps also the public schools, to differ greatly from what we see now. Existing differences are important only if we continue to prevent meaningful school system change. It's especially true of the private sector outcome of significant changes in school system governance and funding policies because private school choices might be able to differ greatly from the current private school menu that is very much the result of the public school system's public finance monopoly. Under such daunting conditions, private schools survive much more readily if they offer instruction, such as religion, that public schools cannot offer. In a school system that did not discriminate against private school users, private schools would be much more likely to compete head to head with TPS, trying to be better at providing mainstream secular instruction.

One of the reasons private schools, as a group, struggle to be more effective statistically than public schools is that the expensive, wait-listed prep academies are undermotivated. Like the nearly ubiquitous wait lists of chartered public schools, the wait lists of elite private schools[19] buffer them against the normal relentless market pressure to perform at a high level and to keep getting better. Because of the entire private school sector's low market share,[20] a lot of private schools don't get enough competitive pressure from other private schools.

Most private schools must provide schooling for much less per-pupil funding than public schools, including much lower teacher salaries. So, the less expensive parochial private schools typically struggle to hire the best new teachers and keep experienced teachers. To teach children without public schools' micromanagement of their lessons, poor discipline, and politically correct materials, some private school teachers willingly accept the typically much lower private school teaching salaries and accept or prefer the teaching of church doctrine. But the lure of significantly higher public school salaries and widespread low interest in non-secular curricula causes a lot of new teacher pass-through. It also forces some private schools to cut corners on acceptable minimum qualifications to fill slots at low salaries. Private school materials and facilities also suffer from the typically large private school per-pupil funding disadvantage.

The next chapter provides an overview of what can be done to change those debilitating conditions.

---

[1] Many state commissions (Franciosi 2004), and much increased per pupil funding.

[2] http://www2.ed.gov/pubs/NatAtRisk/risk.html

[3] Dworkin, Anthony G., Lawrence J. Saha, and Antwanette N. Hill. 2003. "Teacher Burnout and Perceptions of a Democratic School Environment." *International Education Journal* 4:2, p 108–120.

[4] Levitt, Steven B. and Stephen Dubner. 2009. *Freakonomics*. NY: HarperCollins

[5] The central premise of the currently dominant approach to school reform and school system reform is that until the reform frenzy initiated by the 1983 "Nation at Risk" National Commission Report, public school educators were

not nearly sufficiently accountable for ineffectiveness, or adequately rewarded for extraordinary effectiveness.

6   Roselli, Anthony M. 2005. *Dos and Don'ts of Education Reform*. New York: Peter Lang Publishing.

7   Example: De La Rosa, Michelle. 2009. "Consolidation Not all Bad: Bigger School can add Electives," *San Antonio Express-News* June 10, 2009; p 1B, 5B.

8   Hanushek, Eric. 2004. "What if there are no Best Practices," *Scottish Journal of Political Economy* 51:2, May 2004; p 156–172.

9   Robinson, Eugene. 2012. "Teachers not Responsible for Education Crisis," *San Antonio Express-News* 9/19/12, p A13.

10   Peterson (2010, 86.

11   National Academy of Sciences, National Academy of Engineering, and Institute of Medicine. 2007. *Is America Falling Off the Flat Earth?* Washington, DC: The National Academies Press. https://doi.org/10.17226/12021. See also page 39 of a 2001 National Commission Report: https://fas.org/irp/threat/nssg.pdf

12   (Dumbing Down our Kids, Language Police, and Mad Mad World of Textbook Adoption).

13   https://en.wikiquote.org/wiki/Otto_von_Bismarck.   https://en.wikipedia.org/wiki/Sausage_factory: "A legislative body, whose practices in creating law are *often analogized* [emphasis added] to the goings-on of a sausage factory."

14   (Mad, Mad World, Jonathan Rauch, Ravitch (2), TX School Board)

15   More: https://www.ucdavis.edu/news/troubled-children-hurt-peers-test-scores-behavior/

16   For devastating critique, see Sowell, Thomas. 2018. *Discrimination and Disparities*. NY: Basic Books.

17   Howard, Philip K. 2005. "Class War." *WSJ* 5/24/05, page A12.

18   Peterson 2010, 93.

19   See the Coulson PBS series (http://www.pbs.org/wnet/school-inc/) for a discussion of the interesting puzzle; why waitlisted private schools don't charge more, don't expand, or attract competitors.

20   Because of public schools' public finance monopoly.

CHAPTER FOUR

Guideposts for Transformational Reform

Periodic "Nation at Risk" declarations re-confirm the persistent ineffectiveness that we should expect from the public school and private school classrooms of a change-resistant system grounded on heroic assumptions. To replace those heroic assumptions with appropriate evidence- and logic-based, non-heroic assumptions, we need a clear assessment of the key factors that must guide enactment and implementation of productive, transformational school system change.

There Are Differences in How Children Learn and How Educators Succeed

First and foremost, we have to address and exploit, as much as possible, actual differences in what engages schoolchildren in productive learning and the differences in educators that will make them much more effective in some instructional settings than others. I included the "as much as possible" caveat because factors such as technology gains and population density will affect our ability to provide each student the learning circumstances that will work best for them. Fortunately, as technology gains occur, more and more content can be delivered effectively online to more and more children. That will cause population density to matter less and less, but likely never not at all. It will always be the case that more schooling options will be available where more people are close enough for parents to effectively choose from many options that use some direct interaction. F2F schooling and online schooling are not necessarily all-or-nothing choices. Mixtures of F2F classes and online courses through course choice and blended learning are becoming more popular.[1]

So, the best menus of schooling options can exist where many people live in close proximity and have good transportation networks. That maximizes the potential to use choice- or assignment-based sorting to connect each child with the educators best equipped (including passion) to address diverse learning engagement factors. Since subject theme and pedagogy are the key engagement factors, education entrepreneurs would likely offer multiple pedagogy-specialized and subject-theme-based schools, especially where high population concentrations will support numerous F2F alternatives. For example, one subject-theme specialized school might aim to teach everything from politics, economics, English, reading, and math through sports stories. Such a school would attract educators and children that are sports fanatics.

I chose a sports stories theme as an example because I know that many of the people that will read this are going, "Yuck." Even if that includes you, you **know** there are many sports fanatics. A sports theme would ultra-engage some children in the related academics. Faced with such a schooling option, a few would seize it, and everyone else—indeed, the vast majority—would choose an online, or nearby comprehensive, F2F traditional public school (TPS), or another specialized alternative. It might take a big population concentration for there to be enough child sports fanatics to make a sports theme school viable. In the school systems that address and exploit student and educator diversity, the least diverse menu but steadily improving situation will exist in small towns and rural areas. In a place where only one brick-and-mortar option is financially feasible, the TPS will be the best *available* fit for children for whom the improving online options remain a worse fit.

The Central Problem Is the Political Process

> I don't make jokes. I just watch the government
> and report the facts.
>
> —Will Rogers

> Rather than treating children like pawns in our
> political games.
>
> —Cami Anderson, former
> Newark superintendent

Even a leading defender of the public school system's monopoly on public funding, longtime American Federation of Teachers president Albert Shanker, noticed that

> public education operates like a planned economy, a bureaucratic system in which everybody's role is spelled out in advance and there are few incentives for innovation and productivity. It's no surprise that our school system doesn't improve; it more resembles a communist economy than our own market economy.

However, we know from Shanker's key role in launching price-less chartering that he didn't understand the crucial role of price-lessness in creating the low-performing "planned economy" schooling practices and outcomes he lamented.

The political process is the central cause of persistent low performance, and that process will determine which productive version of transformational change we can enact and sustain. The policymakers matter, but ***not nearly as much as the decision-making process***. My occasional, brief opportunities to interact with mostly Texas and Utah legislators repeatedly confirm that. After each episode, I thought to myself, even the non-conservatives are mostly awesome people. We're not going to elect better people? So why do they typically enact rapidly growing, bloated budgets and create so many dangerous, nutty, or counterproductive laws? And for schooling, even the Republican lawmakers support a public finance monopoly for public school systems and equal schooling for unequal children even though it doesn't yield them any support from groups, such as the teacher unions, that support the status quo. There are twenty-five states, including Texas and Utah, where all statewide offices and both houses of the legislature have been mostly controlled by Republicans for a while. The education establishment groups that are widely alleged to be the key impediments to school system reform almost never support Republicans. Republicans have nothing to gain by pandering to them, yet some of them often appear to for reasons that may require some research to fully grasp (chapter 12).

Referring to my interactions with Utah's conservative lawmakers (the majority), I told some colleagues that they proved that every state needs a constitutional spending limit (then the subject of our discussion). The political process has repeatedly driven those very conservative lawmakers to raise state spending very fast, nearly as fast as revenue growth lets them. If they can't even limit their state's spending growth to economic growth, much less a more justifiable small multiple of population plus inflation, every state definitely needs a constitutional cap on spending growth.

On the school system reform front, the most those very conservative, well-meaning Utah legislators would do, in 2007 (and not since), is two very narrowly targeted, low-dollar-amount tuition vouchers, hardly the transformational change that all the Utah indicators (and most of the conservative legislators), every state's indicators, said was needed. Only the special needs voucher law still exists. As of 2021, Texas Republicans haven't come that far, though arguably in 2015 and 2017, only the House Speaker and the House Education Committee Chair prevented passage of significant school system reform ("protecting many members from recording a tough vote") by refusing to allow consideration of Senate-passed legislation.

A lot of people don't understand that the political *process* is the reason that rapid funding growth and mostly good intentions create and sustain Nation at Risk bad, low-performing school systems. Political control is evident in the persistence of a central planning process to decide which instructional approaches will exist, where, how, and for whom. In every state, the early, misguided local attempts at school system reform yielded a much greater reliance on a state government role—state politics—after local political forums consistently yielded disappointing results. And when the expanded state role failed to yield noteworthy school system improvement, national politics yielded a larger federal role. The Every Student Succeeds Act (ESSA) of 2015 is the latest edition of federal involvement. ESSA replaced the No Child Left Behind (NCLB) Act of 2001, which replaced the Goals 2000 Education Act of 1994. Early disagreement on whether the ESSA would curb the federal government's role may be the latest noteworthy symptom of the futility of changing political forums. Legislated mandates are often so complex that they are subject to widely different interpretations, often intentionally. So far (via periodic re-enactments of the ESEA[2] through NCLB), the greater federal role (see chapter 5) has not yielded noteworthy school system improvement.

The search for a political forum that will identify the key elements of significantly better school systems and then implement them created a fragmented central planning system that may be even more resistant to non-trivial change. A cynic might argue that the next likely step is greater authority for yet higher-level political forums. I say "cynic" because higher means international politics (e.g., United Nations), which seems unlikely, bordering on insane. So why mention it? Well, not long ago, the current federal role would have seemed unlikely, bordering on insane, and international politics does actively create schooling policy entities and guidelines. Another policy option other than the needed recognition that the role of politics must be severely curbed is a better mix of political forums, or a reassertion of local control, which always sounds much better than the past experience with it that initiated the ongoing state and federal frenzied acts of futility.

Parent trigger legislation enacted by seven states,[3] weighted student formula (WSF) in use in many states, and shifting local control from school boards to mayors are recent iterations in the desperate search for a better mix of political forums. Eric Hanushek (2012) argued that "the underlying motivation for WSF is built on a presumption that districts are making patently bad decisions." The attempts at a better mix of political forums have not significantly improved school system performance, though to be fair, there has not been time to generate sufficient evidence, especially for WSF and parent trigger combinations. Since the central problem is the political *process*, I am not optimistic that shifting central planning authority among levels, or re-fragmenting, fragmentary control will make any positive difference.

Parent trigger legislation is especially curious. It specifies that attendance-area majority coalitions can trigger outcomes such as reconstituting the school's staff or TPS conversion into a chartered public school (CPS). So, trigger laws create a new political forum at the TPS attendance-area level. Empowerment of attendance-area political forums is another sign that there's still too little recognition (too much denial) that standard central planning struggles—political determination of what is taught, how, where, and to whom—are common denominators of school system inefficiency. Attempts at externally driven school reform without school system reform have some value. But the costly trigger has a low upside because troublesome governance and funding practices (the system) remain intact and because new educators will have the same daunting task as the vanquished staff: make one size fit the diverse children of an atten-dance area.

The trigger process can do more harm than good. For example, suppose that a majority coalition exercises its trigger rights to change a TPS that has an instructional strategy that works well for, say, a 40 percent plurality of a very diverse student body. The unhappy 60 percent will pursue change that could destroy the existing good fit for the other 40 percent. It would be far better to use school choice to help the unhappy, heterogeneous 60 percent enroll in different schools while the other 40 percent stay put and probably see students transfer in from schools that have different strengths.[4]

Something like the opposite of those percentages is a very likely reality at the TPS that are good at what they are doing, but what they are doing is a bad fit for many children assigned to that school. Often, a majority of parents believe their assigned TPS's mainstream approaches are working well for their children: "we love our pub-lic school." However, a significant minority may want an alternative because the assigned TPS is not working for at least one of their chil-dren. But the happy majorities block the school-choice policy that would let the unhappy minority leave. They see the new policy as a threat to the public school that they believe is working for their chil-dren, a key political process problem called tyranny of the majority.

While a parent trigger law empowers school-level coalitions politically, tuition vouchers, tuition tax credits, and education sav-ings accounts economically empower parents individually. Pulling the trigger requires a lot of time and money for meetings and to con-test court challenges, all to put parents in the same difficult position at the school level that they are already in at the school district and state level, having to agree on which type of uniformity will seem to yield the best overall outcomes. Promises that policy reform will yield "no child left behind" or "every student succeeds," with an appear-ance of fairness, is the political imperative that converts noble inten-tions into persistent low performance. (Jefferson: "Nothing is more *unequal* [and inefficient—my addition] than the equal treatment of *unequal* people.") The TPS to chartered public school (CPS) con-version[5] underway via the first pulled trigger may yield better results than the district-school management combination that it replaced. But like the majority-rejected, assigned TPS, the CPS operator will be unable to offer any specialized instructional approaches. To serve the diverse needs of a school attendance area, the charter operator must create a comprehensive school.

Political Imperatives and Limitations Imposed by the Political Process

Unfortunately, the same political process that's the central problem must yield the solution. With sufficient political will and wisdom, widespread productive school system reform can begin with one key political forum recognizing its shortcomings as a *process* for deciding what's taught, how, where, and to whom. Evidence that central planning always yields severe disappointment will have to be enough for at least one big school system to assign a substantial role to decentralized planning. Even if we get optimal decentralized planning conditions from the systems willing to move forward without direct evidence generated by someone willing to adopt it before they do, it will take a long time before school system improvement can guide the more risk-averse systems. Poorly conceived attempts at enactment and implementation of decentralized planning will amount to heroic assumptions about how productive change can occur, politically. To succeed, reformers must work within the limitations of political realities and inherent political process constraints.

At Least Fiscal Neutrality

In the increasingly fiscally stressed circumstances of most states, the fiscal impact of transformational change is almost certainly a key constraining issue. Zero state and local fiscal impact, or a fiscal savings effect, may be a de facto requirement to secure enough support for enactment of change that will elicit significant opposition regardless of the urgency of change and purported high benefit-cost ratios. That constrains the dollar value of private school subsidies (vouchers, tax credits, education savings accounts), and it may require slow phasing-in of some provisions of a proposed reform. Phasing in must not be confused with the failed longtime strategy of seeking incremental, legislated change in existing programs.

A Carefully Crafted Transition Period

An often-neglected issue is the crafting of a transition process (see chapter 14) that can easily be the difference between political feasibility and infeasibility. For example, certain groups that might otherwise be part of an effective opposition coalition might be won over or kept on the sidelines with policy provisions that address their concerns or prevent losses they expect. Then to craft the most efficient, politically feasible school system, we have to realistically take into account the relative strengths and weaknesses of collective decision-making processes at different levels (state, local, and national), and the processes of decentralized planning approaches.

A SIMPLE Basis and Rallying Point

Several political factors, including the basis of many long-standing, existing policies, argue that simplicity is a political imperative for key transformational policy reforms. One key reason is our overextended electorate. Few people recognize the likely political accountability effects of typical voter refusal, bordering on inability, to substantively study all of the candidates and issues on a combination of long election ballots and diverse election dates. For example, in San Antonio, Texas, voters fill over 80 elective offices, ~240 candidates to study if each office is on a primary and general election ballot (2 for each office in the primary, 80 more from the other party in the general election). Hopefully, interstate and intrastate variability in ballot length and ballot frequency will facilitate measurement of overextended electorate effects. I believe those effects are large everywhere. Even news and politics junkies don't have time to adequately study all of the candidates and issues on several, often long ballots. Probably, most voters will only pay close attention to races that can clearly, directly impact them. That creates a lot of swayable,[6] low-information, low-motivation potential voters.

In order to overcome the normal change-resistant political reality that the status quo delivers large benefits to vocal, powerful interests, while the benefits of change are uncertain and widely dispersed over many people, reform leaders need some support from the large majority of voters that pay little attention to most ballot choices. So, for the political issues that don't seem to directly impact most voters, it better not take paying really close attention, much less independent effort, for voters to grasp the key issue to be resolved. Even without our overextended electorate, the mix of concentrated costs and dispersed benefits makes even awful public policies very change-resistant.

Kolderie (2014), Ravitch (2010), Tyack and Cuban (1995), Hill (2008), and Wolk (2012) reached a similar conclusion. Their different perspective argued that our change-resistant political process, alongside the complexity of our school systems, would thwart efforts to legislate school system transformation. Since they didn't mention the consumer choice, free enterprise, and market-driven price change agents that drive decentralized planning, their transformational school system reform scenario is a comprehensive rewrite of the current schooling industry central plan. For example, *Education Week* founder and education entrepreneur Ronald Wolk said, "The best hope for success…is to first redesign schools," which is part of his explanation for why improved performance driven by higher common standards "would require a miracle." Their takeaway: school system tinkering is all that is politically feasible. They see better school system performance arising mostly from working within the existing system to reform schools individually.

I agree that the political process is very unlikely to *directly* produce a central plan overhaul, good or bad. My takeaway: change only the few central plan elements that make it difficult to establish and sustain independent alternatives to the current menu of schooling options. Openness to alternatives probably mostly developed by education entrepreneurs will reduce the market share of existing schools, public and private, and force competitive changes at least in existing private schools. Openness to alternatives will narrow the student diversity range at the traditional public schools and thus make TPS classrooms much more teachable. The latter effect of a 1998–2008 privately funded, universal tuition voucher program made the Edgewood district (San Antonio, TX) schools significantly better than they were before 1998 and much better than they have been since the 2008 end of the program that offered vouchers to all Edgewood families.

I believe a ***nondiscrimination principle*** can be a simple, sufficient catalyst for gradual transformational reform. Implementation alongside price decontrol would deliver all seven of William Ouchi's seven keys to school system reform.[7] Professional message crafters can probably improve upon this definition of the nondiscrimination principle: Don't discriminate against families that believe that a private school is a better fit than the assigned TPS for ***some of their children***. Nondiscrimination is a simple rallying cry that might sufficiently reduce the basis for disagreement that could exist at the several approval levels where a policy change proposal might be stalled or gutted. The key to achieving nondiscrimination is elimination of the public finance monopoly of the public school system. ***With pure nondiscrimination, different children may get different levels of publicly funded tuition assistance, but each child gets the same level of tuition assistance regardless of which school parents see as the best academic fit.***

I emphasized ***some of their children*** in my description of the nondiscrimination catalyst for critical key school system changes because "fit" and "work for them" are key elements in the call for lower market entry barriers for alternatives to the assigned TPS. The needed reforms are mostly not about the horrific conditions of some public schools, potential racial/ethnic bias, or access to schooling with religious content. And the quest for nondiscrimination—an end to public schools' public finance monopoly—is not about being for/against public schools or public education, which far too many people see as synonymous. It is about being able to find a good instructional fit for a child when the assigned TPS turns out to be a bad fit, and it is about the need to create opportunities and incentives to relentlessly offer instructional fit innovations and improvements.

From talking to people, from attending conferences, and from my study of the privately financed tuition vouchers available to residents of San Antonio's Edgewood district, I noticed that families financially empowered to opt out of the assigned TPS often chose an alternative to the assigned school for some of their children, *but not all*. Something like this was frequently evident: "The assigned public school was working fine for Johnnie, but not Suzy." *Even America's best TPS are not a good fit for every child assigned to them*. There are no universally best instructional practices (Hanushek 2004; Berner 2017). That's why we need a dynamic menu of schooling options as diverse as each area's schoolchildren; diverse in terms of how they learn, and other engagement factors such as subject themes. Probably better deployment and execution of existing instructional approaches is more important, at least at first, than more and better lesson content.

We know from nearly 200 years of central plan tinkering that collective decision-making through the political process will not yield that dynamic, diverse school system. Because voluntary specialization in areas of strength is necessary to remain competitive when market entry barriers are low, a dynamic, diverse menu of independent schooling options is the likely outcome of decentralized planning orchestrated by market-driven price change.

Shared Financing of Tuition Must Be Allowed!

Nondiscrimination creates a viable market process, and strengthens political incentives, to address student diversity when the regulatory regime leaves room for useful differences between the current system's schooling options and future alternatives. Also, schooling option diversity will be severely constrained if the government decides that all of the subsidized options must be free (tuition cannot exceed the government-funded per-pupil payment). Such price control restricts the menu of schooling options to instructional approaches that cost comfortably less than the state-funded per-pupil payment plus whatever school operators can consistently acquire from donors. To avoid always-devastating price control, it must be possible for schools to receive public funds indirectly through tuition vouchers, tuition tax credits, or from education savings accounts (ESA) ***and to charge a market-determined tuition co-payment***.

Schools need a co-payment when, for example, a school uses an instructional approach that costs $9,000 per pupil per year, and the annual per-pupil public funding is, say, $7,500. For families that see that as the best available deal (the expected effectiveness improvement is worth that $1,500 out-of-pocket payment—chapter 9 discusses the co-payment equity issues), the family ***or a third party*** must pay the $1,500 per child per-year difference between what it costs to run the school and the per-pupil public funding. There are many synonyms for the term "co-payment" that appeared in the 2002 *Zelman* US Supreme Court decision on voucher use. In Chile, a co-payment means shared financing occurs. Families ***or a third party*** pay private school tuition by topping off or adding on to the per-pupil government funding (tuition vouchers, tuition tax credits, or ESA).

Possible co-payment (shared financing) is critical because then market forces set the co-payment level, perhaps at zero for many schools. The tuition levels—the shared financing, market-determined total for each instructional approach—signal school operators and investors which instructional approaches families value the most. If, in the name of free schooling for all, co-payment (shared financing) is not allowed, instructional approaches that cost more than the per-pupil public funding will be very rare. They will exist only to the extent that school operators can secure large, long-term commitments from donors. And those that exist will often fill quickly and thereafter be effectively closed by lengthy wait lists to all but a lucky few lottery winners.

With the price control that exists when we ban co-payment, many possible schooling options will never get off the drawing board. New instructional approaches can be quite costly at first, or need to be lucrative initially to coax investors into supporting exploratory innovation in schooling practices. A high initial price can restrict early adoption to higher-income households and low-income scholarship recipients, but *the alternative is for them to not exist at all, or barely exist with access only to lottery winners*. An alleged equity basis for opposing permission to co-pay means you want lower-income families to have better access to schooling options that mostly cannot exist without a co-payment! Huh? That means that banning co-payment, which many school choice expansion policies do—and Chile is rescinding co-payment permission—has only a symbolic political benefit, little or no actual schooling access benefit (more detail in chapter 9).

When innovations get off the drawing board and then become established as a good fit for many children, they typically become cheaper with experience, and after competition sets in. Typically, innovations gain life as luxuries for the wealthy and then gradually become widely available to everyone. Prohibiting high prices at the front end aborts the whole process, a process that typically greatly benefits everyone, probably, eventually, the least advantaged the most.

Competition will establish when a school's instructional approach can sustain a co-payment large enough to fund the school's operations. Imitators will attempt to enter the market for a particular instructional approach when the public funds, plus a sustainable co-payment, yield an above-normal profit (revenue per pupil > per pupil cost). That market entry process competitively drives per pupil revenue down to just the amount that the most efficient producers need to barely earn a normal rate of return on their investment. How many schools' co-payment levels fall to zero will depend on the per-pupil public funding level. When Chile allowed public-private shared financing of tuition, the vast majority of co-payment amounts fell to zero or to nominal levels.

When the public per-pupil payment plus a competitive co-payment yields a loss (per pupil revenue < per pupil cost), some producers of the money-losing instructional approach must exit the market. Because that gradually creates excess demand for the remaining producers, tuition levels rise until that exit restores profitability. The profit-loss, entrepreneur entry-exit, price change process is how decentralized planning through the information and incentives delivered by the price system regulates the content, price, and availability of each instructional approach.

Do No Harm—Beware of Toxic Combinations

Economic theory and evidence from other markets tell us the current situation could be made worse. Iatrogenic treatment worsens a condition. Roselli (2005) argues there's been a lot of that. And it seems likely for some of the possible combinations of governance and funding policies that foster some entrepreneurial delivery of specialized schooling options. Based on what economists call the theory of the second best, we need to be wary of reforms that allow some additional autonomy and market openings but retain key restrictions. Hybrid measures can be worse than the opposite pure central, or more decentralized, approaches. For example, increased openness to for-profit schooling options alongside shortages created by government control of tuition prices is a likely scandal-fostering, toxic combination created by state laws that allow for-profit CPS. The outcomes of profit motive with price control would very likely be very different from the outcomes of increased openness to for-profit schooling options alongside market determination of tuition prices and thus price-system orchestration of market entry of profitable schooling options.

More on the Significance of Simplicity

Co-payment raises an equity issue that is a good example of the significance of simplicity, for better or worse. The current system has a simple answer to the concern about differences in the ability to pay for schooling: guaranteed access to free (funded by taxes and donations only) nearby taxpayer-funded schooling. It is simple and easy to understand, which makes it change resistant. Income is not a barrier when schooling is free (no additional charge beyond taxes most people must pay even when they have no children or pay private tuition), until a family wants to choose a higher performing TPS by residing in the desired school's attendance area. That simple, deceptively obvious virtue obscures severe trade-offs, including on the equity issue. Chapter 9 will argue that the less obvious equity implications of the simple proposed nondiscrimination policy are better than the equity effects of the simple free, assigned-neighborhood public school strategy: that a system of dynamic and diverse, mostly free schooling options with means-tested co-payment assistance would be much better on both efficiency and equity grounds.

Another example of the dangers sometimes lurking in the attractiveness of simplicity is the uniformly comprehensive neighborhood public school concept discussed earlier. That concept satisfies the political process' appearance of fairness imperative by offering the same schooling options to everyone. At the same time, it seemingly makes life easier for everyone. Attendance zones assure every child a slot in a free neighborhood public school, which simplifies enrollment, transportation, and administration for operators of multiple TPS. Since the uniformity seems to absolve families from the need to carefully compare the free school choices, it even appears to simplify relocation to another area. But the implicit business plan to provide uniformly comprehensive schooling to everyone has been a gold-plated disaster.

Meaning of "Schooling Is Different"

There are noteworthy differences between schooling as a commodity and the goods and services delivered efficiently by market interaction of producers and consumers. Many people believe that some of those differences justify or even require government financing and production of schooling for children. Those differences include spillovers, the importance of objective, detailed information, the significance of customization, client-producer coproduction of intellectual growth, and the possibility of disruptive, sudden midyear school closures.

Schooling Spillovers from Students to Everyone Else

One of those big differences is the potential for positive spillovers from students to everyone else, including especially the collective desire to train children to become responsible citizens. The actual spillover effects will depend upon what the students actually learn. Those potential spillover effects of schooling children, and how proposed school system reforms could affect that, will be a key element of the political debate. Some scholars argue that parents will pay tuition, or a tuition co-payment, only for instruction that yields direct benefits for their children. So, they argue that a new system's private schools will omit citizenship-oriented content to keep their tuition price competitive. From that, it can seem to follow that the societal need for citizenship-oriented content requires taxpayer financing and some regulation of schooling content. Scholars such as Milton Friedman, E. G. West, and James Tooley disagree. They argue that the primary source of spillovers from each student's academic progress to everyone else, including the skills to exercise citizenship responsibilities, is acquisition of basic skills that also yield the bulk of private benefits of schooling that virtually all parents will buy for their children. Corey DeAngelis argues that some of the possible spillovers can be negative, so that a net positive effect cannot be taken for granted. Indeed, he finds that compared to private schooling, politically correct schooling of the current public school system cohort will yield a $1.3 trillion net negative spillover effect.

The well-argued objections of DeAngelis, Friedman, Tooley, and West notwithstanding, there is a widespread sentiment, scholars included, that schooling is a public good, that society must finance schooling to avoid the development of an unaffordably (Nation at Risk) large, undereducated underclass. So, because of widespread failure to grasp that schooling is a merit good, not a public good, and because of greater concern for possible absence of citizenship-fostering content than for brainwashing via government control of schooling content, government intervention went beyond the means-tested tuition assistance suggested by equity and merit good arguments. This 9/26/60 presidential debate exchange between Senator John

Kennedy and Vice President Richard Nixon captures the concerns and trade-offs perfectly:

> Kennedy argued, "There is no greater return to an economy or to a society than an educational system second to none." Nixon agreed, but expressed deep concern over "giving the federal government power over education…the greatest power a government can have."[8]

So, now the US has a system of government-owned, public-employee-staffed public schools with a public finance monopoly. Ironically and tragically, the resulting fifty-one US school systems have the feared undereducated underclass that didn't exist in the US prior to the advent of public school systems in the mid-1800s. Prior to that, literacy rates were higher than now even though children from low-income families were at the mercy of charitable provision of schooling, there was some discrimination against girls, and for some time, there was little secondary education.

The distinction between a public good, that schooling is **not**, and schooling as a ***potential*** merit good is critical because it objectively stops the automatic rejection of market-based delivery of schooling, something like "We have to provide schooling publicly because it is a public good." Real public goods, such as national defense, cannot be delivered by entrepreneurs through markets because it is very hard to confine the benefits of a true public good only to those who have paid a full fair share of the good's cost. The availability of public-good free rides results in very little voluntary payment for true public goods, and thus a very low, inefficient level of private provision. True public goods are also non-rival, so each person's level of service does not depend on the number of people served. For example, arrival of immigrants does not diminish the protection of citizens by the level of national defense provided simultaneously to all.

We know from the existence of schooling financed by tuition, and because even online schools cannot serve additional children at no additional cost, that schooling is not a public good. Schooling is a potential merit good, which is a private good that can yield benefits beyond schooling consumers. Purchasers of schooling may not value all of the instructional options that yield spillover benefits to non-students, so merit goods may be under-consumed unless spillover-generating instruction is subsidized.

Significance of Objective, Detailed Information on Schooling Options

Another widely noted difference between schooling and typical market-provided goods is the importance of good information about the alternatives. That is even more important for a school system in which diverse schooling options provide a strong basis for customization. One line of reasoning (Brown 1992) is that many people prefer a system of uniformly comprehensive public schools because such a system prevents having to make complex comparisons of diverse schooling options with perhaps different best-fit schools for different children in the same family. But the uniformly comprehensive options still differ enough to be a top consideration of homebuyers, which means only the lowest quality versions of comprehensive are free. The better versions impose higher housing costs. And nondiscrimination would offer both options: the assigned uniformly comprehensive public school as the default for where-to-live decisions, plus an opportunity through public subsidy portability to opt for some customization through a full-time or part-time (blended learning or course choice) alternative to the assigned public school at little or no additional tuition cost. That's important politically because we can't address the issue empirically until we have some good modern examples of school systems with a lightly regulated, largely market-driven sector.

In a recent discussion of the evolving post-Katrina New Orleans system, differences in the ability to compare schooling options had become an equity issue. The equity argument is that it is unfair that higher-income families are typically better equipped to shop and compare than others. That is probably the key argument for government provision of the information public good.

Beware of information masquerading as relevant evidence. For example, the post-Katrina New Orleans school system suffered significant shopping chaos until a one-application computer-program-driven process (OneApp) of matching families to choices replaced some of the shopping chaos problems with new problems. The New Orleans experience is evidence, but of what? Was the pre-OneApp chaos a "schooling is different" issue inherent in shopping among market-provided schooling options? Did the chaos result from the absence of key competitive market conditions, or was the chaos just a temporary result of growing pains? The latter would be a somewhat predictable, normal adaptation struggle. People are not used to making detailed school comparisons. They are very accustomed to the assignment of students to uniformly comprehensive schools based on place of residence.

My preliminary assessment is that all three possibilities were key factors. Change creates confusion and transitional, temporary conditions, and the post-Katrina New Orleans system is a lousy experiment in market-driven schooling. Two key ingredients of high-performing markets are completely absent. Louisiana charter school law prohibits profit-seeking charter operators, and there is no market-driven price system to orchestrate what kinds of instruction are on the menu, how schools operate, exactly where, and who ends up at which schools. Recall that profit-seeking together with price control that creates shortages is a toxic combination.

Price control is inherent in the zero-tuition, chartered-public-school-centric, post-Katrina school system. Without profit-loss and price change to eliminate shortages or excess supply of specific instructional approaches, New Orleans does not have school choice. It had mostly school chance based on a lottery, and now it has choice-guided assignment among schools via the OneApp software. Newark had the same reaction to charter wait lists. Instead of implementing price decontrol, Newark created their own "one-stop enrollment system."

Because CPS cannot charge a co-payment, the New Orleans school chances can only offer instructional approaches that cost less than the state government per pupil payment plus rare, major long-term donor funding. The absence of a market-determined co-payment possibility means that the school system cannot use co-payments to prevent quality-eroding shortages and to attract competition where its value is greatest. Pre-OneApp, it was very hard to shop for a school because interest would often, perhaps mostly, only yield an enrollment opportunity through a lottery. You better file a lot of applications if you can't tell which school will admit your child. OneApp manages school chance with software that decides which children get which of their ranked preferences. Seventy-five percent get one of their top three choices, but the price control and profit ban severely diminishes the range of possible choices that families are able to choose from.

Step back from the careful search for relevant evidence of properly/improperly informed shopping behavior and consider the likely features of an actual schooling marketplace. Note that schooling is a frequently purchased, big-ticket item. That, alongside potential co-payment creating family skin in the game, motivates careful shopping, producer attention to reputation, and a high enough demand for objective information that it is very likely to be provided publicly and privately. To create and sustain valuable reputations, school operators are very likely to pursue prestigious accreditations and certifications. When start-up and infrastructure costs are high (large fixed costs), definitely with online schooling, and many versions of brick and mortar schooling, a few customers are sometimes the difference between sound finances, including profit where allowed, and loss. That means a relatively few well-informed, discriminating customers are enough to motivate school operator attention to the quality issues specific to the school's planned instructional approach. And bottom-up, subjective school operator accountability to customers will force school operator attention to all valued aspects of schooling, not just the empirically measurable items that can inform objective top-down accountability to political authority.

Coproduction of Intellectual Growth

We hire educators to foster the intellectual development of their student clients. Unlike most industries, educators cannot succeed without the cooperation of their clients. That is, students will not learn very much unless they are engaged in the learning process. Teacher-student coproduction of intellectual growth occurs only to the extent that there is student engagement.

Engagement in public school classroom content is low and declining with student age, reaching a low engagement rate of 33 percent in the last three high school years.[9] Since engagement is not objectively or easily quantified, there is much room for controversy over the definition. That notwithstanding, those low measured engagement rates are consistent with the public school system's learning-issue-diverse classrooms, pressure to make one size seem to fit all, weak and perverse educator incentives, high rates of out-of-field teaching, and the involuntary nature of student assignment to public schools and classrooms within the assigned schools. We need a school system that matches student learning needs with school and teacher strengths. Without that, low official engagement rates will cause our low literacy and numeracy rates.

Abrupt School Closure Concerns

Possible sudden business failure is another factor sometimes cited as a reason for favoring publicly owned schools. Private schools can run out of money and abruptly close before the end of the school year. It is much less likely that public schools would do so, though such outcomes arise as a possibility when budget deliberations threaten traditional funding streams. And arguably, many traditional public schools are so bad that they should close despite the disruptiveness of a sudden school closure. The answer to this concern is twofold. First, many parents will have that concern and demand evidence that closure during the school year is extremely unlikely. Such assurance can come from published public and private information sources or through a requirement that schools insure themselves against midyear bankruptcy. Second, competition would probably force something like the latter in the absence of a formal requirement.

Concerns about an Underclass Invasion of Suburban Public Schools

If the evidence, such as Lance Izumi's "Not as Good as You Think" state studies, is not enough to convince suburban households that their schools are mostly still not great, political necessity may force a means-tested approach to implementation of nondiscrimination. But the correct application of means-testing is to end the public schools' public finance monopoly at first only in the poorest *places*. It would mean that *every* family in those places has access to big private school tuition discounts alongside free public schooling. Not only does that address potentially major political opposition from suburban households fearing harmful transformations of their suburban public schools, it creates a much-needed inner-city economic development magnet. The large and growing body of evidence that keeping middle- and upper-income families with children nearing school age from fleeing inner-city areas has significant economic development and environmental improvement benefits may deliver a necessary swing vote to implement nondiscrimination in the areas most in need of economic development, pollution reduction, and school system improvement. Sufficient school system improvement in those especially challenging places has the great potential to cause more and more states to implement nondiscrimination everywhere, in part by generating evidence from a genuine universal choice experiment.

What Has Already Failed to Deliver School System Improvement

Perhaps the most depressing subtext of a school system that bipartisan and non-partisan authorities repeatedly describe in dire terms is the tendency to recycle or double down[10] on strategies that have already disappointed repeatedly, more of the same—harder (MOTS-H). The continued political correctness of strategies with an awful track record is at least a symptom of the low economic literacy that we can partly blame on the current school system and the overextended electorate situation that strengthens special interests' power to block substantive change. This book's economics lessons on the likely school system outcomes of the nondiscrimination principle described above will not eliminate recycling of failed strategies. The rationale for this book is the hope that it can inform policy entrepreneurship enough to elevate the will and wisdom of the great communicators that can mobilize the intellectuals with a strategy that cannot be defeated by special interests or by demagoguing low-information voters.

Increased Per-Pupil Public School Funding

A tripling of the current system's per-pupil spending since 1965, adjusted for inflation, did not produce noteworthy, much less proportional performance gains. Differences in policy variables explain very little of the differences in the low average per pupil school system outcomes. Skyrocketing inefficiency has been the only noteworthy net effect of more spending (Hoxby 2004), yet new spending is repeatedly asserted as necessary, even via lawsuit. The public school system plaintiffs argue that the poor academic outcomes of their state prove that their state's K-12 spending is unconstitutionally low. Some of those lawsuits were successful. Some legislatures reacted to those judgments with spending increases, though usually not to the sometimes-astronomical levels specified in the judgments. However, the hoped-for academic gains did not follow.

Two examples are especially noteworthy: (1) the non-effect of a huge court-mandated spending increase in Kansas City, MO, and (2) inconsistent declarations by the current and previous Washington state governors. In Kansas City, much-increased spending, including for better-paid teachers and luxurious facilities, ignored the roots of the problem. The extra money didn't make the school system's key assumptions such as "*incentives don't matter*" less heroic, or make classrooms sorted only by age and neighborhood more teachable.

Washington's governor Christine Gregoire (D, 2005–2013), significantly increased K-12 spending. Few politicians confess failure, but Governor Gregoire publicly lamented the costly failure of that strategy. In 2005, there was already a long history of failure to produce improvement by increasing funding as a basis to have known better. With Governor Gregoire's recent lament on the record, her successor, Governor Jay Inslee (D) had an even more substantial basis to know better. So did the voters that elected and re-elected him, and the courts that ruled Washington's K-12 funding to be inadequate. But he announced plans to further increase funding, MOTS-H, in his first term and continues to make that promise!

Not only did increased spending, plus mandating better outcomes (higher expectations), or else, fail to yield significantly better school system outcomes, there have been serious negative side effects. Even though the "or else" promised by the efforts to increase educator accountability has mostly been absent,[11] it sounded threatening enough to cause widespread diversion of classroom time to standard test-taking skill development and a narrowing of the curriculum toward the tested aspects of the tested subjects. There has also been proof of test-taking fraud, which anecdotal evidence suggests may be just the tips of many yet-to-be-discovered large icebergs.

Increased Teacher Training and Smaller Classes

Eric Hanushek (2010) has shown that teacher skill matters, even in the world's relatively low-performing top school systems (the best are still not great). But additional teacher training for those already deemed qualified has not yet greatly impacted effectiveness, nor has across-the-board reduction in maximum class sizes. The rare key ability to successfully differentiate instruction to address a high percentage of the learning factor diversity often (unnecessarily) present in a public school classroom seems to be something that cannot be taught, at least not yet.

More and better training and smaller classes seem like they should yield student gains. But it yields little or no bang for the buck *in our public school system*. Improved training to increase effectiveness in the typical, learning style-diverse TPS classroom, and uniformly smaller classes are very expensive, likely low-value improvement strategies. Site-, subject-, and situation-specific training can yield some gains, at least for a particular teacher with the current crop of students. But when the students in a classroom have only age and neighborhood in common, next year's set may require different kinds of differentiation. When a teacher repeatedly faces a much more homogenous—in terms of how they learn or which subject themes engage them in learning—student population, training and experience can be focused on skill enhancement they will need repeatedly. That would happen in a school system in which specialized schools of choice are common.

Certainly, the number of students in a class can be inefficiently high or low. The coproduction, efficiency-maximizing class size depends on the teacher, the subject, the technology options, and the likely learning issue diversity of the students. A few years ago, I was speaking to a self-described serial entrepreneur. He said but for the daunting task of competing against well-funded, free public schools, he'd probably try to run some schools. I'm citing that conversation because a point he emphasized was the importance of experimentation with class size to achieve and maintain competitiveness. For some teachers for some subjects, it would take a small class to meet parents' expectations. To offset high costs for small classes for some teacher-subject combinations, he'd look for teacher-subject-technology combinations that can meet parents' expectations with larger class sizes wherever possible. Uniform class size limits, such as the twenty-two maximum in Texas, for the youngest children, hinder such optimizing experimentation.

Federal Funding and Federal Mandates

We know from the predecessors of the federal Every Student Succeeds Act (ESSA, 2015) that expanding an already-huge national debt to bribe states and school districts to do certain things does not deliver much bang for the buck. But it has been politically incorrect to curb the federal money. So, the political process yields some mission creep and MOTS-H to sustain or expand federal K-12 spending. The 2015 ESSA version of federal intervention, unlike its NCLB predecessor but like NCLB's Goals 2000 predecessor, doesn't even challenge the heroic assumption that your assigned TPS can make one size fit all. ESSA doesn't provide for private school choice expansion.

The original NCLB proposal fostered private school choice expansion. The congress quickly removed that provision, but the NCLB negotiations retained some federal funding portability between public schools. That had mostly rhetorical value because the absence of significant differences between the choices actually available for selection (different grades of comprehensively uniform) yielded very low public school choice usage rates.

The Trump administration's support of school choice expansion (see next chapter) didn't launch a federal funds portability experiment. The overused "experiment" term is appropriate despite our experience with the narrowly targeted, low per-pupil funding school choice expansions possible from the federal government's small share of total K-12 spending. Parental choice with federal funds would have yielded a so far unseen mix of restrictions and reporting requirements. Since education savings accounts and tuition tax credits are least vulnerable to debilitating regulation, hopefully, Congress and the president will prefer them to the tuition voucher policy. Given the federal government's small share of K-12 spending, nondiscrimination with just portability of federal funds is unlikely to be transformational.

Summary

The political process—political accountability—created our Nation at Risk school system. To have a chance to productively transform some US school systems, we'll have to recognize and avoid factors that convert incentives inherent to political forums and good intentions into bad outcomes. The differences between schooling as a service (a merit good, not a public good) and the services efficiently delivered by markets don't favor the central planning approaches now in place or favor hopes to do central planning better, except politically. Many of the troublesome key elements of the current system have remained politically correct because of their simplicity, combined with an overextended electorate also often lacking some of the economic literacy needed to quickly grasp the advantages of alternatives to the existing system's key elements. The nondiscrimination principle offers an opportunity to escape the consequences of mistaken pursuit of simple policies by the current system (such as free only and uniformly comprehensive schooling) with a simple catalyst that can drive gradual, productive school system transformation. It can do so without the very unlikely legislative overhaul of the current central plan.

---

[1] Despite failure to train teachers in how to take advantage of the growing popularity: see also Lance Izumi's *Moonshots in Education* (Pacific Research Institute, 2015), pp. 216–219.

[2] Elementary and Secondary Education Act of 1965.

[3] http://educationnext.org/empowered-families-can-transform-the-system/

[4] Merrifield 2012.

[5] http://www.edweek.org/ew/articles/2016/03/16/first-parent-trigger-school-leaves-district-oversight.html?qs=First+Parent+Trigger+School

[6] Bryan Caplan's careful proof of the myth of the rational voter does not take account that the volume of expected voter choice is part of the problem: https://press.princeton.edu/titles/8756.html

[7] Ouchi, William (with Lydia Segal). 2003. *Making Schools Work*. New York: Simon and Schuster.

[8] http://www.edweek.org/ew/articles/2016/03/09/education-is-absent-from-the-2016-presidential.html

[9] http://www.edweek.org/ew/articles/2016/03/23/gallup-student-poll-finds-engagement-in-school.html?qs=Student+Engagement+Drops

[10] Will, George. 2010. "Doubling Down on Education," *San Antonio Express-News* 3/18/10, p 7B.

[11] See pages 160 and 178 of Peterson (2010): p. 160: "The country ended up with a system of accountability that was more apparent than real." p. 178: "It [NCLB] is accountability in appearance, not in fact."

CHAPTER FIVE

Improving the Federal Role as Part of a Transformation, Perhaps by Largely Ending That Role

Vicki Alger's 2016 book *Failure* is a detailed proof that federal interventions in education have no specific constitutional basis and that the lack of a constitutional basis for a federal role in education was a widely accepted fact for a long time. A recent report from the government's General Accounting Office confirms Alger's assessment. Alger also showed that the successful efforts to escape that legal barrier led to an ongoing series of costly failures. If some federal interventions at least helped some children (likely), other factors offset those benefits. It must be that the federal rules that came with the money caused other children to gain less than they otherwise would. The descriptions of federal micromanagement in Neal McCluskey's (2007) Feds in the Classroom help us understand why.

Significant overall performance gains are not discernible (flat test score trends) despite long-term, much-increased funding at all levels: local, state, and federal.

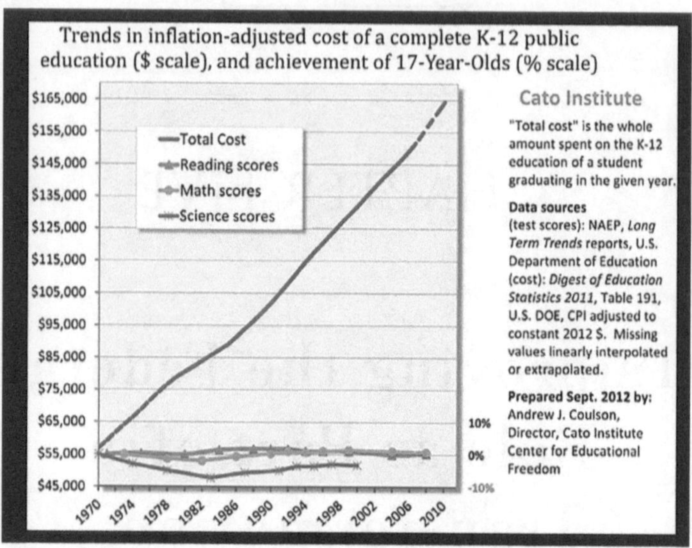

Flat lines are consistent with the title of Myron Lieberman's 1993 classic, *Public Education: An Autopsy*. The flat lines likely mean that policy changes that don't vanquish or provide an escape from the zombie's actions—non-transformational changes—will have trivial *net* consequences. Periodic heroic efforts to succeed against the odds were offset by broader-based systemic decline consistent with the non-viability of the current system's heroic assumptions. The only other way, other than through a zombie system, to get nearly ripple-less flat lines would be if decline-inducing episodic factors took their toll at exactly the same time that new programs, at any level, yield net benefits. Decreased absolute poverty over the period should have increased scores.

There are periodic claims that labor market outcomes, especially for disadvantaged students, sometimes reflect increased school spending even if test scores do not. However, the labor market studies struggle to establish the specific causations behind the correlations.

If increased spending was necessary to prevent test score decline, the slight great recession-induced overall drop (no inflation adjustment) in per-pupil spending—across our fifty-one school systems, lower spending slightly offset greater spending—should have produced noteworthy declines in test scores. But nationally, the flat line persists. Increased spending doesn't increase scores. Spending cuts don't reduce scores—together, a true zombie result. If declining scores followed cuts in the individual states where cuts occurred, that would have been highly publicized and used to bolster court cases that public school system spending is unconstitutionally inadequate. There has been only silence, just as there always had been, until the advent of the labor market outcome studies noted above, after spending increases were found to not improve measured student performance.

The findings of Vicki Alger and Neal McCluskey don't prove that there cannot be useful federal roles. Information clearinghouse and data collection may already be productive roles and would be even more likely to be productive if the effort yielded data that made it easier to compare whole school systems. The bully pulpit might also be productive if the president or the Secretary of Education were to expose key problems such as those at the root of the persistent low-performance problem (chapter 3) and central causes such as pricelessness. Just having a secretary known to be pro-choice, even without choice expansions, has caused a lot of Americans to discover the issue. For the likely readers of this book, it may be very difficult to grasp that a lot of Americans—perhaps the vast majority—have no connection at all to the critical policy issues that consume our attention. Starting a discussion of, say, education savings accounts and tuition vouchers in general company will not yield much more than blank stares and substantially false misimpressions.

The fiscal circumstances of the federal government—a likely growing fiscal struggle against the rising cost of financing our large and growing public debt (even without the inclusion of huge unfunded liabilities), especially if interest rates were to return to historic norms—are reason enough to at least return the US Department of Education (USDOE) budget to the much lower President H. W. Bush, "Education President," pre-Goals 2000 Educate America Act (1993) levels.

Because denial of failure is a virtual political imperative, the failure to make good on the promises of the 1994 Goals 2000 Educate America Act edition of the Elementary and Secondary Education Act (ESEA of 1965) did not lead to ESEA repeal or retrenchment to the ESEA's original missions. Failure caused the federal-level political process to replace it with the No Child Left Behind (NCLB, 2002) Act edition of ESEA. The NCLB-demanded drastic improvements by 2014 didn't happen, which helped produce an NCLB replacement in 2015. In a reaffirmation of the appearance of fairness political imperative, the name of the latest version of the ESEA law has a name that is a NCLB synonym. The Every Student Succeeds Act (ESSA) at least confesses that the NCLB version of ESEA took the federal role too far, though ESSA's ultimate impact on "too far" is a matter of some controversy even after the Trump administration's executive order that state and local control be maximized. The ESSA increases the deficit and the debt to supposedly send money to states with looser strings attached, not necessarily fewer but hopefully looser, allegedly more flexibility for states to figure out how to do it according to the national political consensus on how to revise the primary and secondary education central plan.

Large budget cuts are rare events. It may take a financial crisis— going over the fiscal cliff—to make huge programmatic cuts politically feasible. In the meantime, it may have to be enough to provide an escape route from the effects of federal strings attached to federal funds. Portable subsidy funding from just state and local funds, provided equally to public and private school users (the nondiscrimination recommended throughout this book), would expand the menu of schooling options to include many more instructional approaches not distorted by federal rules.

Hidden Hazards on the Road Ahead

The confusion and conflicting mandates that result from overlaying the result of federal politics and additional regulation[1] onto the legislative and regulatory results of state and local politics is very likely to continue to yield a lot of unintended consequences, well-documented across a wide range of policy arenas in "That's Not What We Meant to Do: Reform and Its Unintended Consequences in the Twentieth Century." Given the very short attention span and aversion to details of many voters, a small-scale federal choice expansion could devastatingly reinforce the existing narrative. A narrative now grounded on studies of tiny, little-known state- and locally-funded school choice expansions becomes a much larger political barrier to productive transformational change if part of its alleged basis includes disappointingly small gains derived from a well-known federal initiative.

A Constitutional and Productive Federal Role

To improve the political feasibility of productive transformational change, we'll need high-quality answers to key questions. To address those questions, we need to be able to make apples-to-apples comparisons of the basis for different outcomes of the US school systems. For that, we need a Federal Office of Education Research, and a National Center for Education Statistics (NCES) that collects data for America's state-level and large metro-area-level school systems, ***not just the public school system data already available through NCES;*** data for whole school systems to allow measurement of aggregate outcomes of the menu of public and private schooling options. That, and a president imploring states to implement transformational reform are federal government roles that may be worth more than they cost.

Little-Noted Federal Intervention Issues

The 2015 ESSA, like previous revisions and reauthorizations of the ESEA signed into law by President Johnson in 1965, is a central plan that aims to bribe states to substitute what is politically correct in national political forums for how states would prefer—based on state political forums—to centrally plan what public schools should do, how, where, and for whom. States can reject the ESSA influence if they are willing to forego the additional federal deficit spending and debt-provided federal money to fund state programs that state taxpayers may not value sufficiently to keep if the federal funds were not available. Or, for programs that states would fund directly if federal funds become unavailable, state officials prefer to take the money through additional debt or out of their taxpayers' federal taxes instead of their state taxes. Most states pursue the federal funding despite the strings attached.

Federal, state, and local political processes may continue to declare implicitly that we cannot trust parents to prescribe schooling content through their private choices. Official assessments may continue to imply that efforts toward "one size fits all" will yield better aggregate outcomes than parents shopping a diverse menu of schooling options to find what will best fit each of their school-age children. ***Far too few people, including frustrated educators, grasp that decentralized planning is the only viable alternative to continued failed attempts to make federal intervention do what state and local political forums could not.*** A frustrated educator, John Mann, made this comment on a February 13, 2018, Wall Street

Journal description of Trump administration efforts to eliminate unwise past interventions:

> I taught high school for 9 years, followed by 8 years on the local school board. During that time, I never saw a single policy, edict, rule, or whatever issued from the Federal Government's Department of Education that was anywhere near the mark. Nothing.
>
> How can anyone think that a one-size-fits-all approach will work?
>
> ***Local educators spend too much time adhering to federal and state rules, and not enough focusing on the needs of local children***. [Compliance focus: Root of the Problem #9]
>
> Solution: Eliminate the Department of Education. Make accountability local.

Indeed, children are diverse and elimination of the federal DOE would be a huge positive step.

Is Local Political Control Best?

I do not share the seemingly widespread belief that "closer to the people" local and state political forums consistently yield better political outcomes than the national political forum. If state and local political forums even occasionally produced good central plans, there would have been no clamor for federal intervention. The better politically correct, local plans would have gradually become the norm. Across the policy spectrum, the benefits of being able to escape especially bad policies by relocating to another area ("Tiebout choice") and being "closer to the people" seem to be, more often than not, offset by reduced transparency, reduced competency, and easier entry for rent-seekers at the state or local level. From Ayn Rand's *Atlas Shrugged* (1957), I've recognized that the economics term rent-seeker, which means using political influence to benefit at others' expense, is far too kind. Rand's term, "looter," is better. We must be extremely wary of anything that empowers and incentivizes looting through the government.

The diversity of children within communities is much greater than between communities and states. Even before large-scale state and federal intervention, the one-size-fits-all central planning approaches produced by local political forums were not notably better than what we're getting from the fragmented political process in place now. So, whether we have multi-center, central planning, or primacy by one political forum, we need nondiscrimination so that decentralized planning can provide schooling alternatives to families not well served by the instructional approaches prescribed by one or more political processes.

Political Control Yields Uncertainties

We can also be certain that a central plan is subject to interpretation. The enforced meaning can depend upon who is president, and meaning can change selectively with exemptions that are often commonplace, such as under NCLB. That's a major source of weak accountability, confusion, uncertainty, and influence peddling (corruption), which are key underlying reasons why it is widely understood that central plans invariably produce terrible outcomes.

The USDOE has, for example, a thirty-seven-page single-space "frequently asked questions" document for just the NCLB-ESSA transition. A recent controversy over the Trump administration's definition of "ambitious plan" is an example of the significance of administrative power to define terms and change their meaning, even significantly, from one administration to the next. The Trump rhetoric, including an executive order demanding minimum federal intervention, seems at odds with Secretary DeVos' policy of meticulously following the provisions of the law, which is arguably what is required of any law.

A recent Cato Institute Forum that didn't even get into the regulatory or judicial weeds, except with some examples, reflected widespread disagreement on key questions. The forum discussed the broad topic of whether ESSA would actually yield more state and local political control, something I tentatively regard as a good thing because it means the involvement of two political forums (state and local) rather than three, and because we can learn a lot by comparing the outcomes of the many state and local political forums. The Cato Forum participants were not convinced that ESSA will yield a lighter federal touch.

Samples of Federal Political Process Outcomes

There is, of course, the stealth appearance of widespread teaching of extremely controversial Critical Race Theory that asserted: (a) persistent systemic racism; and (b) future race-based discrimination as a correct response to past discrimination. And Arne Duncan's USDOE provided plenty of stunning examples. In a 2012 speech, Secretary Duncan said he would not "micromanage 100,000 schools from Washington," but the Thomas Fordham Institute said, "that is precisely what Duncan is doing." That was in addition to the institute's complaint that Duncan's USDOE had put a federal fingerprint on the Common Core Curriculum Initiative that had previously avoided the taint of alleged federal involvement to further centralize and standardize schooling policies. Fordham's Mike Petrilli also voiced disappointment with the Obama administration's efforts to eliminate the small, restriction-laden voucher program for the District of Columbia. Complaining about a government official being moved by the political process is bizarre. Government is force focused by politics.

The political process can foster bizarre behavior. This example, from a USDOE "Dear Colleague" letter is worth a second airing:

> The administration of student discipline can result
> in unlawful discrimination based on race [even]
> if a policy is neutral on its face—meaning that
> the policy itself does not mention race—and is
> administered in an evenhanded manner, but has

a disparate impact, i.e., a disproportionate and unjustified effect on students of a particular race.

What is more amazing than the legal analysis that followed is the need for a legal analysis. We can now have court cases over the meaning of "unjustified." And so the political process made public school system leadership positions even more challenging, having to adjust school practices, if not policies, to guard against the appearance of injustice, often at the expense of other students.

With nondiscrimination in per-pupil public funding, plus the possibility of co-payment to curb space shortages, we can implement policies that deter and punish racist behavior without legislating consequences or costly litigation (even if justified to punish individual racists). With nondiscrimination, parents can punish schools that impose "unjustified effects," either through misapplied discipline or inadequate discipline, by moving the victims to another school. Innocent alleged perpetrators are not the only victims.

The Obama USDOE made equal access to advanced placement a right delivered only if the numbers don't reveal disparities in enrollments. Another Dear Colleague letter provides a good case in point about how the appearance of fairness imperative yields standardization and uniformity, and how it creates uncertainty.

> OCR assesses the types, quantity, and quality of programs available to students across a school district to determine whether students of all races have equal access to comparable programs both among schools and among students within the same school.

Paul Petersen's (2010) *Saving Schools* contains several examples of how the combination of politics, force, and uniformity can create huge problems. It is costly to codify behavior that could be made to mostly occur naturally. Force—assignment to a school combined with the public school system's high exit cost—compels us to fight[2] over the definitions of acceptable inmate behavior, especially when the definitions arise from law applied widely, such as to a whole state or country.

Few would disagree with the need to assure, ***formally if necessary***, the education of children with disabilities. But a different school system might have made it unnecessary to create a federal law, the Individuals with Disabilities Education Act (IDEA), and made it possible to avoid much unpleasant, stigmatizing labeling of children and arguing in court over the meaning of phrases such as "least restrictive environment." Many so-called disabilities are just differences in how children learn that became disabilities because they don't fit the current system's mainstream pedagogy. A specialized schooling alternative to the assigned TPS, even with a modest co-payment, might be greatly preferred to the IDEA road to a "least restrictive environment" on a TPS campus. Many disabilities—perhaps most—probably don't even need recognition by a Weighted Student Formula (WSF) category. We can imagine that a "least restrictive environment" definition that causes "over 1/3 of the emotionally disturbed to spend over 80% of their school time in a regular classroom" (Petersen 2010, 95) is often very costly to the other children in such classrooms. They become unintended victims, part of an ignored trade-off to help the disabled. Regardless of how one might define cost, the IDEA "declared that cost considerations are irrelevant" (Petersen 2010, 91), something definitely inefficient and arguably irrational that can arise only from a process that spends other folks' money.

Likewise, another controversial practice discussed by Petersen (2010, 101), bilingual education, could be left to profit-motivated enterprise to address, perhaps encouraging customized uses of Education Savings Account funds. Instead, by making the periodic reality of English as a second language a political-legal issue, we have often poorly conceived practices that one critic described as yielding "illiteracy in two languages."[3]

Pleasant Surprises?

Roza and Hagan (2017) celebrated that ESSA has a financial transparency reporting requirement that "presents an opportunity for state education agencies (SEAs) to build an information system that helps districts and schools leverage their dollars to do the most for students." Dr. Roza has repeatedly documented large, school-level differences in per-pupil spending, with an implicit, sometimes explicit, assertion that equalization at the school level could be even more helpful than at the district level, where nearly all of the equalization attention has been seen. Maybe. It depends on exactly how the reallocated money is used and what is eliminated in the schools that have to swap more expensive inputs for less expensive inputs, such as experienced teachers for new teachers. There will be unintended consequences, hopefully mostly good. If the improved ability to track dollars to the school level increases school uniformity, that will likely yield more harm than good. There's already far too much equal treatment of unequal children.

If we could sharpen the ESEA focus on its original mission of providing assistance to the disadvantaged, we might reallocate some USDOE dollars to finance means-tested co-payment (alongside tuition voucher, tuition tax credit, ESA, or privately funded tuition payment) of private school tuition discussed in detail elsewhere in this book (see also chapter 9). Such a use might even be worth the increase in the federal deficit to do it (not compared to past USDOE budgets, but more spending compared to eliminating most current USDOE functions), though reining in the national debt will require curtailment of more than low-value federal spending. Productive results of overspending the federal government's means will have to be offered to states.

Summary

Probably, most helpful to productive school system reform would be an elimination of the USDOE, with a few pieces saved as part of other agencies or departments, and the president using the bully pulpit to ***urge states to follow the best research on the key governance policies of high performing school systems***, and to urge scholars to address the key outstanding questions. Until the dire federal fiscal circumstances make it politically feasible to include USDOE curtailment among the necessary huge budget cuts, appropriate active federal roles include means-tested school choice funding for the economically disadvantaged, including especially co-payment assistance where a child's best instructional fit costs more than the state and local government per-pupil funding. Perhaps in cooperation with the Department of Housing and Urban Development (HUD), the focus could be on means-testing places, not people, which would attract higher-income people to some lower-income places and thus create much-needed income-diverse places and student bodies.

Finally, even in a continuation of much of the status quo, hopefully the federal government will end the interventions that make it difficult: (a) to escape the comprehensive uniformity imperative for assigned public schools; and (b) for proposed alternatives to the assigned TPS to exercise selectivity when it is consistent with the school maintaining a chosen, distinctive mission and only on the distinctive mission basis.

---

[1] See Coulson, Andrew J. 2006. "Why Federal School Vouchers are a Bad Idea," Washington, DC: Cato Institute.

[2] McCluskey, Neal P. 2007b. "Why We Fight: How Public Schools Cause Social Conflict." Cato Institute Policy Analysis #587. http://www.cato.org/pubs/pas/pa587.pdf; Arons, Stephen. 1997. Short Route to Chaos: Conscience, Community, and the Re-constitution of American Schooling. Amherst: University of Massachusetts Press.

[3] It was an unnamed Hispanic caller to a radio talk show.

CHAPTER SIX

A Dynamic Customization/ Matching Process

The vast majority of those expressing an informed opinion at least pay lip service to the wrong-headedness of a business plan to attempt delivery of one-size-fits-all formal instruction to a diverse student population. Children have different learning styles, and some of the many possible subject themes (business, sports, health, etc.) would significantly improve all-important student engagement for a large subset of students. So, we need different strokes for different folks, which means we need a process that properly matches actual and still-to-be-invented different instructional approaches with different educator strengths and student learning (including engagement) factors.

Since the political process demands the ***appearance of fairness***, the current US system addresses the challenge of student diversity through assignment to a comprehensive campus with the same set of choices for all students as the other comprehensive campuses. And the classrooms of our uniformly comprehensive traditional public schools (TPS) address diversity with the appearance of fairness, by sorting each attendance area's students only by age and through training aimed at empowering public school teachers in the art of differentiated instruction. For mandatory classes, administrators assign students to teachers, but not necessarily with students' learning factors and teachers' strengths and weaknesses as a major sorting basis. This chapter addresses the track record of the current strategy for addressing student diversity, how it might be improved, and discusses the other approaches to the customization/personalization of instruction widely cited as necessary to significantly improve school system performance.

The Uniformly Comprehensive Approach

That approach produces disappointing results and serious side effects[1] such as corruption, fraud, and student alienation. But policy reform or technology improvement could change that. Inertia is always a major factor, so attempts to address student diversity through comprehensive public school campuses, and the problems that such campuses cause, will persist as a major factor even with more supportive conditions. Perhaps it will survive as a choice on a much more level playing field with other approaches. Maybe uniformly comprehensive public school campuses will be a much better fit for those that remain when such campuses no longer house the children for whom that approach does not work, the latter probably being the children that will do better in a smaller, mission-focused specialized school.

How might we improve the effectiveness of comprehensive campuses without the important but politically difficult step of sharply reducing discrimination against families that believe that the assigned TPS is not the best available fit for at least one of their children? Blended learning via multi-source course choice is one possibility.[2] Because of transportation challenges exacerbated by the large catchment areas of comprehensive (therefore big) public schools, adding the blended learning option to our current system will likely amount to a mix of online instruction and F2F instruction on the assigned comprehensive campus. But it need not be, especially if student-parental choice is not constrained by public school approval of the off-campus course options.

Another route to improved customization for TPS users is much-improved instructional software. A leading proponent, Utah state senator Howard Stephenson (active at American Legislative Exchange Council meetings, where I met him), calls it micro choice. Such software allows students in the same classroom to learn content in different ways, at their own pace. It changes the role of front-line educators from classroom-based, teacher-instructor to coach-facilitator. That will create a lot of skill obsolescence and thus a lot of resistance, but not necessarily overwhelming if micro choice is phased in, perhaps more gradually than the rate at which software improvements create productive micro-choice-based opportunities for academic gains. It will help with the differentiated instruction challenge, but clearly in a way that is inferior to situations in which specialized settings reduce the need for differentiated instruction.

To properly think about how much we can expect from better instructional software, we need to keep the micro-choice-through-technology tool in perspective. To do that, let's review the classroom-level roots of the current system's persistent low-performance problem and see which of them are potentially addressed by increased use of high-quality software-delivered instruction. Also keep in mind that the potential benefits of increased reliance on technology and the benefits that will be realized by its actual use in public school classrooms may be entirely different things. There is already an extensive record[3] of status quo defenders using their political clout to block adoption of new capabilities delivered by technology. And the history of computer use to broadly improve TPS instruction is anything but encouraging.

If blended learning and improved learning software produce noteworthy improvements, public school districts can perhaps address student diversity within the remaining significant constraints, without constructing mega-campuses widely regarded as too large. With or without catchment areas, smaller schools avoid some of the negative side effects of large schools.[4] And smaller, therefore closer together schools expand each child's F2F course choice menu.

One of the key roots of the current low-performance problem is rampant out-of-field teaching. Can technology improvement make curricula educator-proof so that a learning facilitator lacking, say, a math degree can foster math uptake from learning software as well as someone with a math degree? I doubt it, but the change in educators' roles (less direct instruction) will likely blissfully reduce the out-of-field teaching effects of the virtually ubiquitous single salary schedule.

A heavier dose of technology *can* ease the teacher burnout issue, including distaste for contact with parents, in part by redefining front-line educators' role in the instructional process. The adult(s) in the room with the students, or online, may no longer deliver lectures or other types of traditional lessons, or at least do it a lot less often. Instead, the adult(s) may roam the room to lend assistance where the software does not completely address student struggles, or not all types of struggles. Encounters with parents may become less contentious because the technology uses *can* facilitate more customization than is possible through human attempts at differentiated instruction.

Then there's the current system's struggles to incentivize effectiveness gains. The current system makes it difficult to measure merit objectively and then perhaps properly (perversely because of that difficulty) compensates the vast majority of public school system educators without regard to their hard-to-measure individual effectiveness in the current system. Technology can help us measure some aspects of merit, but that may not increase its impact on educators' paychecks.

Teacher micromanagement is one of the roots of the persistent low-performance problem. A heavier dose of technology could push that either way. Increased micromanagement is possible because software-based instruction can make it easier for the authorities to specify *exactly* what a course will present to students. But use of technology can also ease the impact of teacher micromanagement on students with the dictated content coming to students in a variety of speeds or forms, perhaps with different subject themes and pedagogies.

A heavier dose of technology cannot take the politics out of deciding what is taught. Improved delivery of politically correct content is not an acceptable substitute for engaging though perhaps controversial content or content that parents want their children to learn even if it differs from some of the content other parents view as essential. And it may take a menu of instructional approaches to achieve much-improved engagement of a much higher percentage of schoolchildren.

A Silberman-Wolk Public School System Revolution

Charles Silberman (1971) advocated personalization through experience-based, mostly self-directed student learning. In the envisioned intellectual growth development strategy for all, students work alone or in small groups with supervision by advisers. Silberman seemed to believe that personalization could be achieved by students within a system of uniform public schools. He did not mention increased use of private schools as a key part of a personalization strategy. He sought a central plan overhaul that ends sorting children into grades, and that greatly reduces direct instruction of students in traditional classroom settings.

More recent proponent of personalization through experience-based, mostly self-directed student learning, founding *Education Week* editor Ronald Wolk (chairman emeritus of Editorial Projects in Education) recognized the transformational challenge. It is huge even though Silberman and Wolk seem to believe that personalization through experience-based, largely self-directed student learning can coexist with efficiency-impeding, long-standing public school system traditions such as single salary schedules, school cartels known as districts, neighborhood-based assignment to public schools, a public finance monopoly for public schools, school uniformity, and pricelessness. Wolk did not specify what need not or should not change, but he did note a key central planning (without mention of the term) impediment to change: "The reason nothing important changes in education is because if one significant change is made, everything would have to change." Likewise, a recent effort to measure some aspects of governance noted:

> Some of this apathy [my query: or is it despair
> about potential for governance change?] arises
> from the reality that the structures, rules, and

> institutions of American public education are so
> slow and cumbersome to change. Even seemingly
> small matters, like altering when the local school
> board holds elections, can prove impervious to
> change.

And Osborne:

> Changing a centralized bureaucracy with many
> moving parts is extremely difficult, because
> everything is connected [Osborne 2017, 148]
> and thus part of the resistance to change.
>
> You wouldn't believe some of the simple
> things that we can't get done. [Osborne 2017, 180]
>
> The ability to make change in a complex sys-
> tem like this is incredibly challenging. [Osborne
> 2017, 190]

They independently discovered why centrally planned econo-
mies, such as the former Soviet Union, have five-year plans. You can't
continuously centrally orchestrate total change.

Wolk argued that just the degree of proposed change in the
delivery of content is enough that it would take an expensive ad campaign to gain adequate voter support. A public school system that
achieves personalization by having students demonstrate competencies at their own pace in ways they choose is a very different learning
process from the classroom batch processing most voters experienced
as children.

That proposed transformation would impose an instructional
approach that may fit more children than the current batch-process-
ing, direct-instruction approach, but it is not likely to adequately
fit all. I may be one of the skeptics the ad campaign would target.
Personalization through experience-based, largely self-directed student learning would likely work very well for many children, but I
believe that it would work very badly for others, for example, children
like my two adopted boys. I believe it would be very tough to keep

them focused on academic growth-relevant, project-based learning. However, I recognize that I may have just revealed my ignorance of that pedagogy's facilitation process, a likely widespread problem among parents, which may be a key reason why an effective ad campaign would need to be extensive and thus expensive.

We must think about political determination of (a) the expected competencies (desired outcomes); (b) how proposed policy would change how the system assesses the students' various desired competencies and how the proposed policy would change how the system measures educator effectiveness; (c) where the new schooling process would occur, how much public school retrofitting and new construction should we plan on to facilitate personalization through experience-based, largely self-directed student learning; and (d) how cost factors might impact who has access to what. Once you aim to personalize, you raise the tough political issue of unpredictable non-uniform per-pupil costs (outside a weighted student formula) and the superficial, seeming unfairness of unequal treatment of unequal children, even though "there is nothing more unequal than the equal treatment of unequal people" (Thomas Jefferson). Justice Felix Frankfurter agreed: "It is a wise man who said that there is no greater inequality than the equal treatment of unequals."

Political control through a central planning process means that political correctness will continue to decide what public school students should know. Can the self-directed learning process take the boredom, controversy, and distortion out of schooling content deemed politically correct? I don't know. We have to remind ourselves that even the most seemingly uncontroversial, value-free instructional content—for example, basic math—is still controversial.

Personalization through experience-based, largely self-directed student learning seems to be an even greater challenge for assessment and top-down accountability than the batch instructional approaches of the current system. Even though the specification of the desired competencies may be sufficiently uniform to have a standard exam, there is still a timing issue. Since the different competencies are to be attained at each student's preferred pace, which standard content should be on which student's exam at the exam time, and how do we compare students? How can a central authority create seemingly appropriate student assessments?

For a centralized assessment of a teacher-facilitator, how then will we know whether more competencies could have been attained sooner for more students? Will this mode of instruction help us more accurately measure merit, reduce the resistance to recognizing it tangibly, and make it easier to finance merit-based pay increases? The answer to each seems to be no. And if indeed no is accurate for any of those connected merit pay challenges, will absence of merit-based pay be more or less problematic with personalization through experience-based, largely self-directed student learning than with the current system's preference for classroom-based batch processing of rows of diverse students? What about educator burnout? Personalization through experience-based, largely self-directed student learning seems likely to be helpful on that issue.

Can personalization through experience-based, largely self-directed student learning occur adequately in existing public school facilities? What kinds of facilities are ideal? Is experience-based, largely self-directed student learning an F2F-only process, or can it occur for some students online, through software or through e-mail with online facilitators and online discussion forums?

Will continued equal treatment of unequal educator skills through the single salary schedule that curbs tangible incentives, that causes the current system's rampant out-of-field teaching and causes spot shortages in hard-to-staff places be less problematic when educators do more one-on-one advising and do less direct batch instruction? I don't know. My instincts as an economist ($\equiv$price theorist) tell me that resource allocation under price control will always be very inefficient. But it may be less inefficient than in the current system.

Overlaying a redefinition of preferred instructional approaches or improved instructional software on the entrenched traditions and practices of the current system may be helpful and may be all we can achieve in light of the system's resistance to change. That overlay, and resistance to change, may yield significantly smaller academic gains than the less complicated—though perhaps more ambitious—selling of the nondiscrimination principle.

Customization Through Openness to Entrepreneurial Initiative

Nondiscrimination in public funding opens schooling to entrepreneurial initiative, which typically fosters niche-based one-upmanship and new niche development. Then, individuals and groups implement ideas on how to better serve a certain population segment or better deliver a particular service. Sometimes an innovation makes a long-standing practice obsolete. It takes a formal assignment algorithm or parental school choice to match students to specialized schooling.

Nondiscrimination means that the price system orchestrates resource allocation within and between markets. In the case of copycat entrepreneurship (competition for successful innovators) and markets' typical relentless incremental one-upmanship, the price level of existing goods and services signals each person where their talents and interests will earn the largest income or profit. For individuals, the full rate of return is a combination of tangible factors such as income, and intangible factors such as job satisfaction. Market entry occurs—competition increases—until the resulting drop in prices causes market entry to no longer be attractive. The importance of price change that reflects instructional approach scarcity is why choice restricted to free public schools is unlikely to produce anywhere near comparable long-term academic outcomes as parental choice among schooling options, public and private that receive approximately the same per-pupil subsidy payment for a particular child.

In school systems with large, nondiscriminatory per-pupil subsidies[5] combined with price decontrol, competition will drive the private co-payment share of the tuition price of the least costly instructional approaches to zero. Recall that "nondiscriminatory per-pupil subsidy" means that the funding supporting private school users is similar to the subsidy level supporting public school users. That level is way above the full per-pupil cost of many existing private schools. For many of the new instructional approaches, competition would immediately, or gradually, force entrepreneurs to accept the public per-pupil subsidy amount as full payment of tuition. In countries such as the US, nondiscrimination near current per-pupil subsidy amounts (national average > $13,000/year) would yield an oversupply of many popular instructional approaches unless schools can offer to accept *less* than the per-pupil subsidy amount as full payment, with families being able to spend the difference on other education expenses, including perhaps later, on higher education expenses. The next chapter describes how the Education Savings Account (ESA) public subsidy strategy allows such deferred spending.

Because some costly instructional approaches will be sufficiently popular and costly to produce, competition will not force the tuition price of those approaches down to the per-pupil subsidy level. Market conditions will allow the entrepreneurs offering such high-cost, high-value instructional approaches to charge parents a tuition payment (co-payment) large enough so that the combination of co-payment and per pupil subsidy will be sufficient to cover the school's expenses, including a competitive rate of return on the school owner's investment. Recall that chapter 9 addresses the equity issues raised by subsidized schooling that is not necessarily free. It hurts no one to have high-value, high-cost options on the menu of schooling options.

Highly motivated, entrepreneurial due diligence doesn't eliminate all the possible bad ideas. When a seemingly useful innovation is actually a dud, implementation will lead to financial losses for the entrepreneur and his/her financial backers. Customers may suffer as well. For example, an entrepreneur-initiated school's failure to be sufficiently popular to pay its bills would force its patrons to find a new school, perhaps after the students have fallen behind where they would be had they chosen a different instructional approach.

That's sad, but consider our current system's alternative to that periodic small-scale failure alongside periodic significant instructional approach innovations that improve instruction for big subsets of the student population. Closure of a poorly conceived or managed private school is much less costly to children than the current system's approach of keeping low-performing schools open and repeatedly assigning children to them. Political correctness can yield long-lasting, large-scale failure either by entrenching low-performing instructional approaches like batch processing of same-age but otherwise academically diverse children or by widely imposing, in the name of fairness, an instructional approach that is effective for a lot of children but leaves a lot of children behind. Ted Kolderie (2014) argued that chartered public schools (CPS) should serve as innovation laboratories, in part to avoid the current system's propensity for costly, large-scale semi-permanent experiments (for example, the "whole language" approach to teach reading to *every* child lasted much longer than it should have). But political determination of what CPS can charge and donor dependence severely reduces CPS ability to perform that function.

The Silberman-Wolk self-directed student learning approach is likely in the latter category, effective for many and perhaps also ineffective for many. In school systems open to entrepreneurial initiative, some entrepreneurs would offer and fine-tune the experience-based, largely self-directed student learning approach, among many other approaches already in limited private-sector use, and others stalled on drawing boards because few families can pay a high tuition rate on top of the taxes that support the public school system. In school systems open to entrepreneurial initiative, new schools would form to offer experience-based, largely self-directed student learning approaches until the added supply and new competition drives the tuition price down to the amount barely sufficient to adequately fund those approaches. At that point (with the long-run equilibrium price established), the tuition price will reflect the true minimum cost of that instructional approach. Open school systems produce that true minimum cost price level through competition from new schools no matter what the per-pupil subsidy level is. In a market open to new competitors, the subsidy level only affects the size of the market. The subsidy level affects how much new school formation it will take until the price level falls to the true minimum cost. If the subsidy level is quite high, the tuition price—the co-payment amount—will stabilize at zero, which could yield excess supply of some of the cheaper instructional approaches.

Parents will pay an out-of-pocket add-on or seek a third-party funding source (likely means-tested) when the expected results of experience-based, largely self-directed student learning, or any other instructional approach, are sufficiently superior to the expected outcomes of other instructional approaches to justify the co-payment, if any. Many of the alternatives may be less expensive. More simply, parents will choose the best instructional *value* for each of their children.

According to Paul Kihn, a former assistant district superintendent, a few districts have acknowledged that they cannot provide appropriate (a good fit) schooling for all children. Kihn recommends a paradigm shift to "2.0 districts": "They must become deeply specialized in some, *but not all*, areas of schooling." As part of 2.0 district reinvention, Kihn recommends TPS specialization in at least "neighborhood-based schooling," plus specialize in "academic gaps in the citywide system." Kihn mentions only CPS as providers of instruction that districts should leave to others. He does not describe the key elements of the neighborhood-based schooling instructional approaches, but it seems to mean focusing on the instruction that will work well enough for mainstream children, for which school proximity will be a key choice-making factor. With the genuine competitive pressure that districts would face with the loss of districts' public finance monopoly, and the freedom to specialize, we would see a lot of 2.0 district initiatives. That might yield considerable diversity in how districts would see themselves on the much more level playing field that would exist with nondiscrimination in per-pupil public funding.

Exactly how nondiscrimination could work, or fail to be achieved, matters quite a bit and certainly needs to be specified and clarified. Before that is addressed in chapter 8, the next chapter explains why central plan optimization, currently the primary method of pursuing school system reform, has a low upside.

---

[1] Powell et al. 1985, Segal 2004.

[2] Teacher training issues: "Moonshots in Education" (Pacific Research Institute 2015), pp. 216–219.

[3] Christensen, Clayton M., Michael B. Horn, and Curtis W. Johnson. *Disrupting Class: How Disruptive Innovation Will Change the Way the World Learns.* McGraw-Hill, 2008.

[4] Longtime education analyst David Kirkpatrick pointed out that "hundreds of studies have found that large schools are less effective and more dangerous than small ones." *School Report* 9/20/07.

[5] None do now, except for a few states that fund TPS and CPS on an equal per-pupil basis.

CHAPTER SEVEN

Central Plan Optimization

Amazingly, a well-articulated, lengthy, soul-searching article about the decades of failure to achieve significant school system improvement doesn't even mention, much less seriously consider as a possibility, that school systems might achieve rapid performance gains if what was taught, how, where, and to whom was determined the way nearly all of the US economy settles those issues.[1] The author, Paul Reville (2016), does not ask if we should adopt policies to allow and foster decentralized planning of the production of instruction for school-children through market-determined tuition and input prices. The key input, teacher labor, is currently subject to price control through a single salary schedule. Just for being the norm for the economy, decentralized planning should receive serious consideration, but the article implicitly assumes that what I call central plan optimization is the only way to move forward. The same thing is true of three recent books hoping that the existing funding and governance processes will quickly yield radically different outcomes.[2]

Paul Reville's "urgent call to action" asserts widespread "disillusionment," a word that should not apply to something—central planning—known to never work. How can disillusion result from the failure of strategies that always fail? The article mentions the centerpieces of all of the recent, noteworthy failed central plan improvement strategies, perfectly sensible-sounding things such as higher standards, better data systems, greater pressure (promised accountability), and the public school choice contained in the No Child Left Behind (NCLB, 2002) proposal.

How can such a separate reality persist in so many highly educated brains (see chapter 10)? Many of the same people—probably the vast majority pursuing school reform or school system reform—probably have a visceral negative reaction to the term "central planning." But they have not recognized that central planning is the governance mechanism of the schooling industry. That and tiny islands of price-less, uncoordinated capitalism—chartered public schools—determine what is taught, how, where, and to whom. Central planning's serious shortcomings are responsible for the low performance of school systems worldwide, which is why the best systems have aggregate outcomes only about 10 percent better than our Nation at Risk outcomes.

So, a widespread conviction persists that much-needed improvement can only occur through the same central planning processes that created the urgent need for huge improvements.[3] Maybe the problem is that reform advocates cannot identify governance options they believe are likely to work better. Is Reville's call for better leadership a call for better central planning? Probably. But maybe Reville allows that better leadership could also mean the political wisdom and will to pursue a more level playing field between centrally planned schooling and entrepreneurial alternatives.

I'm discussing the Reville article because he didn't get into what educators should do. Countless others describe the unacceptable outcomes of the current system, then call for better integration, better communication, more buy-in, better data and better use of it, etc., and then urge educators to change their behavior without calling for any changes in the incentives that produced the regretted current behavior.[4] Those are all well-worn euphemisms for better planning. But K-12 schooling needs a new "business plan," one that exploits the critical information and powerful incentives delivered to independent decision-makers connected by a price system.

The failed approaches cited by Reville amount to central plan tinkering, a familiar concept. David Tyack and Larry Cuban (1995) dubbed it *Tinkering Towards Utopia*. The Tyack-Cuban subtitle, *A Century of Public School Reform*, could have been "More of the Same—Harder Yields Nation at Risk Performance Levels." Blair Lybbert noted that the widespread persistent reliance on unproductive tinkering was an attempt to "introduce positive change to the system without fundamentally redesigning it." Osborne called it "more-longer-harder" (Osborne 2017, 2). Hess (2010) called it "the same thing over and over." I cited the term "more of the same—harder" in my *The School Choice Wars* (2001). ***So, apparently, frustration with recycling of failed approaches has existed for a long time. It has been the only game in town, and it will keep yielding costly frustration until productive, transformational change becomes politically feasible.***

Tinkering is not relevant to a Nation-at-Risk-sized problem, which is what bipartisan and non-partisan authorities have repeatedly told us we have. That bolsters my point that a simple basis for exit from the assigned public school may be the only politically feasible, credible, potential route to the major school system improvement we have repeatedly been told we need. Ironically, Lybbert's insightful phrase about the failure to consider transformational change was part of an article in which he argued that increased flexibility about eligibility for graduation would amount to a radical change. Maybe it's possible to achieve radical change without a transformational catalytic policy reform? I doubt it.

I have no objection to higher standards whenever the existing standards expect less than the system (the current system or another), or a proposed system, can deliver. And I have no objection to creating greater accountability for outcomes achievable through the evolved business plan imposed on the system's participants. If tinkering is all that is politically feasible, by all means, let's find tinkering that hasn't already produced disappointing results and assess its potential by any means available. The absence of empirical evidence should not be a showstopper. If other grounds for assessment argue that a new policy could be worthwhile, we don't want to insist that someone else has to try it first, then wait a long time to have the empirical evidence of worthwhileness.

Because the chaos that constant experimentation yields is costly, and central plans are especially resistant to change (Wolk in chapter 6: "The reason nothing important changes in education is because if one significant change is made, everything would have to change."), only big changes are worth the effort and the chaos risk. To minimize the recycling of failed approaches, we need a prominent study to carefully (no broad-brush indictments!) document the reform strategies that have attempted, and failed, to deliver noteworthy school system improvement.

Though I believe that we should abandon small-scale and large-scale central plan revision in favor of decentralized planning (trigger transformation with simple policy changes), this chapter addresses the people determined to address the Nation at Risk problem—pursue significant performance gains—through central plan transformation. To do that, I will use one of the five—the best one—prominent schooling reform proposals to overhaul the central plan to illustrate why central plan optimization has a low upside. The three-headed, fragmented central planning of current US school systems has an even lower upside, which may be a key reason why the central planning outcomes of many foreign school systems top ours. But the key point of this chapter is that even the best central plan transformation proposals will not significantly improve school system performance. Decentralized planning through free enterprise and school choice orchestrated by market-determined price change will produce the best results.

Large-Scale Central Plan Optimization

Of the five calls for major changes in school system performance that I am aware of, I have already discussed the Wolk-Silberman proposal (WSP). Though the WSP doesn't name any noteworthy funding or governance changes, longtime scholar and *Education Week* founder Ronald Wolk believed the proposed policy changes are significant enough to require a major public education campaign to make it politically feasible, to cause the public to support its implementation through existing governance processes.

John Merrow's (2017) seeks radically different public school system behavior without any specified catalytic policy changes. Merrow calls for an informed public uprising to demand better behavior from the administrators and teachers. Kolderie (2014) and Osborne (2017) seek more and improved chartering, alongside (Osborne) policy overhauls at the district level driven by examples from New Orleans, Denver, and Washington, DC. To them, allowing the combination of market-determined prices and profit needed to unleash free enterprise and the innovation they seek is sad or evil, something to be avoided. The public sector is not known for innovation prowess, but Kolderie and Osborne expect innovation from school boards and administrators. They believe that narrowly defined powers and responsibilities plus freedom from ordinary political pressures will yield innovation and improve governance. They believe that if insulation filters out the pressures to pay attention to adults' interests, the authorities will fully focus on the students' interests. And then the political process will yield something very different from the behaviors and outcomes produced by the current system's political process. They seem to agree with me that the political process is the central cause of poor school system performance.

They don't recognize that we've tried that no-accountability central planning process and that our current system still creates decision-maker insulation with policies that depress parental involvement and school district election turnouts. The low performance of limited local political accountability combined with no market accountability led to increased state and federal intervention and the multi-center central planning process we have now. More, different, or fewer rules is how central planning works. Persistent disappointment produced more rules. Indeed, we have what many people describe as a compliance-driven, not performance-driven, public school system. Market accountability would yield more professional autonomy than multi-center central planning, but genuine market accountability cannot exist when price controls create shortages and stymie the informational role of the price formation process.

The Hill-Jochim Central Plan Proposal

Only the Hill-Jochim proposal calls for significant funding and governance changes. The proposed changes don't appear to have a downside, so I believe it is the best central plan optimization proposal. Some school districts are already attempting some of the key Paul Hill and Ashley Jochim central plan revision proposals.

Is it too soon to judge the Hill-Jochim (HJ) Portfolio Management Plan's effectiveness, or do the on-the-ground portfolio management realities insufficiently resemble the HJ proposal? In other words, did the school district cooks omit some of the key ingredients of the HJ cake recipe, or has the cake not yet baked long enough? Probably some of each, but in addition, I will argue that the plan is fundamentally flawed because of the fundamental flaws of central planning. The HJ plan might still yield better outcomes than the current system, but even if that is the case, it may not be worth it. The transition might be so costly that the improvement is not worth it. And perhaps worst of all, it is likely that any major change precludes other types of major changes for a long time, some of which likely have a much higher upside than even the best possible central plan.

In an *Education Week* article, "Beyond Chartering," Paul Hill and Ashley Jochim describe the highlights of their new book, *A Democratic Constitution for Public Education.*[5] It basically asserts a superior central plan for primary and secondary education. Hill-Jochim, in effect, argue that if the central planners have the clearly defined roles they describe, including, especially, clearly and correctly limited powers, K-12 schooling will become the first ever high-performing price-less or price-controlled industry. They assume the central planners will spell out the ideal per-pupil payments that taxpayers will finance and then make lots of wise, complicated, controversial decisions, even though such brilliance from the public's perspective, including efficiency, has been rare in all circumstances driven by the political process.

The central rationale for the Hill-Jochim plan is that chartered public school authorizing is often either too lax, or over-reaching. Their answer: "The only way to eliminate these problems is to clarify the government's role in public education and limit its powers." "Clarify" and "limit" are common themes for getting positive results from the political process. To do that, HJ said there needs to be "one agency responsible for all of a city's [public school] students." So, they believe we need to further centralize central planning to make it productive. Through the central planners' wisdom alone, they would know what schooling should cost (that subsumes a lot of cost guesses—materials, building, teachers, etc.), including weighted student formulas (WSF) that set different per-pupil payments for different student characteristics, properly documented. Because there are some obvious cost differences for some broad classes of children, a WSF can be a solid starting point for subsidy payments that parents can then top off if they need to and wish to, in order to match an instructional approach to the specific attributes of their children. But we know that a WSF amount that must be accepted as a full payment is predictably a failed price-control experiment. It took the Florida legislature only one year to recognize the impossibility of specifying exactly what it should cost to educate all of the different kinds of special-needs children. At the end of that year, Florida's McKay special-needs voucher law was changed to allow parents to co-pay to top off the state-provided voucher amount. It is also true for mainstream children that it is unwise to specify exactly what it should cost to educate each one, but it is less immediately obvious.

Underneath, the "one agency responsible for all of a city's students" school districts would still exist, but in the HJ plan, school boards would only have two roles: (a) develop a menu of schooling options and (b) employ a CEO. Supposedly, school boards would not need market price information to know the optimal menu of schooling options. They'd know which types of school choices are missing from that menu, and that the missing schools would be financially feasible. That presupposes brilliance and insulation from controversy in creating the weighted student formula and that schools' costs would only depend upon which WSF-recognized types of students it enrolled, that there is only one useful pedagogy for each recognized student type and that pedagogy has consistent, predictable costs. To keep schooling free, cost cannot depend upon how a school proposes to educate the children that choose it from the menu.

In a portfolio management model, the school board's CEO also wisely tracks school performance, identifies underserved children and neighborhoods, and forces replacement of non-performing schools, having all of the necessary information to do that in a decision-making process untainted by the political pressures likely to arise from the CEO's powers. The CEO would also know when a new instructional approach has been created that is superior to what is done by some of the existing schools, and then demand that those existing schools be closed to make room for superior new approaches. The school board would know when the CEO was not doing that, and then quickly hire a replacement who would be more diligent and have better foresight. Are you repeatedly saying to yourself, "Yeah, right"? You should be.

The technical reasons for the dismal track record of central planning by an expert, politically accountable group mostly revolve around two immense, never surmounted challenges: (1) the difficulty properly aligning planners' incentives and the public good, even to the fuzzy degree that instructional approach possibilities can be prioritized without market price information; and (2) the immense difficulties of administratively processing all the information relevant to wise resource use. Like many of the jokes about economists (I am one, Hill is not), Hill simply assumes wise resource allocation by the central planners with the newly clarified powers and duties, and with insulation from ordinary politics. Why/how that can suddenly be the case, Hill does not say beyond the need to clearly spell out the authorities' duties and also spell out the things beyond each official's purview. If they have less power, suddenly they become wiser and lacking the power to do the counterproductive things that are now commonplace, they will be left with no choice but to do the right things. Even if that were credible, we'd have a stagnant industry. They can only choose instructional approaches they are aware of. How will the planners know the right mix? By what process will innovative approaches—only the good ideas—displace tried and true but suddenly inferior instructional approaches?

I know Paul Hill, retired founder and longtime CEO of the Center for Reinventing Public Education. He has the ability to produce the best possible central plan. Unfortunately, his vast knowledge and experience makes him susceptible to what Friedrich von Hayek said, in a book, was the fatal conceit of central planners. Paul Hill knows so much that he believes the immensity of the task is doable through a wise, clearly tasked central authority. The best argument, which may prove compelling, for the Hill-Jochim proposal is that we will need the best possible central plan if we are not wise enough to recognize the severe limitations of central/political control of primary and secondary education. Hopefully, we will be wise enough to implement the funding and governance changes needed to adopt the alternative of decentralized whole-population planning through dynamic market price signals and free enterprise, to create, improve, and sustain the optimal mix of specialized schooling options.

In a recorded interview that describes the Hill-Jochim book, Hill asserts that a key objective of the proposed HJ strategy is "to make public oversight safe for schools." That aligns with my assertion that the central cause of ubiquitous Nation at Risk school system performance levels is that the political process decides what the public school system does. And the public funding monopoly of the public school system severely constrains what private schools can sell.

Indeed, as Hill's statement strongly implies, public oversight is now not safe for schools. Hill stated that public oversight (the political process) has "tended to erode school freedom." Indeed, there is widespread micromanagement. So, within the HJ-envisioned, expert-chosen menu of public school options, there is school choice, and the schools are not told how to teach, except when the instructional process is part of what caused a school to be included in the portfolio. But even for schools still accountable to their customers because they have seats to fill, the HJ system sets limits on the portfolio schools' freedom even without actual rules proscribing certain actions, or without central office overseers empowered to veto school-level choices. For example, an innovation might cost more than the budget (based on what the experts believe should be the per-pupil cost) can support. That is quite likely for many innovations, especially early on, before experience and competition lowers costs. So, an innovation can easily be cost-prohibitive even if a small additional allowed cost would yield a huge improvement in student outcomes and then, with experience, become less costly. Is it politically feasible to temporarily fund some of the portfolio schools at higher per-pupil levels than others to facilitate at least initially costly innovation? Given that the appearance of fairness is a political imperative, such unequal funding will be hard to achieve and hard to keep focused on just the intended purpose. And conveying that discretion violates the HJ imperative that public officials have very few clearly defined powers.

Given the political correctness of, and desperation for, improvement without threatening too many elements of the status quo, we should not be surprised by the broad support for the portfolio management concept, in general, "despite minimal evidence of success" (Henig et al, 2010). "Politicians from the right and the left (including presidents George W. Bush and Barack Obama), and prominent educational funders, have held up these districts as models for district reform." Indeed, it may be the best possible way for the political entities called school districts to discharge their duties.

Henig et al. correctly observed that "the successful operation of a portfolio model [still] depends on good government. It is not a way to sidestep the challenge of creating and sustaining smart bureaucracies." And, "politics—the interplay of interest groups, partisan maneuvering, and influence trading—will have as much, or more, to do with the way portfolio management unfolds in practice as will market forces." Because I cannot fathom how the typically brilliant Henig and co-author Henry Levin (an economist) can see market forces significantly influencing the portfolio strategy's outcomes (except negatively by stifling innovation and creating shortages), I thought about not including those last three words in the quote. It was not an isolated slip of the fingers on their word processor. Elsewhere, they imagine that "portfolio management is not just another market-based model that runs on supply and demand." The TPS-CPS combination is widely, mistakenly seen as a "mixed market approach." Nonsense!

Portfolio management does not run on supply and demand! The portfolio managers prohibit profits, set prices, and choose the providers of free instruction. That setting does not resemble the typical market setting wherein producers exit or enter depending upon the profit potential signaled by prices set by the lightly regulated or unregulated interaction of buyers and sellers. Indeed, as Henig and Levin note, "the government [political process] makes the key decisions." It is a price-less environment. Absent a true market setting, actual and aspiring portfolio schools may act "like private contractors in other urban services or in the defense sector" and "find it easier to use their inside knowledge and access to ensure their position than to rely on the innovation, quality, and consumer responsiveness" that we get in uncorrupted market settings.

Kolderie's Split-Screen Strategy and Osborne's Reformed Bureaucracies

Both Kolderie and Osborne see an increased role for increased chartering, provided it is 100 percent nonprofit. I agree that there is immense potential in charter expansion, but not with their views on how to facilitate increased chartering. My proposal to expand the role of chartered public schools (CPS) would work by phasing in deregulation of market entry and allowing co-payment of tuition (price decontrol). That would yield market accountability and eliminate the existing toxic combination of profit potential, entry restriction, and price-control-induced shortages. At the end of the phase-in, we'd be able to rely on potential profit to yield the market entry that right-sizes each niche's output. And profit potential incentivizes investment and innovation. Nonprofit CPS are fine under those circumstances, but then for-profit CPS are an essential, rather than toxic, part of the mix.

Kolderie and Osborne do not recognize the significance of price control (co-payment ban). They view profit as an unsavory element of schooling. Such attitudes are a costly symptom of low basic economic literacy, present even among the senior professionals of many fields. The current K-12 system is partly to blame. Because differences between good and bad capitalism (Baumol et al, 2009) are not well understood, many people do not differentiate between an honest, competitive profit, and a profit that results from rent-seeking (gaining at others' expense through political power), or as Ayn Rand's *Atlas Shrugged* (1957) aptly put it, looting through political influence. Honest, competitive profit results from moving resources to higher value uses; that is, by creating wealth.

Kolderie and Osborne see net benefits from increased chartering provided there are some additional rules and better oversight from charter authorizers to police bad behavior. Indeed, the latter is critical as long as shortages of CPS space largely eliminates accountability to parents. But improved authorizing is of limited value in this regard. Some undesirable corner-cutting is just a matter of deciding how to deliver the product, so not subject to policing-based correction.

And policing almost never comes close to eliminating profit-enhancing, counterproductive behavior. Shortage-created opportunity to increase profit or to allow increased spending on salaries in an ostensibly nonprofit CPS will channel some of the innovation that free enterprise is famous for into schemes to cut costs without arousing the ire of the authorizers. The "bad capitalism" propensity to channel innovation from productivity-increasing activities to beat-the-system schemes is a large part of the explanation why some countries are much poorer than others, and for recent "riches to rags" cases such as Argentina and Venezuela.

Much of the remaining critique of the improved central plan outcome proposals of Kolderie and Osborne is similar to the Hill-Jochim critique. They expect radical behavior changes from the public school system educators—market accountability outcomes (especially Kolderie)—from injecting their proposals into little-changed, political-lite-accountability-only school systems that ultimately empower the most-motivated, best-organized special interests, which are typically the people employed by the system directly or as vendors.

The Moonshot for Kids Project

An aptly titled moonshot competition[6] arrived in 2019 to finally, this time, for sure, devise a significant central plan improvement. An early 2022 net search indicated no moonshot news since a late 2019 announcement of ten finalists.[7] Maybe newsworthy moonshot outcomes were put on hold by the pandemic. If the moonshot competition is another example of hope triumphing over vast experience, we must not let it distract us from pursuit of school system reform.

Documented Governance Confusion

Extensive discussion of central plan governance illustrates and supports the consensus that it is important.[8] But as a sort of proof of my point that central planning has a low upside because central planning has never surmounted fundamental flaws, a recent effort to measure several aspects of school system governance did not offer any hypotheses about how each measured aspect affected academic outcomes; no mention of the fundamental flaws. That effort did not cite any established theories that motivated the measurement of what they quantified. So, they believe governance is important but do not say why or how, a section in A Taxonomy of Education Governance entitled "Why Governance is Important" notwithstanding. Looking at the various scatterplots of school system governance attributes reveals no obvious simple correlations between academic performance and measured fundamental aspects such as state vs. local control and fragmentation/consolidation of authority, and standard incomplete measures of school system performance such as aggregate test scores. So, measurement of the governance aspects believed to be worth measuring provide no guidance to a central plan revision process, at least not yet. Now that we have data for the measured aspects of governance, we will hopefully find it of sufficient importance to develop governance theories for them. Absent an established body of theory as a basis for hypothesis development, studies can only fish for reasons for their importance. Provided that there are sufficient data for a fully specified model, we should at least test the hypothesis implied in many activists' longtime clamor for local control.

If you look at score levels and score trends, you could argue that there are some significant differences between the fifty-one US school systems. The new governance aspect data described above can make possible more of the fully-specified models needed to test the importance of actual school system differences. For example, two states were similar a few years ago, but one shot ahead. For central plan improvement, it would be helpful to compare those two states' recent policy changes. And the differences between the scores can be used to explore which policy differences between the states account for the score differences. But *state comparison can ONLY reveal the importance of ways in which the fifty states and DC actually differ*. Even had the authors attempted to measure extent of market control (decentralized vs. centralized planning), empirical assessment of that all-important aspect would very likely be stymied by insufficient variation in a market-control independent variable. My apologies for the lapse into stat-speak. A hopefully useful, insightful translation is that our fifty-one US school systems may not contain enough variety in the extent of market control to learn from those differences the importance of market control. Likewise, widespread similarities in political control may preclude assessment of some significant governance policies. I believe the debilitating similarities in the fifty-one US school systems are more significant than the differences, a hypothesis supported generally by the small deviations around low average test scores. But we have yet to test/measure the importance of the specific similarities.

Summary

Central plan optimization may stay the only game in town for a long time, so we had better get a lot better at it. Indeed, Van Schoales (President of A+ Colorado) called for a reinvention of central plan optimization after recognizing its utter failure ("The End of Education Reform").[9] This book presents an alternative to that futility. Widespread failure to recognize central plan optimization's low upside was a major reason I wrote this book. To be more than naive about our desperation for significant school system improvement, we have to (a) learn the ways in which governance can be productively changed; and (b) wisely change the incentives of educators if we are to rationally expect a significant, permanent desired change in their behavior.

The next chapter describes the different policy vehicles for opening up school systems, for achieving nondiscrimination in funding to get out of the central plan optimization rut. And then chapter 9 challenges the notion that equity is an advantage of providing services through taxation and political control.

---

[1]   For a book-length version of the same lament, see Roselli (2005).

[2]   Osborne, David. 2017. *Reinventing America's Schools: Creating a 21st Century Education System*. NY: Bloomsbury; Merrow, John. 2017. *Addicted to Reform*. NY: The New Press; and Kolderie, Ted. 2014. *The Split-Screen Strategy*. Edina, MN: Beavers Pond Press.

[3]   Ibid.

[4] Ibid.

[5] A recorded interview provides further details. In the edexcellence interview, Paul Hill says that private schools are not included in the managed portfolio, but that he is open to revising the strategy to include them.

[6] https://fordhaminstitute.org/national/commentary/moonshot-kids.

[7] https://www.americanprogress.org/press/release-10-finalists-announced-moonshot-kids-competition/

[8] See, for example, McGuinn, Patrick (ed.). 2013. *Education Governance for the Twenty-First Century: Overcoming the Structural Barriers to School Reform.* Washington, DC: Brookings Institution Press. There are six editions of Sergiovanni et al.'s *Educational Governance and Administration.*

[9] https://www.edweek.org/ew/articles/2019/04/26/education-reform-as-we-know-it-is.html.

Chapter Eight

The Appropriate Public-Private Subsidy Mix

My primary aim is to clarify how the subsidy mix can differ, why differences are important, and why there is much disagreement. A secondary aim is to clarify the grounds for my policy preferences. I have found that doing so is the best way to foster debate and to ferret out hidden assumptions (often hidden from its owners) and avoid hidden agenda perceptions. And since there are strong feelings on this subject, I will name some non-evil, deliberative, intelligent proponents of policy preferences sometimes described as severe. Arguably, the implied TPS "business plan" is severe (often described as such—recall the heroic assumptions discussed in chapter 2), objectively so because a public finance monopoly for government producers is not the way we produce any other private (rival, exclusive) goods, even when they are merit goods. However, since supporters of the school system status quo are numerous, there is no need to single out any of the status quo's supporters as evidence that supporters of the status quo are not evil.

First, we need to be clear that private subsidy arises through charity, and that taxes finance public subsidies. That public subsidy policies arise from a political process is the main reason why scholars such as Milton Friedman, James Tooley, and E. G. West prefer school systems with no more government role than would apply to any entities that offer services to the general public. They and others argue that zero public funding has and would again produce better schooling outcomes than any likely system with public funding and political determination of what will be taught, how, where, and to whom. In this policy area, Milton Friedman is best known for his advocacy of universal eligibility for tuition vouchers that would create a playing field between public and private schooling options that is much more level than the current public finance monopoly of the public school system. Less well known is that Friedman supported a tuition voucher policy, including market-based co-payment, just as a first step (chapter 14 is a discussion of transition issues) toward getting politics out of school system governance, ownership, and funding.

Many people do not share Professor Friedman's reverence for market mechanisms, his high confidence in the adequacy of private subsidy for those least able to pay, and his abhorrence of the political process. But I've never heard Professor Friedman described as a reckless decision-maker, delusional, or evil. Sadly, such characterizations do exist, even among the scholars and activists that favor major changes in the fifty-one US school systems. For example, a prominent proponent of limited school choice said it would be "evil" to ***allow*** subsidized schools to charge subsidy co-payments (something I strongly support as an absolutely critical element of school systems); that is, for example, to allow families to supplement a tuition voucher with private funds to pay the tuition of a private school that charges more than the voucher amount. Milton Friedman's views and those of many others are proof that rational, deliberative, well-informed decision-making can lead to a conclusion that school systems will produce better outcomes, including for the least-advantaged, when politics plays a much smaller role, perhaps zero, in deciding which instructional approaches will be produced, how, where, and for whom. We should challenge assumptions, especially heroic assumptions, weak logic, and incomplete command of evidence but not accuse serious people of perverse preferences, recklessness, or malicious intent.

The fifty-one US school systems are currently at the other end of the public vs. private spectrum from systems where the only subsidies arise from charity (100 percent private). In the US, the political process is the key determinant of what each public school system produces, how, where, and for whom. Entrepreneurial initiative, consumer choice, and market-driven price change have only relatively minor impacts on primary and secondary education, even when delivered by private schools. In many countries, government policies prescribe much private school behavior. In the US., the public finance monopoly of the public school systems yields privately subsidized, church-run, nonprofit dominance of the private sector offerings, especially the choices within the means of the vast majority of families.

The numerous thoughtful proponents of the status quo, perhaps with increased per-pupil funding and continued efforts at central plan optimization (chapter 7), believe that schooling is too important to leave to the uncertain outcomes of the market and that the schooling of children, as a merit good (widely, mistakenly believed to be a public good), lies outside the range of goods and services that are best dealt with through the whole-population, decentralized planning achieved by markets. Others, including me, argue that schooling is too important to leave to the certain adverse outcomes of the political process.

Status quo proponents may further believe that private subsidy alone will not adequately support the schooling of children from low-income families. That belief is very likely a key basis of the widespread, strong condemnation of analysts eager to see government funding and rules reduced to zero. Belief that private subsidy alone will be inadequate is especially strong for folks that define "adequate" as equal opportunity. Since even very high levels of taxation cannot generate enough public subsidy funding to eliminate the advantages afforded by greater earnings, proponents of "equality" of opportunity have fallen back on the current policy that makes it extremely costly to purchase more schooling for your child than what the per-pupil public subsidy amount provides to everyone through the assigned TPS. If you opt out of the assigned TPS, you have to pay for schooling again, unless you can secure a slot in a CPS with an instructional approach that is a good fit for your child. It's a leveling-down approach because it holds back some without benefitting anyone. A more efficient public subsidy approach is to provide for a portable high minimum, i.e., the nondiscrimination funding policy advocated throughout this book. When a family privately supplements their nondiscrimination share of public funding, it does not make the families unable to do so worse off. You are not made worse off when someone else spends more on the schooling of their children. If anything, in the long run, it makes lower-income families better off through the positive spillovers generated by efficient schooling, and by attracting more and better entrepreneurs (innovation) and educators into school systems. There are a lot of thoughtful people with public subsidy preferences between the US status quo and the Friedman-Tooley-West preference for zero public subsidy. I will describe my public subsidy policy preference before I discuss the specific non-zero public subsidy policy options that are available.

An Ideal School System Reform?

Even if efficiency is the sole objective, there is no such thing as a perfect school system policy or a perfect policy reform. And because we have to start from where we are at, rather than from a clean slate, the best possible policy and how best to move forward from where we are at may not be the same thing. In this section, I aim for honesty in stating my perspective, including, especially, how I weigh the trade-offs involved in some key school system policy choices.

If I had a clean slate to work from, my preference for a public subsidy policy would be ***tax credits for households and businesses that donate to providers of means-tested private subsidies, and bankable, nonrefundable education tax credits for households for each child they opt out of free (no tuition) public schooling***. Means-tested private subsidy could, for example, help finance co-payments for lower-income families. That assures every child of a well-funded, competitive schooling option regardless of family income. I'm tempted to exclude politically correct (by definition) free public schools from my start-from-clean-slate preference, but such a system may not be politically stable. Complaints about widely unequal opportunity may yield a replay of the nineteenth century, when a lower-performing, public-school-dominated school system replaced a higher-performing, lightly subsidized, private-school-only school system.

Education tax credit nonrefundability is important because courts typically rule that such credits do not amount to government spending, which is much more susceptible to debilitating regulation than refunds of taxpayers' own money. Bankability means that families get credits against taxes paid after their children are no longer in school, which is important and proper because families pay the taxes that fund the public school system throughout their lives, including indirectly through school taxes paid by businesses. Families pay relatively little of the schooling cost while their own children are actually in school. For example, suppose family A's estimated school taxes average $4,000/year. Suppose A's use of private schools saves the state an estimated $160,000. Suppose that such families are eligible for a 90 percent nonrefundable education tax credit. I recommend against 100 percent. Coulson's (1999) research demonstrated that skin in the game is critical. Starting with the first year that one of the children uses a private school, the family gets a $3,600 (90 percent of $4,000) tax credit and continues to receive that amount each year until the credits earned total 90 percent of $160,000. That would likely take many more years than their children attend school. Without bankability, the family gets the credit only while at least one child is in school. The resulting much smaller subsidy of private school users will preserve much of the existing huge private school entry barrier. Allowing the tax credit only while the family has children in school would still create a much more level playing field than we have now, but the discrimination against private school users would still be significant.

Starting from the status quo, I believe in approximate nondiscrimination in public subsidy of schooling options at a dollar amount that fosters enough competition to force *some* of the private schooling purveyors to set their tuition so that the out-of-pocket cost to parents is no more than Y percent of the nondiscrimination subsidy level. The assigned TPS, and CPS where available, continue to be free. Why ***approximate*** nondiscrimination?[1] (1) Some of the public funding must service debt and finance pension payments to retirees; and (2) Y > 0 percent because it makes sense, and we have evidence (Coulson 1999) that schooling consumers make better choices and cause the choices to improve when they have some out-of-pocket cost, some skin in the game. So, the public subsidy for private schooling options should be specified as X percent (X = 100-Y) of the private school tuition (after funding pensions and debt service), or the nondiscrimination funding level, whichever is less.

Suppose we decide that 10 percent is the minimum appropriate skin in the game. Then Y = 10, and X is 90. Then suppose we discover that school system ABC's current public funding yields enough for debt service and public pension commitments with, say, $9,000 per K-12-aged child left over. Then $9,000 is the maximum per-pupil, annual private school subsidy payment to be paid to private schools that charge tuition of over $10,000. For a school with a tuition level of $8,000, the subsidy amount is 90 percent of $8,000, or $7,200, forcing a co-payment of $800. Table 7.1 provides additional examples with the public funding at $9,000 or 90 percent of tuition, whichever is less.

Table 7.1: Tuition and co-payment when skin in the game must be at least 10 percent.

Full Tuition	Public Funding	Co-payment Amount
$8,000	$7,200	$800
$9,000	$8,100	$900
$10,000	$9,000	$1,000
$11,000	$9,000	$2,000
$12,000	$9,000	$3,000

If competition does not force some of the co-payment amounts below $1,000, the per-pupil public funding level may be too low; private schooling options are not sufficiently affordable for low-income households. "May be" is a judgment call that will likely depend upon the availability of private or public funding for means-tested co-payment assistance, i.e., financial help for-low income families to enroll their children in TPS alternatives.

The open-ended co-payment possibility—the skin in the game—also has the ***critical*** effect (decentralized planning cannot replace central planning without co-payment possibility!) of putting the price system in play. Price decontrol creates incentives to make risky private investments in innovative schooling approaches, it makes high-cost, high-value schooling possible, and it allows price change to properly size each instructional niche. New schools will enter an instructional niche until that process competes the co-payment amount down to the level where efficient producers of that type of instructional can just barely earn a competitive return on their investment.

That so few people understand the critical need to have the price system in play is a key failing of the current school system, a massive economic education failure. The price system orchestrates most economic outcomes, typically, efficient outcomes. That's a fundamental fact about our world that everyone should have to learn. Many of the so-called market failures are still better than the result of the government intervention produced by the political process, which is the result of the typical political failure to achieve maximum efficiency.

With the co-payment possibility, central planning would still guide the public school system, but decentralized planning would orchestrate the school system's independent school options. I am confident that private subsidy payments—and maybe public— would significantly defray the co-payments of low-income families. The resulting trade-off I urge everyone to willingly make (discussed in greater detail in chapter 9) is a much larger, dynamic menu of schooling options—actual school *choices*—with some families, including some low-income families, preferring a low tuition option to the free public school options. If co-payment is not allowed (if TPS alternatives cannot receive public funding unless they take the public funding as full payment), if the price system is not in play, there will be far fewer schooling options (lacking nearly all of the options that would exist if schools could levy a co-payment). And, without the possibility of co-payment, shopping for an appropriate schooling slot becomes much more a matter of chance than choice because of long wait lists (shortages) for many of the fewer schooling options that would exist.

Public-private shared financing of tuition is the norm at public universities. The long-term funding trend at several major state universities is for public funding to gradually disappear. Fiscal pressures alongside solid performance by the new choices provided by the transformed school system, including not leaving low-income families behind, could yield the same outcome for the K-12 school systems. It's a likely slippery-slope process that could gradually increase the co-payment share of the tuition amount. That has happened in higher education because the smaller the public subsidy's share of the total tuition amount, the easier it is to further cut it.

The political prominence of the call for free college tuition may be a sign that public subsidy of higher education has fallen too far. Likely a key reason for that outcry is that the higher education co-payment share and the tuition level rose together. That double whammy is less likely for K-12 schools, because with nondiscrimination (ending the public-finance monopoly of the public school system), it will be much easier to launch a credible private school for children than a credible university for adults. That is, increased demand for K-12 private schooling is much less likely to yield a large, sustained rise in tuition rates than an increase in the demand for higher education. Of course, it is ECO 101 that price increase is an immediate effect of a demand increase. But because that immediate price increase intensifies competition, higher prices are not necessarily a lasting effect of increased demand.

The increased demand for private schooling that would result from ending public schools' public finance monopoly could increase the average tuition rates of existing private schools. That's because current private school tuition rates often do not reflect the total cost of running the school. Most current private schools are privately subsidized, mostly by the churches that own and run them. Since churches probably cannot subsidize a much larger number of students, expansion of the private market share of school systems would force tuition rates to reflect total schooling costs.

Public Funding Practices and Strategies

Within my general preferences and perhaps yours, there's plenty of flexibility in resolving key features of the school system. The public subsidy method can range from direct payment to schooling providers, based on enrollment, to education tax credits (refundable or nonrefundable), tuition vouchers, and education savings accounts. So that a lawsuit will not cause exclusion of church-run private schooling options from public funding based on the nondiscrimination principle, direct government payments for private schooling is probably not an option in the US. Parent-directed government payments (tuition vouchers) to church-run schools are constitutional (*Zelman* 2002), but direct payment very likely is unconstitutional.

A tuition voucher is a per-student certificate with a specified public dollar value that eligible parents can submit to a private school as a full or partial tuition payment. Eligibility for the voucher may vary by a student's origin (targeted district—recall Plan B from chapter 2, or he/she was assigned to a formally designated "failed" TPS) within the school system, or by the age or socioeconomic status of a student. The cash value of the voucher may depend on socioeconomic status (a proposed basis) or a by potentially detailed criteria widely referred to as a weighted student formula (WSF) that increasingly impacts a wide variety of public subsidy practices.

Nondiscrimination has not nearly been the norm for setting the dollar value of rare tuition vouchers. Enacted voucher legislation and rejected voucher proposals typically set the voucher dollar value at well below the per-pupil public subsidy level of public schools. So, we have little direct empirical evidence from which to predict the school system effects of a potentially transformational public funding policy based on the nondiscrimination principle.

Another common key constraint has been that schools cannot cash vouchers unless they accept the voucher amount as full payment. That's the typical language of a co-payment ban. That imposes a price ceiling on publicly subsidized private schooling. That constraint keeps all publicly subsidized schooling free (no out-of-pocket cost, no co-payment), and it keeps families of greater means—but not greater by enough to fully self-fund private school tuition—from spending more on the education of their children than families of lesser means. Those are two things that some people feel very strongly about, perhaps because they are not fully aware of the consequences.

Without public-private co-payment of tuition (shared financing, i.e., a \$4,000 voucher + a private check for \$1,000 to pay a \$5,000 tuition), central planning plus uncoordinated capitalism (true chaos) will continue to be the way we decide which instructional approaches are available, how they are made, where, and for whom. Recall from chapter 2 that the world's best systems—mostly price-less—do not perform much better than our Nation at Risk level. From that, and an enormous body of indirect evidence, we know that central planning, perhaps plus chaos, are unlikely to ever yield a high-performing school system. Centuries of evidence indicate that industry-wide and economy-wide central planning eventually (usually quickly) yields disastrous results. Reliance on central planning—price-less decision-making—is definitely an example of a critical effect that probably the vast majority don't know they are causing. A co-payment ban (no public-private sharing of tuition) yields de facto price control. With market-driven price formation and change, a decentralized planning process based on the full knowledge and strong motivation of every market participant can replace central planning. Without market-driven price formation and change, we have to rely on central planning by a politically correct, possibly perversely incentivized, inherently underinformed and misinformed handful of experts.

That strong objections to some shared financing of tuition quite often survive the unveiling of hidden assumptions and a somewhat complicated explanation of the major impacts is a key reason to prefer public subsidy policies that are not as easily restricted into price control as tuition vouchers; for example, tax credits or education savings accounts. Tuition tax credits reimburse approved private spending on schooling at a certain rate up to a specified maximum. For example, a state legislature may enact a 50 percent tax credit for private school tuition up to, say, $10,000. A family that spends over $10,000 on tuition will enjoy up to a $5,000 reduction in their tax liability if the tax credit is nonrefundable, or shed the tax liability plus get a check for the difference between $5,000 and their tax liability if the tax credit is refundable. A large, refundable 100 percent tuition tax credit can achieve the zero out-of-pocket cost objective for the families for whom that is important without capping what private schools can charge families lacking the means to fully self-finance tuition of all of the popular schooling options; that is, without devastating price control. Refundable tax credits can achieve nondiscrimination without the complication of banking nonrefundable credits. However, as noted in the explanation of my start-from-scratch policy preference, the courts typically rule refundable tax credits to be government spending, making schools enrolling recipients of refundable credits more susceptible to regulation of their practices. That's a key reason to strongly consider bankable, nonrefundable education tax credits.

Another increasingly popular public subsidy practice is an education savings account (ESA) for children that leave their assigned public school. ESA holders can spend the funds in the account on approved education-related purposes via a special debit card. ESA eligibility may be restricted to certain student subgroups, for example, as in the tuition voucher, to students that had been assigned to a public school with a formal "failed" designation, or low-income families, or every family in designated low-income places, or with a special needs diagnosis. Via weighted student funding, some eligible students may receive larger annual ESA deposits than others. Only two of the still rare ESA programs lack narrow eligibility limits. Though the Arizona[2] and West Virginia[3] ESAs have almost no eligibility exclusions, the ESA funding falls far short of the nondiscrimination standard. The West Virginia ESA amount—a $4,600 annual deposit—can fully finance the tuition of many alternatives to the assigned TPS, but not every alternative. Some of the schooling alternatives will require co-payment. Maximum flexibility is a central aim and key virtue of ESAs, so there is no history of co-payment constraint, no price control. And because ESA funds can be spent on a wide variety of education-related services, ESA use is hard to regulate. Public subsidy via ESA fosters the formation of the market-driven prices that can drive the decentralized planning that underlies the economy-wide norms of efficient market outcomes. Indeed, an ESA policy typically assumes co-payment, and it avoids price floor effects (private schools all charging at least the subsidy amount) by allowing the ESA funds to be spent on a variety of education-related services (not just tuition) and by allowing unused balance carryover, all the way to higher education expenses when unspent funds remain after the secondary education years.

In terms of my policy preference, an ESA that gets an annual deposit of X percent of the approximate per-pupil nondiscrimination public funding level runs a close second to the nonrefundable, bankable tuition tax credit described above. The ESA and nonrefundable credit policy preferences described immediately above have competing advantages and disadvantages. The preferred ESA policy is simpler, and it allows use of leftover funds to finance higher education. But nonrefundable tuition tax credits are least susceptible to debilitating regulation of private schools.

A tuition voucher worth the nondiscrimination amount or X percent of tuition, whichever is less, is still quite acceptable if schools can accept the voucher as full *or* partial payment. But an effort to enact such a voucher runs the considerable risk that the critical partial-payment option is omitted from the legislation, or that a political fight over that issue prevents enactment.

Private Funding Practices and Strategies

The key private subsidy issues are the subsidy recipients (producer, consumer, or third party) and the eligibility basis, especially when the recipients are the consumers. Private subsidy is typically targeted, either based on need (family income and/or special needs) or merit/potential (scholarship funds), or a mix of the two.

Hard-to-Avoid Bad Practice of Subsidizing Producers of Instruction

Milton Friedman warned against directly subsidizing producers. The producers might prove undeserving of it, or less deserving of scarce funds than market newcomers. Choosing which producers to subsidize in the first place, the correct subsidy amount for each, and then deciding which should be renewed is a lot of work that is largely avoided by subsidizing only consumers and then observing some basic protocols, for example, some consumer skin in the game, and deviations from subsidy uniformity based on student cost (weighted student formula) or pedagogy cost for the best fit for a student. Churches, the current major sources of private subsidy funding, largely avoid that work by subsidizing their own schools. From society's perspective, that may not be the most efficient use of those funds.

Probably because of the high per-pupil cost, private funding of private school scholarships, such as the $52.4 million money spent providing vouchers to Edgewood residents, hasn't greatly increased the use of private schools beyond the level made possible by churches subsidizing their own schools.

In the charter sector, donor wannabes have no choice but to send their money to the CPS owners. With current CPS policy, spending the subsidy money on grants to families that enroll in a CPS makes no sense. Affordability is not an issue. CPS slots are free. The family problem is to find a not-full CPS that seems, with little study (hurry—openings can be very short-lived) to be a better-than-TPS fit for one of their children.

A key reason to create policies that make it easy to subsidize consumers is that it is difficult to reallocate resources from less to more deserving producers. Subsidy-losing schools may have to close, forcing children back into a TPS, perhaps the one they were glad to leave. The more deserving producers may not serve exactly the same children. Reallocation is a continuous, incremental process when schools get subsidy funding one student at a time.

Donor Dependence Yields Shortages and Sometimes Scandalous Quality Erosion

Common chartered public school (CPS) situations illustrate some of the key private subsidy issues. Across the forty-five US school systems (forty-four states + DC) that allow independently initiated CPS, donor dependence is common, perhaps the rule rather than the exception. No state's charter law allows tuition payments. So, every CPS must survive on their state's formula-determined, per-pupil payment, plus whatever they can solicit from donors. For some of the popular CPS-delivered instructional approaches, the state's per-pupil payment is not enough to run a small school, much less deliver enough seat capacity to meet the demand at the mandated tuition price of zero. Those shortages attract donor support, but even with billions of dollars in US donor funding, wait lists (space shortages) are still common, perhaps the norm.[4] New schools in areas with few or no CPS are probably more attractive investments than school expansions to address shortages. Such donor dependence keeps some potentially useful instructional approaches from getting off the drawing board, and donor dependence often leaves the amount available far below the level demanded.

Such shortages are problematic in their own right, and they create profit opportunities in scandalous corner-cutting. Economists agree (yes!) that quality reduction is a likely outcome of policies that yield persistent shortages. Beyond the economists that study the consequences of shortages, quality reduction is rarely anticipated. I've never heard that concern raised by CPS proponents. However, opponents are starting to make a big deal out of the quality reductions that are deemed scandalous.

I've heard the scandal issue mentioned as something that CPS proponents believe will be solved by CPS-TPS funding equity. No doubt the increased funding for CPS that would result from funding equity would increase the supply of CPS slots, which could decrease the corner-cutting quality-reduction incentives. But eliminate them? I doubt it. Existing weak to nonexistent CPS accountability to customers is at the core of the temptation to increase profit by cutting corners, sometimes scandalously huge corners. There are already some states with funding equity. A project that collected scandal data by state would shed light on the hope that funding equity would eliminate the scandalous behavior.

Market-Determined Co-Payment Eliminates Donor Dependence and Shortages

Allowing market-determined co-payment—ending the zero-tuition mandate—eliminates the inefficiency problem evident from the long wait lists, and it strengthens the producer accountability to customers. Co-payment permission eliminates producer donor dependence. The co-payment possibility would allow CPS to charge what it takes to run a popular school with enough capacity to meet demand. But that creates an equity issue. Chapter 9 argues that the co-payment equity issue is probably imagined to be much larger than it really is even if the equity considerations do not include that the co-payment possibility frees donor funds that had been paid to CPS to make them available to instead finance means-tested co-payment assistance.

How much of the donor money now paid directly to CPS would instead go into co-payment assistance funds, mostly need-based grants, but perhaps some based on merit/potential? Because then the money would go directly to needy children, not sometimes-large businesses and sometimes mismanaged CPS, I believe more donor money would support CPS (and other new schools made feasible with tuition vouchers, tax credits, or ESAs) through co-payment assistance than now helps all CPS users (needy *and not needy*) indirectly by sending their donations directly to CPS operators.

Conclusion

The likely continued limited availability[5] of charity funding and its uses (means-tested, special needs, etc.) will be a key determinant of the efficiency and political viability of a system in which public subsidy policies do not favor public school users, and in which co-payment allows families with greater earnings to buy more schooling than lower-income families can buy from just their own earnings. Is it wrong for families to work to earn more schooling for their children?

This chapter describes past uses of public and private subsidy and potential uses to improve the outcomes of school system reforms that include school choice expansion and perhaps increased reliance on market-driven price change to orchestrate what instructional approaches the school system will produce, how, where, and for whom. Equity concerns are likely a major reason why we have not pursued market routes to improved efficiency. That's the subject of the next chapter.

1   Suddenly "approximate" because "approximate non-discrimination" is not much of a slogan.
2   A 2018 vote prevented expansion.
3   The Nevada ESA program is stalled by a court ruling that the legislature needs to use a different funding source.
4   http://www.publiccharters.org/sites/default/files/migrated/wp-content/uploads/2014/05/NAPCS-2014-Wait-List-Report.pdf
5   "Limited"—not enough to significantly increase the number of TPS alternatives by subsidizing school operators.

CHAPTER NINE

Equity Issues

The current US school system creates a simple, but superficial illusion of equity. Every child is assured a 100 percent taxpayer-financed ("free") neighborhood public school (TPS) slot. And equal opportunity, except for families that can pay twice—taxes to support TPS and private school tuition—seems like an obvious effect of the current system. Each assigned TPS offers the same package of instructional approaches, though perceived differences in the quality of uniformly comprehensive campuses are large enough to yield significant differences in housing costs between districts and attendance areas.

Contrary to the long-standing public education hope and promises, we know that the policy of assigning children to a "free" TPS has been an efficiency and equity disaster. Incredibly, some still view exit from the assigned TPS as equity-reducing, even if it improves TPS classroom teachability and increases public school system per-pupil funding. The exit of families able to pay private school tuition or the housing cost premium of homes near the preferred schools concentrates poverty near the schools left behind.

The current system's low absolute overall performance level is a bigger disaster than the gap between low- and high-income student opportunities and outcomes. The infamous achievement gap may be mostly due to lower-income family students' greater dependence on formal schooling for intellectual growth. Even the best TPS are a poor fit for many of the children assigned to them, yet for those children, viable significantly better alternatives are rare. CPS are affordable, but they are relatively rare and often available only by chance (lottery). Many children, especially those from low income families, are not learning nearly enough to achieve a high level of economic opportunity, or to perform their duties as citizens. Much is made of economic opportunity being a function of zip code—neighborhood affluence—but the neighborhood effect is mostly a function of family influence, *not* consistently better schooling delivered to children from affluent neighborhoods. That is also true in other countries. Family pressure, informal tutoring, and spending on formal tutoring, not superior schooling, is responsible (Carnoy, Garcia, and Khavenson 2016) for the slightly higher-than-US-average test scores earned by many foreign countries.[1]

This book has already discussed efficiency issues for different ways to expand the menu of schooling options with additional privately produced schooling and increasing access to them. Chapter 7 discussed the potential to better serve all children, especially disadvantaged children, through central plan optimization. Below, I discuss the equity implications of nondiscrimination in school finance with the possibility of third-party tuition co-payments, and without them.

Nondiscrimination in School Finance— Co-Payments Prohibited

Recall that nondiscrimination means that each child's share of public funding is roughly equal regardless of the chosen school. A co-payment ban means that the chosen TPS alternative receives the public funding that follows a child only if the school accepts the public funding as full payment of tuition. That keeps subsidized schooling free, but the resulting price ceiling and floor at the current public funding amount would create excess capacity at the schools with the least expensive instructional approaches and create shortages at schools with practices that cost more than the per-pupil public funding level. The latter include schooling options that would eventually come down in price to at or near the per-pupil subsidy level. The price ceiling effects would keep some innovative instructional approaches from surviving the developmental stage where the high cost of resources, especially appropriately specialized personnel and the possible need for an initially high price to attract investment require a high price until competition drives the price down to the long-term minimum cost per pupil. That copycat-entrepreneur, market-entry process is the only way to discover and achieve a tuition price at the long-term minimum cost per pupil.

As an explanatory and cautionary note, recognize that the US norm that the per-pupil public funding amount is much larger for students attending the assigned TPS than elsewhere, which is highly inequitable with or without the possibility of co-payment. Such discriminatory public funding creates problems worth a brief mention. In some US choice programs, the portable amount is so small that— alongside a co-payment ban or cap—it does not induce any new school formation. Even if program participation is not limited to target groups such as low income, special needs, or students assigned to a public school formally designated as failed, the portable public funding amount is only enough to induce existing private schools to fill their excess capacity. Programs with larger but still highly discriminatory public funding amounts may cause some school expansions, but not nearly enough new schools to create a dynamic menu of schooling options as academically diverse as the area's schoolchildren. Such non-transformational, surgical strike programs don't make the school system any worse, but it creates a misinformation risk. The "on the cheap" part of "school choice on the cheap" may be overlooked in generalizations about whether school choice has been a useful policy. It's a non-trivial risk. Proponents of the current school system have been willing to paint with a broad brush to resist reform with disinformation.

It's curious that the inequity of free schooling created by the current system is much more widely recognized than its massive inefficiency. The current US system discriminates against families that believe a private school, or a CPS, is a better academic fit for their children. And we know that the current system tends to concentrate children from low-income families in the TPS that combine the bad business plan common to all TPS with students least able tolerate a plan built on heroic assumptions. Despite that, we see stiff resistance to the nondiscrimination that would gradually yield alternatives to public and private schooling environments that have persistently failed many children, especially socioeconomically disadvantaged children. Nondiscrimination would likely yield private school improvement through competitive pressures and improved per-pupil funding. Nondiscrimination would make classrooms of TPS and unspecialized CPS (about 50 percent of CPS) less academically diverse and thus more teachable.

One of the major objections to third party co-payment of tuition is that the already well-off will benefit more from that than the less well-off. Even if that were clearly true (likely false), is it wise to see the potential for widespread but unequal gains as a reason to forego the gains? The interest groups that believe that the tax dollars raised to educate all children belong to just the students and educators of the public school system are not the only people voicing those strong objections. Even states with political majorities opposed by the pro-K-12-status-quo interest groups, including many states with no collective bargaining and thus weak teacher unions, have done little to erode the public funding monopoly of the public school system.

With nondiscrimination but without the possibility of co-payment, we would have a menu of free schooling options, but a very different menu from the one we would have if co-payment is allowed. Without the possibility of co-payment, instructional approaches with per-pupil production costs above the per-pupil public funding level will struggle to come into existence and then struggle to remain available. Many of the instructional approaches that will exist will only be available by chance; thru lotteries to address shortages. Shortages and no (parent) skin in the game will erode the quality of many schools. Previous chapters discussed how shortages (wait lists) substitute school chance for school choice and how shortages virtually eliminate producer accountability to customers, which creates the potential to increase profits by cutting corners. Educators in schools with the least expensive instructional approaches will be working in partially filled schools and classrooms, sizes below the most efficient level. That's the big-picture equity trade-off. ***Prohibiting co-payment yields a smaller, lower-quality, less-diverse menu of actually available schooling options to keep all of the schooling options that receive public funding "free"; that is, when available at all, available for no additional cost than taxes that must be paid.***

The biggest downside to a zero co-payment policy is not obvious to very many people, even most school system scholars. Only with co-payment potential can the price system influence which instructional approaches are available, how they are made, where, and to whom they are available. Even people credentialed as price theory professionals—people typically referred to as economists—rarely note the power of a market-driven price system to efficiently create and fill each industry's niches. The reason for that may be that it has been old news for over seventy years. Because price system effects were widely discussed and were a huge source of controversy in the 1920s to 1940s, most economists and the general population have taken for granted how freedom-to-choose-driven price change eliminates the shortages and surpluses that result from constantly changing production circumstances and consumer preferences, while relentlessly fine-tuning the use of scarce resources to meet the highest value wants and needs. Nobel laureate Friedrich von Hayek (1945) argued that if someone had invented the price system, it would have been heralded as one of the greatest inventions of all time. But resource allocation and income distribution through market-driven price change is a natural process. The process amounts to self-interest-driven, decentralized planning. It does not produce perfect outcomes anywhere, but best possible in most industries. And it serves as a great starting point for some careful, mostly externality-driven[2] adjustment in the rest. Banning co-payment keeps decentralized planning orchestrated by market-driven price change from replacing the central planning process that nearly always produces disastrous results. That's a very high price to pay for the meager advantages of a small menu of only free subsidized options over a much larger, more dynamic menu of schooling options with many free and nearly free school choices among them.

Nondiscrimination in School Finance—Co-Payments Permitted

Assumed equity benefits are the driving force behind widespread knee-jerk preference for "free only" (no tuition, no co-payment allowed), taxpayer-subsidized schooling options. Sure, we need to be certain that low family ability to pay is not a barrier to a solid schooling experience. But we need to recognize that, as a society, we will never have the means to provide every child free access to every instructional approach that might be a better fit for them. The per-pupil subsidy level (taxpayer funding) should be high enough so that some private schools will accept just the subsidy as full payment, or just nearly so to keep some skin in the game. And the subsidy level should be high enough so that many other schools will accept it as a substantial partial payment; that is, a large share of the total tuition. In the US, we are already there with per-pupil taxpayer-financed revenue of over \$13,000 per TPS student.[3] Many school systems spend much more. ***What is missing is portability, breaking the public finance monopoly of public schools.*** Many private schools already take much less than \$13,000/year as full payment,[4] perhaps the vast majority now, and then likely more so in a school system with a more competitive private sector.

Insisting upon "free only" can seem to yield greater low-income family access to the menu of schooling options. But reduced access may be the actual overall result. Certainly, the many not-free options that would be available with co-payment would exist without co-payment only to the extent that a long-term donor funding commitment makes it possible to provide those options. And donor-dependent instructional approach availability typically fails to match the amount demanded without co-payment. Because of price-control-created shortages, the true menu—what is actually readily available (no lottery) to choose with "free only"—may be much smaller than even the potential number of suitable schools present with co-payment, certainly much than less those actually present without it. So, with the price control implicit in "free only", the menu is smaller, lower-quality, and less dynamic than it would otherwise be. Better access, just for some, to fewer, lesser schools will mean much less overall access to many families. As is the case now with the public-finance-monopoly price-control combination, families looking for an alternative to the assigned TPS will mostly not know what would otherwise be available to them.

Complaints about the co-payment barrier to low-income family access border on bizarre. It is very hard to imagine how more choices will make anyone worse off. Without the co-payment, many of the choices would not exist at all (no access), and the rest would likely be accessible only by lottery, often with a very low probability of being a winner. And the lottery process changes schools too; not accountable to customers and not as good a fit for the average lottery winners.

Allowing co-payment eliminates donor dependence for the instructional approaches that cost more than the per-pupil public funding level. The equity advantages of free-only are likely to be tiny because I believe that with co-payment allowed, charitable foundations will shift their subsidy dollars from schools to low-income families. And achieving those current equity advantages for the households that win the lotteries will have high equity costs, fewer, lower-quality choices. When donors directly finance instructional approaches that cost more than the per-pupil public funding level, they indirectly subsidize all of the children that attend the school, including the children from the higher-income families quite capable of bearing the co-payment, which is the market-determined amount in excess of the per-pupil public funding level.

Since my family adopted some local special-needs children, this obsession with free-only has been very costly to us. There aren't very many CPS near us, and they're all full, with wait lists. Lacking a good fit, we're not on a list. But if there was a seemingly great fit, and our family were to win that school's lottery, that would be our situation. We'd get free schooling perhaps at the expense of a family of lesser means. We can manage to substantially supplement the per-pupil public funding level if that would yield a great fit, but we struggle to pay full private tuition for the best fit we can find, on top of our school taxes. Our area's TPS don't look like a good fit for our adopted boys. If co-payments were lawful for Texas CPS, significant persistent wait lists would be gone, and we'd be able to shop from a much larger, dynamic menu of schooling options.

Only if the charitable foundations fail to adequately fund academically appropriate co-payment costs (needed for best-fit schooling) for low-income families do we have to make a policy choice between the co-payment ban outcome of cheaper, by-chance access for some low-income families to a smaller, lower-quality menu, and increased access to a much bigger and higher-quality menu for the vast majority with co-payment permitted. An additional or substitute approach to funding means-tested co-payment assistance, used by Chile for twenty-five years, is a tax on co-payment to finance means-tested co-payment assistance.

Even without major new privately or publicly funded co-payment assistance, low-income families are probably better off with the bigger, better menu of schooling options made possible with co-payment permission. The Edgewood voucher experience destroyed the presumption that low-income families will not pay tuition. Many low-income Edgewood families found the money for co-payments from their pockets and from student-focused philanthropic sources. Furthermore, we don't help low-income families by taking the co-payment option away from the families with the means to use it. Given resource scarcity, equal opportunity (except just in terms of absence of restraint and equality before the law) can only mean taking opportunity away from some. As Thomas Jefferson noted and I cite often, "There is nothing more unequal than equal treatment of unequal people." Nondiscrimination in school finance would yield a high minimum level of opportunity, including many free and eventually free or nearly free schooling options for everyone.

As President Reagan argued (and perhaps others before him), "You cannot strengthen the weak by weakening the strong." In fact, restraining the strong often hurts families of lesser means. Banning co-payment hurts low-income families by stifling some development and introduction of instructional approaches that might initially cost more than the high minimum subsidy available to all, but eventually fall in price and become widely available. An initial high price paid by high-income early adopters, then a falling price until what started as a luxury is available to everyone is a product development norm. Schooling would be no different if price control implicit in free-only did not short-circuit the process at the front end. There is much less innovation because many products do not get off the drawing board. There is an old saying about price control: "It is magic in that it makes things disappear." It can also keep some things from appearing in the first place.

Furthermore, because insisting on free-**only** reduces private spending on schooling, which reduces total spending on schooling, we hurt choice-worthy educators and ultimately children by reducing the incentive to become an educator. To conclude this chapter, I examine the potential to support low-income families from a conservative estimate of current donor funding.

Early Equity Math for a Transformed System

Suppose, through nondiscrimination, we provide a high minimum level of per-pupil public funding to anyone wanting to exit their assigned public school, and we allow co-payment. So, private schools can charge whatever the market will bear. Some schools would do that—gasp! Markets would then set tuition rates, often at or near (with the "skin in the game" policy urged in chapter 8) the per-pupil public funding level (free), but sometimes above. Competitive market entry would drive tuition rates down to the level needed to finance efficient operations, including a normal rate of return on investment. Purveyors of poorly conceived instructional approaches would not be able to recruit enough schoolchildren to cover their expenses. But purveyors of some well-conceived instructional approaches would be able to get enough families to supplement the per pupil public funding. That would require *a third party co-payment*. For example, suppose the per-pupil public funding is $8,000/year, and school T's instructional approaches cannot be offered for less than $9,000/pupil/year. To avoid the current donor dependence of such schools (the current norm of schools like T, for example, KIPP CPS are highly donor dependent, thus massively undersupplied), T will need to charge a $1,000/pupil/year co-payment. Ending donor dependence frees the donor money currently paid directly to schools for means-tested co-payment financing. So, the $1,000 can come from parents' private funds *or* accounts created from means-tested public funding (original justification for federal intervention) or philanthropic giving. T will get enough parents and donors to pay the $1,000 if T's instructional approach is significantly better than the alternatives for a significant number of our diverse schoolchildren.

How far will existing donor funding go in supporting low-income family access to schools like T? In 2014, approximately 20 percent of children were from officially impoverished families. How many needy families would seek co-payment assistance? We can get an idea from the universal school choice that existed for about six years in the Edgewood District of San Antonio, Texas. The Edgewood voucher amount was large enough so that most of that area's private schools took the voucher amount as full payment. That yielded a peak participation rate of 16 percent. Sixteen percent of US public school enrollment (50 million) is eight million. If poverty has proportional representation in the likely eight million seeking an alternative to the assigned public school, the potential US annual demand for third-party-financed, means-tested co-payment is 20 percent of eight million: 1.6 million.

What would be the average co-payment funding available to potential low-income leavers of assigned public schools? The most recent firm number for K-12 philanthropy is $1.5 billion in 2002. Anecdotal evidence suggests that total amount has risen significantly since then, so I'll assume that at least $1.5 billion would be available for annual charity funding of means-tested co-payment. Even if every one of the 1.6 million eligible for means-tested co-payment funding applied for it (every preferred private school levies a non-trivial co-payment), $1.5 billion yields nearly $1,000 per low-income pupil for co-payment; that is, to top off the public per-pupil funding. The per pupil amount funded by charity for low-income households can be higher to the extent that low-income families choose private schools with little or no co-payment required, *or* to the extent that giving for means-tested co-payment (scholarships) funding rises with increased interest in private schools and increased diversity in the menu of private school offerings.

Chile's useful experience with what Chile calls shared financing of private school tuition is that competition causes the average private (family or charity) share of private school tuition to be quite small. So, the bottom line from the very rough estimates above is that the poor will not be disadvantaged by school system reform that opens the system to much-increased free-enterprise delivery of schooling orchestrated by price (tuition) change and price variability within the menu of taxpayer-supported (subsidized) schooling options. Actually, quite the contrary: low-income families will have more options, and with some donor financing of co-payment levies, they'll have more options without significant loss of accessibility due to increased out-of-pocket cost.

I used evidence and economic theory, including the public choice school of thought that uses economic theory to explain political outcomes, to describe a strategy for school system transformation thru nondiscrimination in school finance, and co-payment permission. There will be disagreements on how to move forward. Since ferreting out grounds for discussion and research is a major purpose of this book, some of the next chapters describe how we can use research to address some of the school system design issues. First, the next chapter addresses the key fallacies that impede clear thinking about the actual policy trade-offs created by the school system transformation imperative.

---

[1] See also "Education in the Republic of Korea: National Treasure or National Headache" http://www.edweek.org/go/qc12

[2] Spillover is a synonym for externality. Pollution is the classic example of negative externality that sometimes rises to the level of policy relevance. Merit goods such as contagious disease inoculation and some aspects of schooling yield positive spillovers that are sometimes large enough to be policy relevant.

[3] A bit less if you include the children enrolled already in private schools.

[4] The feasible, average (WSF-based differences) non-discrimination funding level is likely somewhat lower than the result of dividing total spending by the number of schoolchildren.

CHAPTER TEN

Don't Be an Intellectual Prisoner of the Status Quo

It's critical that we recognize that nearly all of what we think we know about schooling—the alleged evidence base for policymaking—is the result of studying cause and effect within existing school systems which are, the outcomes of price-less central planning. Different funding and governance policies might have very different effects. Factors that yield bad effects in the current system could be key elements of genuinely different systems. Improvement is especially likely when theoretical analyses, high-quality simulations, or other industries point in that direction. For example, a Houston CREDO teacher specialization study found negative effects, even though specialization by firms and by business employees within firms is a cornerstone of our free-enterprise basis for efficiently deciding what will be produced, how, where, and for whom. So, specialization can very likely produce positive effects in a school system that decides what will be produced like most of our economy. I believe the CREDO findings show that the differentiated instruction challenge created by sorting children only by residence and age is greater for subject-specialized teachers. So, certainly, jack-of-all-trades teachers could be more effective in a typical TPS classroom than highly specialized teachers that could be more effective in a more market-driven system. It could be that the results of the Houston experiment agree with economics' theory of the second best, which says if you lift one efficiency-reducing constraint but retain others, you may make things worse.

Well-designed experiments—definitely better than the Houston specialization experiment—may be in order. Why "may"? Certainly, there is value in "look before you leap." But experiments have high time costs, and intended genuine experiments have a long history of being compromised (e.g., vouchers: Alum Rock, class size) but then still being cited as significant evidence. Even for the circumstances that deserve the term "experiment" for the issues being examined, the results are typically subject to interpretation, including deliberate misrepresentation via clever spin or by applying the findings to superficially similar but actually significantly different circumstances, i.e., with an overly broad brush (recall the "does not make much difference" President Obama talking point about school choice). Given the short-attention-span, undereducated, and overextended electorate we have, shameless misrepresentation can be a very effective opposition tactic.

For-profit vs. non-profit evidence is another example of potentially misleading examples, and the high potential for deliberate or accidental misuse. The well-known, massive CREDO study included a comparison of for-profit and non-profit chartered public schools (CPS). *U.S. News and World Report*'s description of the CREDO finding that nonprofit CPS slightly outperform for-profit CPS did not include any caveats such as the critical points that the rare CPS that pursue profit do so without control of their tuition price. As Thomas Sowell's *Discrimination and Disparities* repeatedly demonstrates (Sowell 2018, 2): "Whether a prerequisite [factor] that is missing is complex or simple, its absence can negate the effect of all the other prerequisites that are present."

Furthermore, charter authorizers and/or detailed rules restrict entry to settings where the price control yields widespread wait lists (shortages) that largely curb business firms' typically powerful accountability to their customers. Most CPS can easily replace unhappy customers from a lengthy wait list. The CREDO finding about for-profit CPS supports my hypothesis—again, an example of the theory of the second best—that for-profit schooling is not compatible with shortage-creating price control. Those were the conditions present in the situation studied. So, the CREDO finding is not legitimate evidence that for-profit schooling will necessarily yield worse outcomes than not-for-profit schooling. In a normal setting (open markets where supply-demand sets prices), we have every reason, including evidence (Coulson PBS[1]), to believe that openness to for-profit schooling enterprises will improve outcomes; that is, yield a higher performing system.

Examples of wrong, irrelevant, or misleading findings from effects in the current system include studies of the school choice programs that are too small to do more than move children among the choices available from within the existing system, which are the vast majority of the programs, especially the programs given the most attention here in the US. Even the actual studies often fail to note all of the key limitations created by the conditions being studied, and the people citing them almost never do. It's *the* evidence that most supporters of school choice expansion have felt compelled to defend, and their opponents feel the need to discredit when positive and spread with a broad brush when negative. The right reaction is to assert the near irrelevance of small-scale program effects to school system reform. The passage of time since the earliest school choice expansions has shown usefully that small-scale programs do not necessarily produce the hoped for irresistible pressure to gradually expand school choice into a transformation catalyst—that at least a larger-scale start (WV Hope Scholarship) than we've studied would be needed for that.

To set up the next chapter's detailed discussion of specific fallacies that arise from longtime observation of cause-effect in the current system, I will describe some specific examples. They support my contention that intellectual prisoners of the status quo include senior people—in terms of age, experience, and status/credentials—that have been involved in school reform, and or school system reform all of long adult lives. Because my purpose is to demolish debilitating ways of thinking about critical issues, I will mostly decline to name

the prisoners. Probably, the chapter 10 discussion forum at https://
objectivepolicyassessment.org/K-12 will name them.

Leadership Denial/Dissonance—
the Stockholm Syndrome

> a condition that causes hostages [insiders] to
> develop a psychological alliance with their cap-
> tors [system] as a survival strategy. (*Wikipedia*)

The syndrome is pervasively evident in a compilation of essays
from twenty-five "education leaders from around the globe" in
*Leading Educational Change: Global Issues, Challenges, and Lessons on
Whole System Reform* (Malone 2013). I highlighted ***Whole System
Reform*** because it's what drew me to the book. The five chapters—
by school system leaders—in the "Whole System Change" section
defined "whole system reform" to be new programs? None of the
leaders even mentioned slightly shifting decision-making authority
between central offices and school campuses, much less fundamental
change in funding or governance. Of the book's twenty-five chapters,
only the Finland chapter mentions school choice, and only barely to
imply its irrelevance. The essay authors cannot imagine any major
change in the central planning process that decides what will be
taught, where, how, and to whom, or how schooling is financed.

Likewise, the US has a deceptively titled Center for Reform
of School Systems (CRSS), which implicitly asserted that "school
system" is synonymous with public school system. CRSS trains
superintendents and school board members, which can yield better
performance from the existing governance and funding processes.
The CRSS definition of school system reform and the whole system
reform chapter in Malone's *Leading Educational Change* reminded me
of a February 23, 2012, National Center for Policy Analysis school
system change forum. The speakers were high-profile educators and
public officials from the Dallas, Texas area. Every speaker made a
passionate plea for a new system, but no one offered any new ways
of deciding what kinds of instruction to produce, where, how, and

for whom. They just wanted existing decision-making processes to produce different results. They ignored Pete DuPont's school choice trial balloon. I asked one of the sources of the "new system" pleas (a district superintendent) what would be new about her new system vision. In her "new system," governors, legislators, school boards, and superintendents retain their current roles. Public schools would maintain their public finance monopoly, and district schools would still have attendance zones. Seemingly, "new system" meant some new programs and (somehow) much different outcomes from the current governance and funding processes.

Sadly, we cannot accept promising labels at face value. But it is an opportunity to move forward by asserting more productive definitions of the key terms. At least we can be confident that there is a widespread understanding that current practices are producing unacceptable effects. Sadly, though, decades of costly futility with "more of the same—harder, "more-longer-harder" (Osborne 2017), and "the same things over and over" (Hess 2010) has not yet been enough to adequately erode the persistent mixture of determination and hope that better outcomes will come from a process that looks like what we do now. For those of us that believe we need *real* school system transformation, the good news is that the debate may be transitioning from anger to denial. But we're still far from acceptance of the six-part Nation at Risk drumbeat, or that there is only one alternative—decentralized planning through the price system—to the central planning process that never works, much less a commitment to design a genuinely productive new system.

Public school district superintendents' version of denial is that their school board governs effectively, but very few of the remainder govern well. A poll of superintendents found that just 2 percent of district chiefs said they strongly agree that districts across the nation are effectively governed at the board level. Only another 22 percent agree. Yet 73 percent agreed or strongly agreed that their own district was well governed. Widespread superintendent delusion that their district is an exception to the norm is like the diversity excuse widely held by parents. Parents typically believe that the system does not perform well, but they believe their own school is at least okay, especially if the school is in a middle-upper-class neighborhood. Some of the persistence of the parent version of the diversity excuse lies in the possibility that to believe otherwise would amount to implicit admission of child neglect, something the brain will deny against anything but overwhelming evidence. Because legislators are not only wary of that widespread perception, but extensively suffer it themselves, school choice program eligibility is widely means-tested and thus constrained to lack the potential to be a transformation catalyst.

Hopefully, additional documentation that their own island of excellence is a mirage—that even the best TPS, and some private schools, are not as good as they think—will help end the "more of the same—harder" approaches to school system improvement. The initial California edition of Lance Izumi's multi-state series found not a single high-performing California TPS.

Misplaced Criticisms Arise from High-Level Economic Illiteracy

Dissonance is widespread. Indeed, I believe it is the norm, even at the highest levels. But I can only document the errors of prominent, prolific writers. One of those (X) is prominent in a pro-reform think tank and served as a high government official in an education governance role. I criticized X in my *The School Choice Wars* (2001), so X has been at it a while. Here I'll focus on two of X's 2017 rants, a term I believe X ("I unloaded") would agree with. So, X's fallacies are deeply ingrained and widely shared. They are not the result of casual oversight.

In both rants, X asserted the "idiocy" of several prominent pro-reform people, including Secretary Betsy DeVos. Regarding X's criticism of Secretary DeVos' belief that parental choice yields significant accountability for chartered public schools (CPS), I mostly agree with X. But our reasons differ. X doesn't believe that market accountability to parents can be adequate. I believe it can be adequate, but it is inadequate for CPS. My often-stated reason is the shortages/ wait lists of most CPS. Unhappy CPS users are easily replaced, hence the mounting evidence of scandalous behavior cited by X, also Z (see below). Again, X doesn't note—probably doesn't recognize—the large shortage/wait-list basis for the scandalous corner-cutting. Sadly, it is not well known that economists agree (yes!) that shortages yield quality reduction (= scandalous corner-cutting).

As the writings of X's think tank amply document and exemplify, so-called gold-standard studies of America's narrowly targeted and otherwise severely limited school choice expansions have convinced many people that school choice is not enough—that market forces are inadequate transformational catalysts. X argues that "it would be wonderful if the parent marketplace were a sure-fire mechanism for gauging and producing those results. Sadly, it simply isn't." Indeed, the actual school choice expansions haven't been enough. Eligibility is far from universal, and in the countries that have low barriers to TPS alternatives, intense regulation keeps private and public schools very similar. Many of the "school choice is not enough" people overlooked my 2008 article and two Cato Forums that argued that our modern experience with choice expansions, especially the well-known US examples, does not include cases where critical market attributes are present. And it's not just that one key element is absent, though that would be enough. Typically, none of the key elements are present. There is no genuine evidentiary basis to conclude that school choice is not enough, but X has. X is right that CPS accountability to customers has not been an adequate "first line of defense," but it's not true because it cannot work. It's been true because price control yielded widespread shortages (wait lists) that kept it from working. But X is okay with it ("parents as first line of defense, sure") if the political process yields X's preferred regulation, second line of defense. But as X notes, good rules are rare. Counterproductive over-regulation is what we have.

Common among people that believe they understand markets but do not is X's description of an imagined schooling marketplace as a "free-for-all in which pretty much anyone can start a school and authorizers don't shut a school just because nobody is learning anything in it." Even in the severely compromised settings of CPS (price control, rarely allowed for-profit), removal of the formal authorization requirement would not create a free-for-all. Wannabe school operators must commit millions of their own dollars or hard-won donor funding to have a chance to persuade enough families that the school will deliver outcomes that seem likely to top those expected from the schooling alternatives. Admittedly, that CPS typically meet that standard for more families than they have slots for (wait list) may only reflect the ineffectiveness of the TPS alternative. CPS are often not measurably high-performing by the standards set in their charter application or in the judgment of the authorizers. Closing a low-performing but still popular CPS may do more good than harm when the closure makes room for a better CPS or the closure eliminates examples that threaten the political sustainability of chartering. The low level of the CPS alternatives may allow low-performing CPS to survive, but we will not need authorizer-initiated closure to eliminate CPS where "nobody is learning anything," especially when that judgment arises from incomplete, top-down accountability measures of performance such as test scores, especially low-stakes test scores. Factors of importance, such as non-cognitive skills, improved mastery of untested subjects, safety, and extracurricular activity can be some parents' reason for opting for a CPS.

It is worth noting that many CPS deliver poor results for many of the root causes that hinder schooling by TPS. About half of CPS nationwide make no attempt to specialize, pedagogically or thematically. In many states, CPS are not independent of the TPS authorities, and all forty-five (forty-four states + DC) charter laws undermine specialization with price control, and by forcing random admissions. CPS may not admit selectively, even based on a focused mission, though some still manage some selectivity. And since many CPS are former TPS (charter conversions—often failed TPS), inertia may yield an attempt at one-size-fits-all for the parents unhappy with their assigned TPS, alongside continued deeply ingrained sorting by age. So, it is true that many CPS did not produce much more engagement than the typical TPS before their conversion to CPS, and maybe thereafter.

X strongly asserts the public good fallacy: "the view—long since dismissed by every respectable economist—that education is a private good." I have not heard any economist assert that schooling is nonexclusive, and non-rival, which is the meaning of a public good, though no doubt, some have carelessly failed to make the critical merit good versus public good distinction I described earlier in this book. A merit good is a private good whose spillover benefits may rise to a level that makes it efficient to levy the taxes needed to fund a public subsidy. The economists that have addressed this issue in some depth concluded that basic skills acquisition is a potential merit good worthy of the tax effort to subsidize such instruction, if necessary.[2] X said, "I sincerely wish that every parent was a sophisticated school chooser," as if that had to be the case for effective consumer-choice-based quality control. Is every computer or automobile owner a sophisticated chooser? No. Yet market accountability works there. A significant minority of careful choosers is enough, perhaps alongside some regulation of potential major spillovers such as citizen-education content. That every parent is not a sophisticated school chooser is X's justification for political intervention in the form of formal authorization practices. But the even greater lack of sophistication in the making of political choices is an even stronger argument for the superiority of accountability to customers over top-down accountability through a political process.

Indeed, X unwittingly makes that "government failure" argument against quality control via authorizing: "None of this is to justify the regulatory overburden that today plagues most charter schools and authorizers." And even though extensive, that well-intended regulation still does not reliably yield an example for Secretary DeVos to cite, without controversy, as "a stellar example of quality control via authorizing" (X). "The charter sector [already] needs a regulatory overhaul" even though CPS have not been around that long. For X, despite the perverse past outcomes of the political process, such an overhaul should include new regulations. Somehow, this time, the political process will yield X's preferred "trinitarian approach," another central plan optimization approach that would extend the reach of the political process in some states. That approach would widen the scope of the process that yielded over-regulation of CPS, the same process that created fifty-one Nation at Risk performance levels despite, mostly, the best of intentions by the central planners.

It is not idiocy to argue that the government failure outcomes may be worse than even the likely outcomes of the weak customer accountability process actually present for CPS. But those outcomes are certainly worse than the non-existent true market accountability that many people imagine to be present despite ubiquitous price control, market entry barriers (often via regulatory overburden), and hindrance of specialization. And the toxic mix of shortage-creating price control and profit potential prevents market accountability from behaving as it does in most of the economy. The "intellectual prisoner of lousy experiments" aspect of this is that many prominent writers and activists believe that our limited experience with school choice expansions (small ones) has told us how market forces will impact schooling outcomes (more on this in chapter 13). That formed many opinions about likely outcomes of market forces without coming close to testing those forces.

X also lamented the alleged supply-side failure of market forces. X wished that "the charter sector would yield more good choices, while winnowing out the bad ones." But, again, the source of disappointment is the unrecognized failure to unleash market forces. It's worth repeating that price control limits the CPS choices to schooling that costs comfortably less than the public funding plus whatever donors will consistently provide. Long-term donor commitments to existing schools and caps on the number of CPS make it harder for new choices to displace the lowest-quality CPS. Also, in a real market setting, displacement doesn't apply to just the low performers. The relentless pursuit of improvement means that innovation displaces even one-time top performers.

Prominent author-activist Y believes that the school system is obsolete. If accurate, it would mean that the business plan of giving public schools a monopoly on public funding and then sorting children into classrooms on the basis of age and attendance zone boundaries was at least initially a high-functioning strategy for delivering instruction to diverse children. No! The once-high-performing claim contradicts the heroic nature of the public school system's key underlying assumptions (chapter 2) and abundant evidence specified around the time Y said the current system was at its peak, as well as before and since, discussed extensively earlier in this book.

Y (not Paul Hill) is borderline self-refuting, a term for people that assert something and then provide evidence that it is false. Like Ted Kolderie (2014), Y lauds market outcomes but deplores the market-price-setting, profit-pursuing process with low market-entry barriers that produces those outcomes. Y said it is a "tragic mistake" when private schooling replaces public. Why? Consider the track record of the public school system governance. More broadly, look at the process that decides who will wield power: low information voting, poor turnout, and character assassination.

Y appreciates specialization but expects it to arise optimally from a steering body (elected and appointed central planners). With nondiscrimination in public funding, central planners, *and* entrepreneurship yields specialization. "Establishing the board's political independence" ("direct election of school boards is a bad idea") will yield the "political freedom to do what is best for children." That, plus Y's opposition to market control means no obvious accountability, which is a well-worn, to some extent, still ongoing failed central planning strategy.

Y applauds the gains made in Washington, DC, New Orleans, and Denver and then shows that little was gained, much was luck, there was a lot of deception, and it took extraordinarily favorable conditions to achieve the improvement to student performance levels still short of Nation at Risk averages. So, as Robert Pondiscio (2015) said about New Orleans, we can be glad that there was some silver lining to Hurricane Katrina—the devastation yielded a central plan reboot that fostered gains relative to a very low starting point—but "a national model, maybe not." I say definitely not. That and especially Y's detailed discussion of the process that led to Denver's gains support the long-standing explanations for why central planning is inherently low-performing, and that supports my assertion that central plan optimization has a low upside.

Here, in Y's words, is the reason I believe often-touted Denver is also not a national model. If you're in New Orleans, DC, or Denver, be glad that they "outpace other cities' academic growth." It is frightening fact because for example, in Denver, still "only 28% in CPS and 24% (2016 PARCC), overall, met or exceeded college- or career-ready standards." Denver is still 4 percent below the awful statewide average, which makes being outperformed by Denver even more frightening.

Y notes that the political process produces bizarre results, and ***you can't afford to be transparent and truthful***, findings that by themselves should qualify as compelling evidence that we should not rely on central planning to produce a high-performing school system. "In a political world the most logical choice is often the least likely," and "it is political suicide to be clear about the reforms you favor." So, you have to lie to enact the policies you prefer!

The DPS district "was so dysfunctional, the superintendent (Bennett) concluded, that he could not fix it from the inside w/o significant outside pressure." And he got it. But despite the outside pressure from the "A+" movers and shakers, the "centralize strategy… quickly bogged down." "Changing a centralized bureaucracy with many moving parts is extremely difficult, because everything is connected." And reform progress would have been lost after anti-reform, teacher-union-backed candidates won a school board majority in a low turnout election, except that one union-backed candidate turned out to be a turncoat that voted with the reformers.

The reforms were hardly transformational, and perhaps because the gains were modest, or despite gains that outpaced other cities, the reforms produced an "empire strikes back" reaction. Neither the DPS political strategies or the changed schooling processes are a model for the transformational change needed by school systems performing at Nation at Risk levels. It is probably possible to achieve desired market outcomes for schooling without a free market, and a totally free market may yield some controversial outcomes. But to foster a relentlessly improving dynamic menu of schooling options that matches student diversity, we need market mechanisms to supplement or replace centrally planned schooling. Especially, we need scarcity-determined (based on supply-demand) flexible prices (through co-payment), profit-loss, and ease of market entry.

Author Z blames low performance on poverty and obsolescence (not ready for the twenty-first century), which is a strange combination since there has always been poverty. Since many people assert the poverty excuse, we need to thoroughly explore whether poverty is more of a hindrance in some school systems than others. Certainly, there are many stories of high-functioning schools with disadvantaged students. We also need to take into account that hardcore poverty is rare. According to Thomas Sowell's (2007) review of longitudinal studies, the incomes of only 3 percent of the population stays in the bottom 20 percent of the population all of their lives.

Z condemns the system but proposes no significant governance or funding reforms. "The old system is flawed beyond repair... A perpetual state of reform is attacking symptoms, not root causes." Z's fixes: less poverty, more caring, increased spending, including to hire higher-ability teachers, and more money for the highest-poverty areas. Z notes that the system wastes a lot of money, but proposes no changes to improve expenditure decision-making. Despite noting that the current system produces a "demoralized teaching force," "teachers are robbed of autonomy," and high turnover among new teachers, Z makes no other mention of adverse classroom circumstances. Like Y, Z eschews political accountability and market accountability.

Z contradicts his obsolescence assertion by arguing that "before the age of the Internet, the schools we need to create [via a central planning process] for all children could not have existed. No chance." And Z said his central plan will be made politically possible by increased citizen vigilance. Z said we must "get out from under our current way of holding schools accountable," but there was no proposal for how that would occur. I suppose it should occur just because Z, a prominent person, argued that it should occur. To somewhat excuse analyst-authors such as Y and Z, we've run the system, politically, with at least some district control for so long that hardly anyone can imagine any other form of funding and accountability. Z made a plea for radical systemic change but offered no radical change catalysts. Z specified radically changed expectations from unchanged governance and funding processes.

Condemn Outcomes—But Cling to the Causes

Authors such X, Y, and Z, along with many others, should be notorious for clinging to many of the causes of the terrible school system outcomes they condemn. X understands that some huge changes in the system are necessary, but all three are guilty of demanding different behavior from people and decision-making processes without significantly changing the incentives and constraints influencing those processes. I call it the ***should syndrome***. There are solid explanations for why the mostly well-meaning, intelligent people of the current system make their policy enactment and implementation choices, indeed fairly consistently across the fifty-one US school systems and even worldwide. Why should we expect people—from voters and parents to superintendents, teachers, and principals—and decision-making processes (boards, councils, and legislatures) to suddenly make different choices without tangible differences in the circumstances surrounding those choices? It is the height of naivete—a heroic assumption—to expect them to act differently just because a prominent analyst said they should.

My "should" to policymakers (nondiscrimination in funding) does not involve central plan revision (public school system policy). Ending the public funding discrimination against families that believe an alternative to the assigned school would work better for one or more of their school-age children would tangibly change the circumstances in which school system policy and implementation choices are made. Nondiscrimination is something legislators should do because it is obviously unfair to discriminate against the families that believe an alternative to the assigned school would work better for one or more of their school-age children. And arguably, nondiscrimination would yield much more intellectual growth per dollar spent.

A thorough documentation of "condemn outcomes—cling to causes" is at least another book, so I will end this section with just an important example. The teacher unions are a leading purveyor of the heroic assumption that condemned outcomes can be changed without addressing the systemic causes. There are a few versions (Berner, 2017) of the "civil society" reform model. Their version of that model asserts that (a) increased citizen vigilance is achievable despite an already overextended electorate, and (b) increased vigilance will yield the changes they desire, even if their wish lists change.

Teacher Unions Sidebar

Five things are very much worth noting as a long sidebar before I discuss what teachers condemn while their unions fight like junkyard dogs to preserve the causes of those lamented systemic outcomes.

1. This book has not said much about teacher unions because, while (a) they are a key part of an insurmountable status-quo-guarding coalition in some states, and (b) teacher unions are formidable in many other states, (c) they're not strong enough to block productive transformational change in every state, not nearly every state.

2. Anything that works well in even one state seems likely to spread to at least several others. Milton Friedman believed a single demonstration of effectiveness "will then sweep like a wildfire through the rest of the country." Demonstrating effectiveness is not just a matter of proving academic gain. Effectiveness at fostering economic development (something we already have evidence of)[3] can be the factor that causes the rapid spread of a transformational strategy.

3. The teacher unions almost never endorse a Republican in a competitive district and are not noteworthy players in Republican primaries. There are twenty-five states with a Republican governor, and Republican control of the legislature. The leadership of those states has no reason to kowtow to teacher unions, but none of them has significantly eroded public schools' public finance monopoly. That includes the often-noted progress of Arizona, Florida, and Indiana; small in a big-picture sense. Among the top ten, in terms of Republican dominance, only Utah has more than a weak charter school law.[4] Because we can't blame that triumph of inertia on teacher union opposition, we should not use that as a central excuse for the persistence of Nation at Risk status.

4. I do not fault teacher union officials for opposing school-choice-based transformation of school systems. Nondiscrimination would greatly diminish union power by freeing their members' mostly captive clientele. Given the current system's heroic assumptions and the public school system's terrible implicit, evolved business plan for discerning the appropriate instruction for diverse children, I do not fault teachers for their low productivity in the current system or even for demanding union representation as a way to counteract their powerlessness in local, mostly weakly competitive or uncompetitive teacher labor markets.

5. I do fault teachers for not recognizing when their union organization is advancing the organization's interests at the expense of teachers[5] and for not recognizing how cur-

rent school system policies hinder teaching. Anti-reform is a rational attitude for teacher union organizations, but not for teachers. To maximize teacher effectiveness and the satisfactions of professionalism, teachers and students need truly transformational school system change. Better funding of a bad business plan amounts to costly futility. Indeed, with a better business plan, more money may be unnecessary. We better hope so, because the fifty-one US systems are already "gold-plated disasters,"[6] and the potential to find that extra money is quite low. The federal government is deep in growing debt. And at the state level, huge pension obligations and Medicaid spending growth are making it very difficult to expand anything else.

Teachers—Bad Circumstances, Bad Choices in the Current System

A public school system forces teachers to choose between the unprofessional conditions of collective bargaining and the equal treatment of unequal teachers and students, plus powerlessness in school-district-dominated teacher labor markets. Having chosen and achieved the former in most states, teachers and their unions condemn the unprofessional treatment (little voice in **how** to do their work), distractions and dangers from inadequate discipline, teacher bashing, teacher-proof materials, and complain about low pay, with little opportunity to improve their income through achievement. Indeed, there are a lot of meetings, there is excessive testing, teaching to tests, teaching test-taking skills, and teachers suffer unnecessary conflict with parents. Those are surely key reasons for high rates of burnout and early teaching career abandonment.

Seymour Sarason (1990) reported a survey of teachers in which a large majority said they'd reject a large pay raise if it would mean never having to speak with another parent. Certainly sad, but not shocking. It is very difficult to satisfy TPS teachers' diverse clientele with a uniform product. Maybe the "Roots of the Problem" chapter should have included conflict with parents. Teachers are accountable to public officials, not parents. Parent requests represent extra work without additional pay.

Some costly protections have arisen from teachers' decision to rely on union due process, instead of ease finding a new job in a competitive labor market. One is a grinding due-process gauntlet that makes it difficult and costly to fire any teacher—even really bad ones. Bad teacher persistence undermines the intellectual development of children, unless they literally get paid for nothing. Bad teacher persistence creates disheartening, demoralizing conditions for the more effective teachers, that include equal pay raises for all teachers, and knowledge of bad teachers' impact on children. All of that is directly attributable to central planning (including pricelessness) driven by political correctness. The political imperative to pursue one-size-fits-all solutions through uniform government-run schools yields costly equal treatment of unequal children. That, and the public schools' monopoly on public funding precludes the exploitation of tried-and-true decentralized planning to create high-quality, diverse TPS alternatives.

Because so many people have become intellectual prisoners of the system that has been their schooling cause-effects frame of reference, we are not addressing critical issues, in part because of debilitating fallacies. The next chapter describes neglected critical issues and key fallacies.

---

[1] https://www.pbs.org/wnet/school-inc/

[2] Hall, Joshua C. 2006. "Positive Externalities and Government Involvement in Education." *Journal of Private Enterprise* 21 (2), 165–175.

[3] Edgewood on the west side of San Antonio, Texas (http://faculty.business.utsa.edu/jmerrifi/evp.pdf), and several examples at https://www.effective-ed.org/

[4] Because of near-ubiquitous wait lists, charter laws create much more school chance than school choice, which also suffers from CPS tendency to draw students disproportionately from private schools.

[5] See my *The School Choice Wars* (2001), chapter 14.

[6] That phrase is not from a conservative think tank. Democrat former California Governor Gray Davis said it.

CHAPTER ELEVEN

Critical Questions and Debilitating Fallacies

The previous chapter documented widespread, high-level critical issue dissonance. Most of this chapter discusses the specific fallacies embedded in the chapter 10 examples, and others not as glaringly present in the examples I am aware of.

Inertia vs. Sensible Formulation of Key Questions

Inertia creates slaves to numbers masquerading as data or evidence. Statisticians, some of them with PhDs in economics, devour the student test score data generated by the US school choice expansions. It is seen as school choice evidence even though US private school choice expansions are too small and heavily laden with restrictions to matter much to a nation that needs transformational change for fifty-one school systems. And the statisticians prefer data from the choice expansions that are most credibly non-transformational. They prefer expansion policies that restrict access to well below the demand from those eligible so that it takes a lottery to randomly decide who gets financial assistance to exit the assigned traditional public school (TPS) and who must stay in the assigned TPS. Random assignment is the gold standard for statistical analysis, and justifiably so for assessment chores such as testing new medicines.

Because the small, restriction-laden school choice expansions are not large enough to induce significant changes in the school choices, the statistical studies yield tainted (see below) estimates of the gains possible from moving eligible (low-income or special-needs) children among the existing choices of a Nation at Risk, low-performing system. We should not make a big deal out of the differences between the schooling options of a system that needs much improvement. Those differences certainly do not inform the "whether" or "how" of school system reform.

Some of the ongoing statistical frenzy is the result of scholars' need to publish to not perish. It is hard to publish without data analysis. But I attribute some of the eligible student versus TPS stayer comparisons to the inertia created by the Wisconsin legislature's requirement—in the first modern (1990) school choice expansion—that Milwaukee voucher users be compared to similar students staying in Milwaukee's TPS. Ever since, the definition of school choice program success has been a statistically significant test score difference between the choice program participants and stayers, preferably unsuccessful choice applicants.

Sadly, it is not widely recognized that the gold standard for, say, medical research is not so golden for school choice. Comparing the treated (with TPS exit) to the untreated (stay in TPS) usually entails a shortage of access to the TPS alternatives, which adversely affects the behavior of the owners of the TPS alternatives. As noted earlier in this book, economists agree that persistent shortages erode the quality of goods.

Furthermore, the comparisons require that the untreated are indeed unaffected. But a key claim/aim of many choice advocates is that choice expansion will create rivalry that improves all schools. And exit of students not happy with their assigned TPS should improve TPS outcomes by creating more teachably homogenous classrooms, less need for difficult differentiated instruction. So, either the comparison is compromised because increased rivalry and more teachably homogenous TPS classrooms helps the TPS stayers, or the choice expansion is largely irrelevant because the vast majority of students are unaffected. School choice expansion that improves TPS performance will reduce the difference between the test scores of the students that exit the assigned TPS and those left behind, which means that the choice expansion programs that improve school systems the most will seem the least successful, all else equal.

As argued in chapter 1, relevance must be determined through school system comparison, not by comparing the performance of students or schools compromised by being part of school systems desperately in need of major improvement. The right question to ask is whether a policy measurably improves the performance of a school system. So, the observations must be school systems that differ in the policy being studied.

The gold standard frenzy is so dominant that the statisticians, including those with a PhD in economics, have not bothered to include a genuine economic analysis in the publication of their empirical findings. Maybe it is an oversight—stay focused on the empirical model—but maybe it is deliberate because such an analysis makes the findings seem much less important. I expressed my disappointment in the failure to apply economic analysis to one such economist and got my future e-mails blocked. Without the statistical analysis of sometimes wrong, often misleading, and weakly relevant student test score comparisons, the economic analysis is not publishable. Since the privately funded, large Edgewood voucher program did not reject eligible applicants, there was no random assignment data set for me to process. Also, Edgewood leavers did not take the same exams as the Edgewood TPS stayers. So, I was unable to include my nonstatistical student performance assessments and basic economic analysis-based comparison of the Edgewood results to the school system conditions conducive to "gold standard" approaches in the article published, because of the Edgewood program's statistically significant impact on property values. I am tempted to look for a school choice expansion-based student test score data set in need of reanalysis just so I can get the all-important theoretical analysis of the conditions that generated the data into a top journal.

Chartered public schools (CPS) have been subject to the same "gold standard" frenzy (Sowell, 2020) as private school choice programs, with even greater analysis issues. Even within a state, there is more diversity in what wears the CPS label than in the current system's private schools (mostly church-run) that are compared to TPS. But despite the additional diversity that results from lumping different states' CPS together, analysts and editors have been quite willing to publish statistical comparisons of CPS and TPS test scores for the whole US. Those differences are seen as school choice evidence even though most CPS cannot be chosen much past when they first open, especially the more innovative, better CPS. Having to choose quickly, before the school fills, or win a lottery to gain admission yields smaller gains than are likely when parents can carefully match their child's academic characteristics to a school's strength.

Are the so-called experiments with randomly assigned school choice lousy in all respects? No! They tell us that parents seeking a TPS alternative can tell when an existing school will work better for one of their children, even if it is not much better, at least in terms of a scores on a standardized exam. So, choice-based shuffling of children among existing choices is helpful, but to escape Nation at Risk, we need reform that greatly changes the school choices. The studies of small, restriction-laden choice expansions should lay to rest the hope that small, restriction-laden programs will incrementally grow into nondiscrimination. Arizona may be an exception, because Arizona took a large first step with a very CPS-friendly charter law. And West Virginia's just-enacted universal Hope Scholarship may be another exception. But other states' school choice program expansions stalled far from the large, low-restriction programs that school choice advocates hoped for. If we're going to "tinker towards utopia",[1] we better take a big first step.

Many Versions of the One-Dimension Fallacy

Because we are used to a school system in which 90 percent of the schools must aim to serve all but the most severe special needs children, our language and thinking suffers from several one-dimension fallacies. One-dimensional thinking at least seriously infects assessment of teacher quality, student ability, and school comparisons.

Teaching Effectiveness

The "good to bad" range depends on effectiveness at the unnecessarily difficult task of differentiating their instruction to address the wide range of ability levels and learning styles present in classrooms sorted only by attendance zone and age. Discussions of teacher quality typically do not note that some teachers are good with some pedagogies or students but ineffective with others. We do allow for the fact that someone with, for example, a history degree is likely to be more successful teaching history than math, but we still have massive, potentially debilitating out-of-field teaching, out of necessity because of the subject field shortages created by the current system's ubiquitous price control via the single salary schedule. Effective teaching would be more commonplace if we had a system that allowed greater variety in how educators fostered student academic growth, which would be more likely if we recognized the multidimensionality of teaching talent.

Student Ability

One basis for objection to reduced discrimination against the families that believe their child would achieve more intellectual growth in an alternative to the assigned traditional public school (TPS) is that the schools of choice will pursue the best students, leaving only the lowest-performing students in the assigned TPS. For now, we'll set aside the implied utter nonsense that education entrepreneurs would ignore the vast majority of the potential recruits/customers. I'll address that in the next paragraph. Characterizing students as bad, average, and good asserts that students are one-dimensional: uniformly average, high-, or low-performing. No doubt, there are some children that struggle, or excel, in every subject, no matter how the subject matter is presented. But children with subject strengths and weaknesses are the norm, especially if we include pedagogy factors. No matter how schooling proceeds, most children will perform better in some subject fields than others, and for many children, the level of performance will also depend on how instruction occurs. The latter depends on how student engagement factors match up (or don't) with the way lessons are delivered, and often also including with thematic packaging. So, for example, some children will learn more from well-designed software than from a well-trained teacher. And an overriding theme, such as sports, politics, health, business, and many other possibilities, can significantly increase the engagement of some students. Within a best-available-fit schooling environment, we might usefully characterize the students according to their relative performance—for example, to focus remedial assistance—but not usefully otherwise. The current system labels many children as low-performing when they might be much more successful in a better-fit environment.

It is utter nonsense to argue that school choice will leave the lowest performing students concentrated in TPS, minus the beneficial peer effects of the higher-performing students that are gone. For-profit entrepreneurs look for the largest gap between likely cost and price. High-performing children, whether they are generally high-performing or with a specific strength their parents want them to build on, are definitely not the cheapest to educate up to the parents' expectations, which are high, which is likely often a key reason why the child is high-performing. That children with some extraordinary talents might seem to be the cheapest to educate could arise from the current system's preoccupation with the appearance of fairness, and thus little additional attention to the gifted, and perhaps the assumption that the proper objective is for each child to be at grade level rather than achieving as much intellectual growth as possible.

In the needed system that allows shared financing of tuition, there might be enough parents willing to pay tuition on top of a voucher, tax credit, or an education savings account withdrawal, to create an attractive high-performing-child schooling venture for one or more school operators. But the more likely, less risky profitable venture is to offer something more engaging than TPS to the much more numerous parents of children still with strengths and weaknesses but without any extraordinary talents. If the school choice expansion policy doesn't allow shared financing of tuition, the weighted student formula (WSF) that many states use, in some form, will determine which children are the most profitable customers. WSFs usually allocate more public money to disadvantaged children, not the most talented. Likewise, for nonprofit schooling ventures to attract investment, they typically must offer to serve disadvantaged children. However, the current system's well-known neglect of the most talented does attract some investment.

The one-dimension fallacy yields concern that less reliance on teacher willingness and ability to differentiate instruction will yield politically incorrect tracking. Note this reaction to two *Education Week* articles[2] criticizing the current system's implicit heroic assumption that differentiated instruction will be adequate and abundant:

> I agree that effective differentiation is very hard. But, I am deeply concerned about the idea of segregating students by ability. This might benefit the higher-achieving students…

The first of the articles asserted that differentiated instruction is anything but abundant. Can we please comfort/educate the people, especially the educators, burdened by the implicit ***false*** notion ("deeply concerned") that students are just average, "higher achieving," or "low achieving." ***Recognition that ability is not typically monolithic productively changes a lot of world views, and eliminates misleading "deep concerns."***

Making differentiated instruction a lot less challenging does not mean generally segregating schoolchildren into "the dummies" and "the rocket scientists." It means sorting children into groups according to strength/weakness/***passion*** in different subjects. So, for example, Johnny might be among the students able to progress more quickly in math, in part because of ability, and sometimes also because it affects something Johnny likes to do so he works harder at it. Johnny could be average or struggling in other academic subjects.

Another reaction to the *Education Week* coverage of the differentiated instruction challenge said, "Differentiation is very difficult" but argued that we needed to still attempt it in order to narrow the range of differences between children. That statement not only strongly hints the one-dimensional ability fallacy, but sadly, it also implies sacrificing more rapid progress by the better students to keep them from getting too far ahead of their supposedly one-dimensionally weaker peers. I agree, we need to attempt differentiated instruction as the need arises. Even with school-choice-driven *ability grouping by subject*, many classrooms will still contain students with some significant differences, especially in sparsely populated places that will have small menus of schooling options (little specialization). But we can create a system in which we do differentiation under less costly (foster investment in strengths) and less daunting (through *ability grouping by subject*) circumstances. When traditional public schools (TPS) group children only by age and attendance zone, they create "impossible dream" differentiated instruction challenges.

School Rankings Exercises

Our current system definitely has bad schools. They are dysfunctional. Because of the reasons discussed in chapter 3, some schools, public and private, are not good at what they want to do. A good TPS is good at what it aims to do. The instructional approaches of good TPS fit the mainstream pretty well, but the mainstream pedagogy works poorly for a lot of students. Schools given an A have not solved the one-size-fits-all challenge.

Because one size can never fit every child in an attendance area, even the best TPS leave many children behind. They are good for many children, okay for others, but not all. Like teachers and students, schools have strengths and weaknesses, and the mandate of each TPS to fit nearly all dilutes the strengths that exist in their teachers and magnifies weaknesses. So, for at least the so-called good schools—functional, good at what they do—we must ask, "Good at what?" and "Good for whom?" and lament the current system's paucity of better-fit, affordable alternatives for the rest. This is a key reason why choice among uniformly comprehensive TPS is not nearly enough to address the differences in how children learn, and what motivates engagement in the learning process. Entrepreneurial initiative is the economy's tried-and-true way to create and fill the highest value niches and drive relentless improvement.

Imagine trying to meaningfully rank the schools on a dynamic menu of diverse schooling options. No problem for informed parents. The ranking depends on the characteristics of their children, so the ranking could vary, by child. Each family will choose the highest-scoring good-fit school (location and tuition, if any, will matter too) for each of their school-age children.

Ranking diverse schools on the basis of measured, basic skill acquisition does not indicate which schools are more effective, even in a generic sense, much less for any given child. An average score or average student score change comparison may only indicate differences in the target student populations' potential for measurable academic growth or schools' ability to recruit teachers and students most suited to the schools' missions. Anomalies can be useful information. For example, it is not noteworthy when schools that specialize in instruction for the scientifically gifted produce the top math and science scores. It is noteworthy when they do not.

So, state test scores on basic skills would be just one of many factors parents would take into account in choosing a school for each school-age child. Test scores may signal how effective each school is with the students enrolled in what their families deemed the best available fit. Differences between specialized schools' test scores can signal families' gains/losses from moving their child to another school only to the extent that several types of schools are a good fit for their child.

School operators can gauge their potential for improvement by comparing themselves to the schools that aim to do the same things in the same way, schools that can be anywhere. Families do that now, but a system of specialized options would likely greatly reduce that. Among the brick-and-mortar options, only those nearby are relevant. And many schooling markets are not large enough to have multiple versions of each type of specialized school.

Public Money Means Non-Selective Admissions

One of the reasons we have a low-performing system is because the use of attendance zones implies that each TPS should be able to educate almost every child. That provide-every-thing-for-nearly-everyone-in-every-school mindset creates large school management challenges (Powell et al. 1985, Segal 2004). It also severely undermines the exploitation of differences in educators and schools to address the differences in how children learn and differences in the factors that maximize the engagement of children in the coproduction of intellectual growth. Of course, an acceptable school system has a good-to-great, accessible choice for every child. A market-driven price system finds and fills the highest value niches better than any known central planning approach. But that said, the location of some children relative to the various schooling choices, including especially in sparsely populated areas, may necessitate some creativity just to create a good choice, for example, perhaps through blended learning that mixes online schooling with classes at the assigned TPS. No system will put every child in adequate proximity to the best possible schooling choice.

Static World Fallacies Are Part of Blob Speak

"Not Enough Seats" Fallacy

It is amazing that any resident of our dynamic nation and world would believe that the size, number, and nature of the existing choices necessarily define the limits, moving forward. But the anti-transformation establishment (the Blob) will assert something that fools some people into opposing transformational change even if what they are asserting is easily refuted and widely seen as nonsense. We have an overextended electorate, and there are a lot of low-information, low-attention, and low-economic-literacy potential voters. So, for example, enacting private school choice is often alleged to be pointless because the empty seats of the private schools of the current system are just a drop in the bucket, just a fraction of the enrollment in the worst schools. But construction, portable units, conversion of former TPS, and repurposing of existing structures can quickly expand supply, and gradual expansion pressure is likely to be the norm.

Because church-run private schools dominate the private sector now, many people believe that church dominance of private schooling will always be the case. When the Supreme Court was considering the *Zelman* (2002) case, a lot of people thought that excluding church-run schools from indirect funding (tuition voucher) would effectively ban school choice expansion—that school choice expansion would be meaningless if the vast majority of existing private schools could not cash vouchers. Exclusion of church-run schools would have been sad but not devastating, provided that the combination of per-pupil public funding and co-payment made creation of new secular schooling options profitable. By a one-vote margin, the Supreme Court avoided unfairness to families preferring faith-based schooling, and they prevented the discouragement of school choice advocates suffering a static world fallacy.

"Choice Expansion Increases Segregation" Fallacy

Alleging a choice-segregation connection must also win some opposition to school system reform. Segregation is the deliberate, forced separation of people according to race, gender, or ethnicity. Incredibly and sadly, some people, including research scholars, use that same term to describe the coincidental separation that occurs through freedom of choice, or because of cost factors like housing costs and travel logistics. When pushed, as such scholars were at a session of the January 2015 School Choice and Reform International Academic Conference, they'll admit that there is a big difference between forced sorting by, for example, race (true segregation), and incidental sorting by choice (stratification, but *not* segregation). But even though there are well-known, appropriate words for the latter—such as *stratification*—they persist in applying the term *segregation* to school enrollment outcomes where no force is involved. It's a practice that fair-minded people must condemn. It undermines clear thinking about policy reform. School choice expansion can increase stratification, but it does not cause segregation.

So, for example, if a CPS operator puts a school in a minority-majority neighborhood—often deliberately to provide an alternative to assigned TPS that are not a good fit for many of the students sent there and to solicit donations—the resulting often overwhelmingly black and Hispanic student body composition of the CPS of choice (or chance) is called segregated? Such CPS typically have long wait lists, and annual lottery winners mostly consider themselves very lucky to secure a coveted seat. We can discuss and research whether there are any de-stratification strategies that would achieve more benefits than costs, but *please*, let's not use inflammatory language that implies we are imposing a terrible situation on the children enrolled in such schools. Words have meaning, and unforced stratification/separation of children by race, gender, ethnicity, or socioeconomic characteristics is a totally different animal than deliberate, compelled separation.

That concern about choice-driven separation of students by race and/or socioeconomic status persists even though school choice expansion is the centerpiece of many cities' court-mandated integration strategy. Indeed, separation by race and/or socioeconomic status is worse than before *Brown vs. Board of Education* (1954), an outcome that is a key example of the often big differences between widely celebrated aims of free public schooling, and the actual public school outcomes.

For choice expansion to further increase stratification of students by race and/or socioeconomic status, student body composition must dominate many families' choice criteria. Such dominance seems more likely to be the case the smaller the differences between the school choices, such as just choice between uniformly comprehensive TPS. It remains to be determined, through research, whether school choice homogeneity is a key difference between the published studies that allege that choice expansion increases stratification, and the studies that allege the opposite.

"Fix with Better School System Leadership" Fallacy

I can use a recent personal example to help explain this fallacy. Jesse Ortiz and I recently co-authored a chapter in *Improving Lives in Alabama: A Vision for Economic Freedom and Prosperity*. One of the criticisms of our recommendations was that we had not taken account of State Schools Superintendent Tommy Bice's then-new Plan 2020. If Mr. Bice (2011–2016) had suggested anything but more of the same—harder (MOTS-H), or the Rick Hess version, "the same thing over and over," it would have surfaced in the outlets that I monitor, where, for example, I learned of the lionization of a then-new Oklahoma superintendent's MOTS-H efforts to stir the public school system corpse. After Bice spent years as the deputy superintendent, and 4.5 years in the top job, a state senator noted that new leadership is in order because the 2015 NAEP test results rank Alabama last among states in fourth grade and eighth grade math. That, and the criticism of the Merrifield-Ortiz chapter is the new leadership fallacy in action. Even though new school system leadership repeatedly fails to yield improvement beyond Nation at Risk norms, somehow hope for a productive central plan revision triumphs over the repeated failure to achieve that goal. What we need is lawmaking leadership to change the circumstances of public school system officials and current and potential education entrepreneurs.

Apparently, the specifics of Bice's Plan 2020 did not even rise to the level of "somewhat new twist" on recycled failed reforms. It was another failure to address the classroom roots of the problem (chapter 3) of persistent disengagement and low performance; another attempt at school change without substantive school system change. Despite my low expectations for his efforts, I wished Supt. Bice well, which was just before his retirement in 2016. After all, it was his job to make the current system work as well as possible. No matter what kind of reform is undertaken, the public school system will enroll the vast majority of schoolchildren for quite a while, still. It is up to each system's governor and legislators to create higher-performing systems. Mr. Bice's successor, Michael Sentence, lasted only a year, followed after a six-month delay by the hiring of Eric Mackey. No doubt each has a grand "more of the same—harder" central plan optimization plan.

The extremely high turnover rates for state superintendent and urban district superintendent attest[3] to the futility of wresting adequate performance from the current system. Arguably, superintendent (state or district) is the world's most difficult job. Their immense challenge is to satisfy a diverse clientele with a uniform product. And as difficult and expensive as the job is, it is also arguably unnecessary. Schools can be managed individually by their principals. Probably, they should be.

The accomplishments of two recently retired lionized superintendents, Pat Forgione of Austin and Tom Payzant of Boston, make the point that the very best in that job raise their districts up from awful to Nation at Risk norms. The ordinary mortals in the superintendent job suffer normal, terrible central planning outcomes. For example, the article announcing Forgione's exit reported that Austin is 2/500 above the NAEP fourth and eighth grade national averages (48 percent and 57 percent respectively). Then they get fired because you have to do a lot of politically incorrect things (make a lot of enemies) to make significant progress, or they retire because they need a break or see the involuntary exit on the horizon. The standard exit line is "We have a long way to go." Yes, but under the current system, the district is more likely to backslide than advance much further.

Poverty Excuse

Blaming school systems' low performance on poverty is bizarre on several counts. Since there is always at least relative poverty and usually some absolute poverty, the right question about the connection between poverty and a school system is whether a system's governance and funding policies minimize the impact of poverty. That can hardly be claimed about a system—ours—that aims for one-size-fits-all, which may be a political imperative of government-run schools. So, we can expect and verify that the fifty-one US systems' uniformly comprehensive approach is especially ineffective for disadvantaged children. The inevitability of some poverty should eliminate every possible excuse for keeping a system that cannot deliver a dynamic menu of relentlessly improving schooling options as diverse as the children that the system should serve.

The evidence from studies of the current system do not support the claim that the challenges of poverty mandate much increased per-pupil spending. The famous Coleman report (1966), Eric Hanushek's (1992) survey of hundreds of studies, and periodic reconfirmations have found that per-pupil funding is not a statistically significant determinant of school effectiveness. Indeed, none of the school descriptors were statistically significant. So, we have "money doesn't matter"[4] and "schools don't matter" findings. Keep in mind those findings arise from studies of the current system. Money and schools could matter in a different system; that is, with significantly different funding and governance policies. In an efficient system, they would matter.

The "money does not matter" claim means that variability in per-pupil funding is not significantly correlated with measured student outcomes. The reliably quantified school descriptors hypothesized to be significant determinants of student outcomes were only rarely found to be statistically significant. Since only student characteristics are statistically significant determinants of school outcome differences, and the average school outcomes in a Nation at Risk are low, the schools must be equally bad, *some better outlier schools (observed outcomes that did not fit the model) notwithstanding*. Factors such as central planning and pricelessness (source of weak and perverse incentives) are likely reasons that statistical analyses imply schools are equally bad. Since student circumstances typically explain all, or nearly all, of the statistically significant differences between schools' average test scores, differences in existing schools have **not** been part of the reason why a child's future depends on their zip code. We need a school system that minimizes the zip code effect, typically, and mostly a parents' socioeconomic status effect.

My study of the determinants of average student outcomes of districts and states highlights why one of my mentors, Myron Lieberman, used *Public Education: An Autopsy* for the title of his great 1993 book. I found some studies with statistically significant school descriptors, but the rate of effect (regression coefficient) is so small that it would take a huge (unaffordable) jolt to barely budge the system outcomes. "Even highly favorable circumstances produce mostly disappointing NAEP, ACT, and SAT results" (Lieberman 1993, 326). For example, according to one of the studies I examined, a two standard deviation favorable change in teacher salaries (+25.1 percent) and pupil-teacher ratio (-20.8%) would have only increased the average student three-test composite test score to 58.7 percent. So, a huge expense for minimal gain to a level that is still terrible.

"Significance/Value of Political Accountability" Fallacy

Some people, including legislators, believe that political accountability is the only kind. Legislators, especially, should know better. Here is a recent shocking example of that fallacy:

> Republican Senator Kel Seliger (R—Amarillo) worried that while money spent on public education has government oversight, money sent to a private school doesn't. "On this body of money we're going to have no accountability whatsoever," he said of SB 276.

Especially sad and stunning is that the fallacy infects people like Senator Seliger, who is not an establishment stooge eagerly mouthing teacher union talking points. The vast majority of Republicans assert belief in limited government and belief in markets as bastions of rock-solid accountability to actual and potential clientele. I'll save for another time a comparison of bottom-up accountability to foot-loose customers that decide how to spend their own money on competing choices to producer accountability to elected and appointed officials spending someone else's money. Here, I'll conclude by briefly describing two things: (1) what ~180 years of accountability to political authority (government oversight of public money) has wrought in K-12 schooling; and (2) the track record of recent attempts to impose greater accountability to authority.

With the persistent shortages legislators created through price control, there is very little market accountability. That's a disaster because political accountability is at least weak, and at worst, perverse. Even without accountability to special interests, the political process tends towards uniformity, tyranny, and expansion. It's a tendency exacerbated by special interest pressures for favors (rent-seeking), and when voters are overextended, undereducated, and miseducated.

The 2015 Texas Legislature's processing of SB 276 (private school choice) illustrated several persistent fallacies, including the mindless willingness to assert that accountability to political authority is the only kind. In the roughly 180 years since the creation of the first US public school systems, the political process gradually produced a K-12 school system that continues to yield Nation at Risk academic results despite massive funding increases and repeated, strongly worded warnings. There have been six warnings since the 1983 original. Prior to that, there were two 1950s warnings: (1) *Why Johnny Can't Read*, and (2) Admiral Hyman Rickover's book warning of insufficient homegrown math/science talent to safeguard our national security secrets, echoed by a 2001 Presidential Commission (p. 38–46).[5] With only minor exceptions, the political process, nationally and in each of the fifty states, continues to allocate nearly[6] 100 percent of tax money earmarked for K-12 education (public school system monopoly on public funding) to very expensive, inefficient schooling that leaves a lot of children behind. Even excluding the schools formally designated "failed schools," proficiency rates are mostly far below 100 percent, and below basic (illiterate) rates are typically over 20 percent, and often much higher than that.

The Nation at Risk warnings mostly yielded a supposed accountability-standards approach to school system improvement. I say "supposed" because that costly approach didn't yield much academic improvement or much actual accountability for poor performance. Rick Hess, Paul Peterson, and others have documented that the promised "or else" for low performance almost always failed to materialize. And because we imposed the fear of accountability on a low-performing system—roots of the persistent low performance problem were not addressed—fear, frustration, and desperation produced some significant negative outcomes, such as systemic cheating (likely far more than has been prosecuted) and narrowing of the curriculum to test prep and directly tested subjects.

Can we please try an adequate dose of the market accountability that Senator Seliger believes would amount to no accountability? It would be difficult to get less from our dedicated educators and ~$13,000/pupil/year than we get from the political accountability and resulting typically weak, often perverse, incentives that government planning and oversight have produced.

Research can provide forums for attacking fallacies, and for providing the information our electorate and their leaders need to move forward. How to do that is the subject of the next chapter.

---

1   *Tinkering Towards Utopia* is the title of a Tyack and Cuban (1995) book.
2   https://www.edweek.org/teaching-learning/opinion-differentiation-doesnt-work/2015/01; https://www.edweek.org/teaching-learning/opinion-differentiation-does-in-fact-work
3   The six-year average for superintendents of the 100 largest districts is the mathematical result of many very short stays, and a few very long ones. https://www.edweek.org/ew/articles/2018/05/16/how-long-do-big-city-superintendents-actually-last.html Some of the short ones result from aggressive behavior; that is, determination to make significant changes. Message: want to stay a while, then don't rock the boat.
4   Some studies have found a statistically significant connection between per pupil funding and earnings.
5   The 2001 commission's description of an unsatisfactory K-12 system was nearly as brutal as the "act of war" language of the 1983 original Nation at Risk report. 2001: "As things stand, this country is forfeiting that [national security] capacity. The facts are stark."
6   It slightly depends on your view of the independence of CPS, minimal to zero, for sure, in at least half the states.

CHAPTER TWELVE

System Design Issues to Address through Research

School system transformation will require unprecedented policy entrepreneurship, a high-octane combination of political wisdom and political will. A good place to start is political wisdom and will enhancement through better information and better issue framing. Then follow with a systematic, careful pursuit of a high-value research agenda. There is abundant technical brilliance to redirect away from nearly always low-value comparisons of schools and students within school systems. Those scholarly resources need to be redirected to high-value projects, such as the strong efforts at school system comparison discussed in chapter 1, and collection of better data.

"HANG ON! HERE WE GO AGAIN!"

Comparisons of different parts of higher-performing school systems will yield more insights than comparisons of different parts or different victims of lower-performing school systems. An ideal data set would include observations from higher-, medium-, and lower-performing school systems, with consistent measures for all of the key variables. Recall from chapter 2 that the average outcomes of higher-performing and lower-performing do not differ that much.

We Desperately Need Better Data

We need school system reform so educators are likely to produce high-performing, relentlessly improving schools. So, we need to look for important differences in school systems, which means assessing the combined outcomes of all of the schools in a system, public and private. All of the schools in a system means all of the schools subject, directly and indirectly, to the same key governance and funding policies.

For the subset of students with higher education ambitions, we may be able to use college entrance exam scores to compare states' overall K-12 outcomes. To identify the US state-level funding and governance policies that measurably influence school system outcomes, we can use National Assessment for Educational Progress (NAEP) data that, fortunately, reflect the combined outcomes of private and public school students. NAEP data, though, have a potentially serious, almost utterly neglected deficiency. Students have no incentive to make a maximum effort on the exam, something likely to affect scores of older children the most. And there may be other bias-inducing factors.[1] Even if that explains a large share of low scores, even for the youngest children, the average scores are still terribly low. What is dubbed the proficient range includes scores below 60 percent.[2]

Often, potentially transformational programs exist only in sub-state regions. For example, New Orleans and Milwaukee have widely studied, specific school choice policies. Both have a mixture of chartered public school use and tuition voucher availability. Except for my recent controversial (so, unpublished) effort to study the aggregate effect of Milwaukee's or New Orleans' unique mix of school choice expansions, no one has tried to discern if a school choice initiative produces measurably better overall performance in a part of a state school system. The same problem exists for international school system comparisons. Policies worth studying often exist only in parts of nationwide school systems. And for nation comparisons, consistent national-level data may not exist for all of the factors that should be controlled for to reach valid conclusions about the effects of school system differences.

My data struggles may partly explain the widespread failure to assess whole school system (public + private) performance. For New Orleans, I was unable to find sub-state performance data for private schools, or data, like NAEP, for combined, public-private performance. NAEP data exist for Milwaukee, but not for the metro areas most like Milwaukee, which are the correct benchmarks for the effects of the policies unique to Milwaukee. So, in part to illustrate the need for better data, my Milwaukee and New Orleans studies assessed just the impact on the public school system, which is of interest, but the narrow focus is also dangerous.

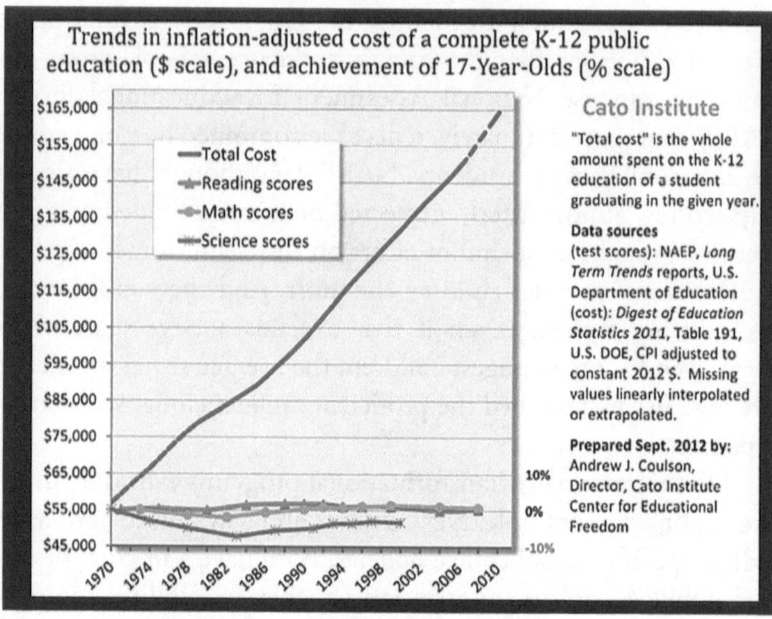

Resting a verdict on whether a program—any potentially transformative new policy, not just school choice programs—is working just on the basis of the impact on public schools means ***we could reject policy innovations that improve the overall system despite little or no deliberate response from the public part of the system.*** That would be a disaster, perhaps a likely one. Public school system nonresponse has been the norm for decades of efforts to improve outcomes (Hess 2002, Smarick 2012).

Remediation data for entry-level college freshmen are another possible basis for whole (public + private) school system comparisons. But even if vetting that source demonstrates that remediation data are useful for comparing sub-state regions in the same state and in different states, we still need to identify additional whole system performance measures. Hopefully, we'll find that some can be developed from currently available raw data, and we can identify important data that would become available if we began collecting some new information. We desperately need to initiate a long-term data improvement effort to help us identify the most promising school system improvement strategies, and before the current deficient data become the basis for a mistaken rejection of potentially useful school system improvement strategies.

Research to Refute Poorly Conceived Research

There has been a lot of well-intentioned, misguided research, much of it technically brilliant. That, and misinterpretation of evidence (often deliberate spin), is the source of many dangerously misleading, irrelevant, and wrong assertions, beliefs, and narratives. It's not always obvious whether episodic nonsense is an honest mistake or shameless and shameful. A good example is an article[3] that uses the 2012 Program for International Student Achievement (PISA) results to claim the US school system works fine—that student poverty is the reason the system is low-performing compared to other countries. Before I describe the apples-and-oranges nonsense underlying their claim, I want to remind you of three things: (1) At the school system level, global best (recall from chapter 2) is not very good. There are some high-performing schools, but no high-performing school systems (states, provinces, and countries). The best whole-system PISA scores are only a bit over 10 percent above our Nation at Risk scores. (2) Low performance by middle- and upper-class area schools is well-documented (Izumi). (3) A Carnoy, Garcia, and Khavenson (2016) finding is that "there is no causal evidence that students in some Asian countries, for example, score higher on international tests mainly because of better schooling."

The offending article example argues that "US schools with fewer than 25 percent of their students living in poverty rank first in the world (PISA) among advanced industrial countries." They compared our best school outcomes to country (school system-wide) averages—shameful and maybe shameless! So, the US school system's low poverty outcomes are comparable to the world's best average outcomes, which aren't far above our fifty-one terrible school system outcomes. And since US per capita income is among the best, the countries with the best school system outcomes may have higher poverty rates than the U.S.

An apples-to-apples comparison is schools vs. schools, or countries vs. countries. We know from a Jay Greene and Josh McGee study that "even the most elite US suburban school districts often produce results that are mediocre when compared with those of our international peers." The article that compared our best school outcomes to country (school system-wide) averages argues that just improving family incomes—leaving our terrible system as is—will make us #1. How would we go about achieving a huge poverty reduction? Hanushek and Woessman (2008) showed that a school system improvement would yield significant income gains.

Moving Beyond Rejection of What Isn't So

To rebut wrong, misleading, and irrelevant findings, an appeal to established theory or common sense will be enough at times. But research may be required, for example, to create direct empirical evidence, and to reject excuses for persistent schooling and policy failures.

Insightful Experiments, Please

Some experiments with genuine market conditions will be critical if we can't move forward on productive school system reform without direct, contemporary US evidence. Waiting for that evidence from real experiments to emerge, be analyzed, and politically processed would yield very costly delays. But we know from the 1979 UK experience that appeals to theory and expertise can be insufficient substitutes for empirical evidence. Theory and expert testimony was not enough political cover for transformational UK change. An appeal to theory and expertise may be enough to achieve some escape-hatch policies (Milwaukee—yes; Cleveland—yes; New Orleans—no[4]) tried in the US and elsewhere so far, but not sufficient for a productively transformational reform. New Orleans was transformed, but not necessarily sufficiently productively. More time will tell.

Why some large districts, or collections of adjacent districts, where all of the standard recipes (higher standards, intention to increase accountability, etc.) have been tried and have clearly failed, have not already tried nondiscrimination is somewhat of a mystery. Such places are a good place for an insightful experiment for their own sake, and to provide insights on widely useful strategies for moving forward. Compared to state-initiated school choice expansion, district-initiated choice can much more easily achieve near-nondiscrimination. Districts can combine state and local money in the funding for those that opt out of a district TPS.

Many places are in a "last resort" policy circumstance. Colorado's Mapleton District said as much. Mapleton's superintendent said choice was needed, yet would not go beyond public school choice. The public school system's monopoly on public funding was more important than extending choice to what free enterprise could offer. Through research, using different definitions, we need to maintain a list of the ready-for-last-resort school systems and sub-systems. The definition of last-resort systems could allow for targeted nondiscrimination for high poverty places (Danielsen, 2017; see my chapter 2), the next best thing to universal near-nondiscrimination. With ***everyone*** in high-poverty places eligible—not just poor people—we'd get solid experimental evidence for decentralized planning involving everyone.

Assess the Poverty Excuse

It is often said (i.e., an example discussed above) that the US school systems are fine for the affluent—that eliminating poverty is the only way to solve the low-performance problem. That may be true of the current system, which would be a key reason to abandon it. Since income will likely always meaningfully impact home environment aspects that impact learning, it is fortunate that there is a growing body of evidence that disadvantaged children can learn in specialized settings that current governance and funding policies discourage. Charter operators have attempted to meet the demand for improved schooling for the disadvantaged, but difficulty financing typically expensive "no excuses" approaches for addressing disadvantage have created huge shortages of such instruction, which typically compromises quality. Price control—not allowing co-payment—is a much greater factor than public funding discrimination against CPS students; that is, per-pupil public funding of TPS is typically significantly higher than per-pupil public funding of CPS.

The poverty excuse also implies that the current system is successful with children from middle- and upper-income families. Even when schooling is better in higher-income areas,[5] the better schools are typically still not great. The roots of the low-performance problem exist throughout the public school system, not just in low-income areas. Current governance and funding policies discourage and severely handicap all but elite private schooling options. Increased spending on schooling or reduced poverty does not make one size fit all or eliminate any of the other roots of the low-performance problem discussed in chapter 3. That evidence needs exploitation and supplementation to confront the poverty excuse for low performance.

I'm not arguing that new research approaches might find that socioeconomic status is a trivial determinant of student academic outcomes. My point is that we need to learn the degree to which the poverty-academic-progress inverse relationship is a function of the nature of the school system. The school system comparisons I've recommended can reveal the average marginal effect of student socioeconomic status and the variance in its significance. We also need to learn the determinants of the within-system significance of family socioeconomic status. So, the rate of change of, say, NAEP scores, with changes in family socioeconomic status is a dependent variable recommended as part of school system comparisons. I'd expect to find that instructional approach diversity significantly impacts the within-system significance of family socioeconomic status. We need to test whether one-size-fits-all approaches are especially bad for the least advantaged.

Document Consequences of Pricelessness

We desperately need some creativity here. Throughout this book, I've noted the likely significance of market-driven price signals, general effects of central planning, and especially the likely terrible schooling effects of pricelessness. There is a solid theoretical basis for that, and lots of indirect evidence, which means there are clear links between price control and disaster for many industries, including K-12 schooling and between price control and episodes of economic turmoil. "Korea at Night" is an especially stark example, a nearly perfect controlled central planning—price control experiment. The northern share of similar people with a similar economic starting point applied central planning. As the satellite photo below shows, even the South Korean crony capitalism[6] version of decentralized planning vastly outperforms the North's central plan.

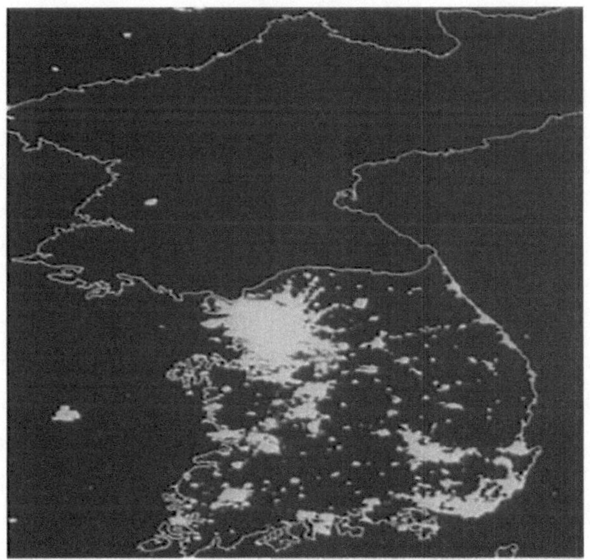

Great visual for the indirect evidence notwithstanding, some direct evidence might be necessary, even to create awareness of critical determinants of what instructional approaches are produced, where, how, and for whom. And that may be needed to create intellectual support for specific policy reforms that yield price decontrol. Failure to adequately explore potentially attractive policy options has been (UK 1979), and likely will continue to be, a leading basis for political infeasibility of transformational change and thus a continued triumph of inertia.

Of particular importance is evidence supporting economists' unanimity that shortages (non-trivial wait list = shortage) erode quality, often sharply (= scandal), is an ongoing phenomenon in K-12, especially in supposed schools of choice that fill through chance more than choice. See further below in the discussion of what we can learn from experience with CPS for a suggested research project that would use differences in states' price control levels to gain some insight on consequences of pricelessness and advertise that critical, mostly ignored connection.

Significance of Means Testing

We should determine to what extent lawmakers' propensity to means-test private school choice access (tuition vouchers, tuition tax credits, and education savings accounts or ESA) is fallacy driven. It may also take some research to better document the many drawbacks of means-testing the eligibility of students. Because narrowly targeting access to a tuition voucher, tuition tax credit, or ESA does not necessarily lower expectations of the effects of a proposed policy change, distorted views of the pros and cons of means-testing threatens much more than the enactment of sufficient access to private schools. Failure to meet expectations, even expectations that a narrowly targeted policy cannot justify, can give a bad reputation (Obama talking point noted above) to an untargeted policy that could produce good results.

So, for improved political feasibility of school choice expansions that might yield more impressive results, we need a thorough theoretical and empirical assessment of means-tested access to private school choice programs. The issues that need to be examined include

1. Means-testing reduces the choice expansion-driven total funding loss of TPS, but the means-test of choice eligibility typically causes a smaller rise in TPS' per-pupil funding. Which is more important to TPS effectiveness: total funding or per pupil funding? While specifically addressing the means-testing issue, we can add to the "Does funding matter?" literature, which so far says that it rarely matters or not at all.

2. Has the terribly low-performing US K-12 system made us a Nation at Risk officially, mostly because of low performance by TPS in low-income areas, or is low performance virtually ubiquitous because of system-wide problems? The heroic assumptions underlying the system suggest the latter, but research must credibly address this issue.

3. Fiscal cost: Means-testing may appear to reduce the state government fiscal cost.

4. Means-testing takes the most likely early adopters of newly developed schooling options out of the market and, generally, probably very significantly lowers the demand for new schooling options. That reduces competition and curbs the expansion and diversification of the menu of schooling options, something much needed to address the differences in how children learn and what engages them in the learning process.

5. Universal school choice expansion would provide middle- and upper-class families an alternative to flight from inner cities to access better suburban TPS. Means-testing sustains the devastating flight of young middle- and upper-income families from inner cities, and leaves the relocated children mostly in still low-performing TPS.

6. The difference between applying a means-test access to school choice program to poor people and limiting access to all residents of lower-income places (Danielsen 2017).

7. Means-testing, by reducing exit of student outliers from TPS—students for whom the mainstream approaches are not working—reduces the outlier exit-induced improvement in the teachability of TPS classrooms.
8. The research may turn up other noteworthy differences between the effects of more targeted and less targeted access to private school choice programs.
9. Compare legislators' beliefs (EdChoice.org surveys) about school choice and means testing to what theoretical and empirical evidence indicates.

Subsidy and Private Regulation Link

As noted earlier in the book, the potential for school choice expansion to increase regulation of private schools is something that can unite strange political bedfellows in opposition to policies that expand access to private schools. That means we need to convincingly identify the specific school system change policy factors that increase the regulation of private schools, both as a matter of policy optimization and political feasibility maximization. We already know that courts tend to rule that nonrefundable tax credits are not subject to rules about dispensation of government funds. Is that enough of a factor to prefer the tax credit route to increased choice, or something to consider as a regulation-minimizing benchmark to pursue through better design of voucher or ESA proposals in light of voucher or ESA advantages over nonrefundable tax credits, if any? It may be that the regulation risk for vouchers or ESAs is not large enough to justify the disadvantages of the politically most likely versions of tuition tax credits. The trade-offs between specific policies for expanding private school choice could vary significantly from place to place. The grounds for such variability would be valuable information.

Transformational Potential of Charter Law

The correct question to ask about laws that allow chartered public schools (CPS) is if/when a charter law can significantly improve school system outcomes. We can use the differences in the forty-five charter laws to discover which charter law features, after controlling for all other potentially relevant factors, explain differences in performances of school systems. The most likely charter-law-based, statistically significant determinants of school system performance are degree of funding inequity and number of potential charter authorizers. Significant regulatory factors could include allowing for-profit charters, content requirements, allowing online CPS, and personnel rules such as requiring union membership in the closed shop states.

Because no state allows the shared financing that would allow market forces to set the CPS tuition prices, we can't directly assess the price control effects of charter law. CPS must fund themselves from just state per-pupil funding and donations. But we can assess the effects of differences in the price control level. For example, states with higher per-pupil CPS funding are likely to have a more diverse menu of CPS offerings, and CPS should have a larger share of total enrollment in those states. That is, the higher the price ceiling, the more instructional approaches are financially feasible without donor dependence. There might be enough data to estimate the quantity supplied for popular instructional approaches at different price control levels. The growing use of weighted student formulae to set different price control levels for different students in each state makes this a more challenging study than it might otherwise seem.

How to Objectively Compare Diverse Schooling Options

A little-recognized, likely challenge of school systems with dynamic menus of diverse schooling options is a fair and useful way of formally comparing schools that teach different things in different ways.

Even in the current system with TPS aiming for uniformity in comprehensiveness (they aim to do the same many things in the same way), the many potential ranking criteria and measurement challenges create significant ranking controversies (Merrifield 2012). Add to that the challenge of objectively comparing all of the schooling options, public and private, and the probability that at least the

CPS and private schools will have diverse instructional approaches, and we may have to rethink the creation and proper uses of the comparisons. Ranking, except perhaps on just the basis of transmission of basic skills, and objective content such as mastery of US history may come to an end. The state can then focus on providing information about how schools differ pedagogically and thematically, and rely on consumer choice to assess continued eligibility for subsidies delivered through parental choice programs.

Establish the Nature of the Choice—Stratification Connection

A direct relationship between choice expansion and segregation is a widely raised concern. The term *segregation* arises from the current system's use of force—attendance area boundaries for traditional public schools and the public school system's public finance monopoly—to mix children in certain ways, intended or unintended. *Stratification* is the appropriate term for changes in the separation of students by race, ethnicity, or socioeconomic class that might result from increased ease opting out of the assigned public school.

Student body composition seems likely to rise in importance as a school choice criterion the more the schools in the choice set are similar in ways likely to be more important to families than composition; for example, few differences in the instructional approach. So, the hypothesis to test is that choice expansion increases stratification the smaller the valued differences in the school choices. If that hypothesis is correct, we would expect efforts to identify the stratification effects of the existing narrowly targeted, nontransformational US school choice programs to find that choice expansion increases stratification the less the choices differ.

Even if that becomes a stylized fact (if existing programs mostly increase stratification), school choice expansions that led to significant diversification of the menu of schooling options could decrease stratification. Larger-scale school choice expansions, such as outcomes of the nondiscrimination in funding policy discussed throughout this book, could fail to decrease stratification. Decreased public funding discrimination could even increase stratification if there is a significant correlation between race or other traditional stratification concerns and some of the specialized instructional approaches that could arise from entrepreneurial initiative. Such a correlation does already appear to exist, but it might be unique to a particular school choice expansion policy, or it might cease to exist if more transformational policies are adopted.

Even lacking significant evidence that school choice expansion decreases stratification when the school choices can differ a lot, the belief that it will has been a basis of many destratification-desegregation efforts. Given the unpopularity of busing as an integration tool, the hypothesis that differences in instructional approaches will mostly be more important choice criteria than student body composition is already the basis for desegregation policies. To spread such policy approaches to destratification, and to know how to improve them, we need a firm grasp of how school system policies influence socioeconomic stratification.

Highlighting Charter Malaise

Some of the projects proposed above may document that. However, those results and other findings specifically aimed at the malaise issue need to answer the question, for chartering supporters and opponents, why the one-size-fits-all problem, and other reasons why the public school system business plan is low-performing, has not yielded a larger charter sector. Nine years after Sheree Speakman's prescient observations (2008) about impediments to charter sector growth, the Center for Education Reform (2017) said chartering had lost its way and needed a course change, not long after Ted Kolderie (2014) voiced similar concerns and hopes for chartering.

> If we fail to address these issues, charters will continue to be small, underfunded, poorly housed recipients of inadequately prepared students who are transferring out of the local public schools. (Speakman 2008, 86)

> The charter governance experiment could be the backbone of the most successful outcomes-driven solution yet. Independently governed, but publicly financed schools might be the best solution *at scale* [emphasis original] to deliver improvements in cognitive skills for students that the traditional system has failed. (Speakman 2008, 109)

> CER (2017): Despite coming to life as a grassroots revolution, the charter school field is now far from its roots. This nascent sector faces the perils of isomorphism before it even occupies six percent of the total school-age population of the US, rendering the potential for greater impact all but lost unless these conditions change. The quest for legitimacy is pernicious.

Maybe price decontrol, by allowing shared public-private financing of CPS budgets, would be enough to end the malaise and curtail the scandals. Malaise, chaos, and stagnation are common outcomes of the central planning that fills the vacuum left by price-lessness. Statistical analysis of models that reflect all of the relevant factors will yield additional malaise prevention advice.

Conclusions

Political paralysis provides the imperative and time to build up political will and wisdom through well-designed research. However, a research agenda should not be seen as an excuse for delaying nondiscrimination unless, despite the urgency of transformational change and the powerful indirect evidence of the need to cede a major role to decentralized planning, the research is necessary to achieve enactment of the needed reforms. Direct evidence to support implementation of nondiscrimination in public funding of schoolchildren will not exist until a school system steps forward to be the first to try it. A key part of the process of making that first try politically feasible is a well-designed transformation transition process. Before we consider those transition issues, the next chapter provides a deeper understanding of competition in K–12 education; imagined and real.

---

1   Recent *EdWeek* story on low-stakes testing.
2   For example, the eighth grade math proficiency level starts at 299/500: https://nces.ed.gov/nationsreportcard/mathematics/achieve.aspx
3   Criticism without direct mention of names is a deliberate strategy to focus on ideas and claims, not the people that made them. Often the articles cited are just examples of widespread fallacy, so it would be unfair to focus criticism on particular victims of a stylized fallacy.
4   The New Orleans changes impacted the schooling of all students.
5   Recall that measured differences in schools explain little or none of the differences in measured performance; 'schools don't matter'; socioeconomic characteristics of students explain all or nearly all of the performance differences.
6   32nd in Economic Freedom (https://www.fraserinstitute.org/studies/economic-freedom-of-the-world-2017-annual-report), especially low on "Administrative Requirements" and "extra payments/bribes/favoritism," where the score is steadily declining.

Chapter Thirteen

Assessing Competition

In school system reform discussions, *competition* is a widely misused and misunderstood word, something that creates a powerful and potentially devastating basis for poor policy choices. For example, consider the typically small academic gains found by the studies of the US school choice policies enacted so far. Almost never stated is that all of the US programs suffer many significant restrictions. Discrimination against private school users, price control, and narrow student eligibility targeting has kept competitive pressures at weak to nonexistent. But since choice yields expectations of competition, the restriction-laden policy's weak effects can cause influential commentators and policymakers to move on, to give up on competition as a useful catalyst, reach a verdict of "guilty" without any genuine evidence. Many have. The Ladd (2000) self-refuted mischaracterization of New Zealand's restriction-laden public school choice as a quasi-voucher convinced many people, including Anthony Roselli (2005), that school-choice-centric reform strategies would not deliver the needed transformation. An equally terrible market accountability experiment, the price-controlled Milwaukee program,[1] was even more influential. Even though the Milwaukee setting lacked several critical elements of genuine market settings, reform advocates Sol Stern, Chester Finn, and Mike Petrilli are among the most prominent people having cited Milwaukee studies as proof that school choice was incapable of fostering the degree of transformation needed. There are additional examples below.

Needed Economic Education

The economic survival of the sellers, and sometimes the buyers (for some products), depends on their ability to secure trade on favorable terms. For example, consumers must acquire food and shelter. Producers must sell their product for at least enough to cover direct expenses. Competition meaningfully exists only if the choices differ, meaning, at the very least, in terms of proximity to some buyers. So-called perfect competition—sellers hawk identical goods—is not competition at all unless, just for the moment, sellers have exhausted all possibilities for a better product or for product differences that address the diversity in buyer preferences. When competing sellers have identical goods, they match each other's price until they can differentiate their version in a way some members of the buying public will value. That's important for school system comparisons because we have not even begun to exhaust the possibilities for better deployment of existing instructional approaches, potential for instructional approach improvements, or variability in instructional approaches that addresses the diversity in student-parent preferences.

Genuine competition yields market entry—new producers—when prices are quite favorable. Net market entry when profits are higher than in other markets that involve similar resources, skills, and risk, and net exit when profits are below normal is a standard ECO 101 textbook prediction. Since market entry occurs until profit levels fall to normal, instructional approaches with different costs will have different prices.

Market entry with new approaches for existing niches, and entrepreneurial assertion of new niches, is central to genuine competition. It is people betting their life savings that they've discerned an unmet need and can profitably meet it. So, potential for profit with a new approach, and widespread profitability for existing approaches, typically increases competition through market entry. That drives down prices and costs to remain viable in the face of the new arrival challenges. That's the "decentralized planning" response to price change. Price change keeps all of the non-obsolete niches filled and incentivizes entrepreneurial creation of new niches. Innovation is a disruption welcomed by the public but is problematic for producers of established but suddenly obsolete instructional approaches. That's why existing schools are often the worst enemy of needed reforms.

Money prices most often define trading terms. Price changes are both a cause of and then an effect of production and purchase choices. Prices adjust to changes in supply and demand and then create feedback effects on one or both. For example, the first obvious immediate effects of fracking technology were new supplies of natural gas. That led to a sharp price decline, which then prompted many natural gas producers to shift their efforts to oil production, where prices took longer to drop significantly. Cheaper natural gas increased consumption by longtime users and caused natural gas market entry by new uses, for example, by baseload power plant planners. The lower natural gas prices made gas-fueled power plants seem cheaper than the coal and nuclear generation that had dominated baseload power generation. Some gas producer exit, plus expansion of natural gas uses, firmed up natural gas prices, i.e. prevented larger price declines. School systems need that tried-and-true dynamic, a price system-driven resource allocation process.

So, what should we make of all of the alleged competition between traditional public schools (TPS: public school choice), between TPS and CPS, between CPS and private schools, and even between TPS and private schools through private school choice programs? Since the conditions of genuine competition are nearly always mostly or wholly absent from those settings, how should we characterize actual behavior aimed at recruiting students, or more often, the potential for or hope for such behavior? Since words need to have clear meaning, I suggest the use of *rivalry* for recruiting effort in situations lacking the conditions that foster genuine competition. Research that measures the differences between different levels of rivalry would establish that difference while also informing us of its magnitude.

Needed Research

We cannot reasonably convict competition of uselessness, or insufficient usefulness, generally, without first studying school systems containing genuine competition as it exists in most of the economy, which we cannot easily do because there are no such contemporary systems. Eligibility for existing US programs that lower the cost of opting out of the assigned TPS is narrowly targeted to particular people, among other important restrictions.

Foreign programs that allow universal choice have regulations that preclude many of the possible important differences between the schooling options. That occurs through restrictions on private school personnel, regulation of instructional content, and price control. For example, Sweden has price control (co-payment not allowed), and Sweden's mandated national curriculum specifies approximately 95 percent of the schooling content of all schools, public and private. Swedish schools cannot differ much except in how they teach the national curriculum. The choices actually available to most families, at home and abroad, may differ only in terms of how well they execute a uniform schooling strategy, the one size supposed to fit all. So, without the increased private school choice through price decontrol and the nondiscrimination discussed throughout this book, there is not much room for even robust rivalry behavior, much less the dynamism of genuine competition.

Establish the Essential Prerequisites of Productive Market Accountability

We certainly need to highlight the market conditions most widely cited for being the basis of positive, relentless change, especially (1) profit-loss potential; (2) low formal and informal entry barriers (level playing field between existing and potential choices); and (3) unregulated price change for independent schooling options driven by changes in supply and demand. Lacking ***any*** of those three converts a recipe for positive relentless change into a likely recipe for stagnation or disaster. No existing school system contains all three, and in many school systems, even in many that have recently enacted school choice expansions, none of the three are present, and there may be other key restrictions such as detailed curricula and/or personnel mandates that apply to all schools.

School choice/chance expansion through charter law is a good example of where the arrival of chartered public schools (CPS) is widely seen as yielding competition. But in many cases, not even noteworthy rivalry behaviors arise. Many of the forty-five charter laws preclude all three of the above-mentioned prerequisites for genuine competition, for schooling outcomes to match the much-lauded outcomes—for example, by Kolderie (2014)—of many other industries. A few of the forty-five allow profit-seeking, and a few have low entry barriers. Every charter law creates political control of prices paid to CPS operators and the zero price to CPS users. So, CPS supply and demand do not decide the price paid by customers or affect a CPS's per pupil revenue. And because the policy-determined price often does not yield a large enough supply of seats to meet the initial demand, the shortage (wait list) means that less-than-tectonic shifts in supply or demand don't even impact CPS' total revenue. Rivalry effects are seen, unproductively, in the length of the wait lists,[2] but not in a CPS's revenues. Often, CPS have no financial incentive to engage in rivalry behavior.

The financial viability of CPS depends on their ability to pay expenses from their state's per-pupil payments, plus whatever they can secure through donations. Yet, a former Assistant Secretary of Education said that "charter pioneer Ted Kolderie foresaw that chartering would introduce the dynamics of choice, competition, and innovation into America's public school system." But chartering didn't do that. Because of price control, recruiting enough students is quite often not a concern (no need for rivalry behavior). As noted above, there is frequently—often usually—a shortage of space. Very few states allow profit-seeking CPS, some cap entry, and all set CPS eligibility requirements beyond the zoning, health, and safety rules that apply to all entities that aim to offer products to the general public. In *The Split Screen Strategy: Improvement and Innovation*, Kolderie (2014) lauded the dynamism of markets and argued that it could be achieved through rejuvenated chartering, but the proposed basis for rejuvenation didn't include any of the key reasons for markets' dynamic efficiency. We should not look to assessments of CPS outcomes to provide insights about competitiveness effects in school systems, especially if the CPS outcomes of different states are lumped together.

Sources of Useful but Potentially Misleading Evidence

The private school activity discovered by James Tooley (2009—"Beautiful Tree") in many third world countries is highly competitive. Studying it can yield some important lessons such as the private sector's ability to deliver low-cost schooling preferred (higher performing, Tooley et al. 2011) to better-funded, free government-funded public schools. But the typical gray market status of those schools, like all other third world commerce, endangered by the corruption that is the central problem of third world countries, forces private school operators to adopt a short-run focus, low investment model, to run their schools. So, the behavior of third-world operators of private schools is worth examining, but with a wariness based on the likely highly significant differences between markets where property rights are secure, and where they are in constant jeopardy.

Likewise, evidence (Coulson 1999, West 1994) from pre-public-school England and the US can be useful, especially to compare those truly competitive but not contemporary conditions and outcomes to the weakly competitive/rivalrous conditions and outcomes present in some of the fifty-one US school systems. We need to learn as much as possible from studying the differences in the weakly competitive/rivalrous conditions present in some US school systems. The combination of examples from other industries, high levels of competitiveness in Tooley's (2009) examples, and behavior in pre-public-school England and US might be enough to build useful simulation models and establish the credibility of those models.

Effects of Rivalry Short of Genuine Competition

Even without the imperative to correct the excessive infer-
ring of competition and the propensity to recklessly paint with a
broad brush, noted throughout the book, it would be quite helpful to conduct research aimed at discovery of the effects of different
degrees of competition/rivalry and attribute school system change
effects to different degrees of rivalry. When does rivalry influence
specific behaviors, unproductive[3] and productive, at a constant rate,
or at an increasing or decreasing rate? A key first step would be to
use research to establish the grounds for expecting any meaningful
rivalry among schools. Some expansion of choice does not assure that
meaningful rivalry will arise. Even where large enrollment shifts are
possible, absence of public school system, individual-educator-level
gain or loss may preclude sufficient incentive to contest enrollment
losses. Possible employment loss may not be highly motivating if system-wide turnover creates numerous job openings to fill, which is
true for educators in most US places. And as an earlier New Zealand
example demonstrated, teachers appreciated enrollment loss because
enrollment losses yielded no staffing changes. And given that outlier
students are the most likely school leavers, teachers losing students
likely also enjoyed less need for difficult differentiated instruction.

Research designs must reflect that it is common for school
choice expansion policies to deliberately curb rivalry pressures by
preventing a loss of customers from proportionately impacting budgets or personnel. School personnel may be entirely shielded from
significant negative consequences of failure to compete effectively.
Even when lay-offs follow significant school-level losses, the vast
majority retained may be unaffected or may benefit.

My Edgewood analysis showed that effects often attributed to
competitive pressures may be due to other factors. As I noted earlier,
the Edgewood district schools were more effective during the 1998–
2008 duration of the privately funded universal voucher program.
They must have been driven to improve themselves, right? Maybe,
but there is no evidence of organized classroom-level responses to
the voucher-induced enrollment losses. I examined the school board

minutes for 1998–2008: no mention of the voucher program or the need to resist enrollment losses. That might be an example of the nonresponse tendency documented by Hess (2002). It may that the political process that produced the does-not-fit-all problem precludes a productive response. Osborne (2017), among others, discovered and documented that it is very hard to make changes, even seemingly minor changes. As Wolk (2012) noted, any significant change forces everything to change. That combination of factors is why it is dangerous to assess reform strategies on the basis of public school system change. It may be unable to usefully reform itself. Public school system ***behavior change*** is the basis least likely to yield major improvements in students' academic skills.

So, why did the Edgewood district outcomes improve with the voucher program onset and begin declining once the voucher program stopped accepting new applications? Maybe there were secret school-level, planned responses, which was possible because a possible competitive response basis not formally connected to the voucher program was that Edgewood teachers could enroll their children in their schools, which some observers said drove the teachers to try harder. Maybe, but holding back until their own children were present is a terrible accusation. My hypothesis is that most of the improved Edgewood district effectiveness was due to greater teachability—less need for differentiated instruction—with the exit of the voucher users; students for whom the Edgewood instruction was not working. I call them sorting effect benefits. We need more and better research that sorts out and measures the different possible effects of student outlier (poor fit) exits.

Discovery of Important Thresholds

There are probably minimum thresholds for most rivalry behaviors and most rivalry effects. Discussion of those would yield value apart from subsequent efforts to identify them. Since there are no general or industry-specific assessments of competitiveness thresholds (no Yahoo or Google Scholar hits), such an assessment for K-12 education would be path-breaking in several useful ways. That may be especially important for schooling because the available data cannot contain any highly competitive settings. Until legislation creates highly competitive settings, or we find them somewhere, discovery of the significance of different degrees of rivalry may have to come just from differences at the low end of the market competitiveness spectrum where multiple thresholds seem especially likely, for example, via differences in market entry barriers (for-profit allowed or not), pricelessness, or regulation of personnel or schooling content.

Confusion with Political Jurisdiction Rivalry

Caroline Hoxby (2000) showed that what is widely called (but not in the Hoxby article) Tiebout (1956) competition has value in school systems. All else equal, more rivalry among political jurisdictions through, for example, having more nearby school districts and greater student mobility, either by changing location or via transportation, is better than having fewer school district offerings to choose from. But Tiebout competition is not nearly the same thing and has a much lower upside than genuine competition among business firms seeking profit and risking loss and bankruptcy. School districts do not compete for students in the same way that businesses compete for customers. Unless a public school district provides for alternatives by giving up its public finance monopoly, it cannot specialize in instructional approaches that only work well for some students even when it works really well for a large subset of the student population. School district survival is not at stake in the rivalry outcomes, and district personnel can't claim profits or suffer losses. That said, the ~90% drop in the number of school districts, nationwide, in the last eighty years has greatly diminished what is still a useful political rivalry for tax base. It is not the kind of rivalry we can rely on for transformational change, but studies have shown that places with more school district choices have slightly better performing school systems (Hoxby 2000). Likewise, school survival is not at stake in public school choice, even in the few places where it substantially exists and occurs in fact, not just in name.

Except, by accident,[4] when private action funded vouchers just for Edgewood residents, Tiebout competition has not yet created private school choice and thus the potential for much larger effects than those measured by Hoxby. But growing interest in driving inner-city economic development with school choice expansion targeted to poor places may greatly increase that form of Tiebout competition.[5]

Some Concrete Examples of Misleading Findings

Failure to Grasp Basics

The Education Choice and Competition Index by Grover Whitehurst and Ellie Klein has a lot of useful information about the largest US school districts, but the title alone amounts to disinformation. It is not unusual for experts in some aspect of K-12 school systems to assume they adequately understand the nature of genuine competition and to even extensively comment on its presence/absence, including in writing. Indeed, the competition fundamentals are uncomplicated. They are well within the grasp of any educated layperson that absorbed their ECO 101 lessons, that does some online due diligence or seeks the counsel of a bona fide economist. But unfortunately, that grasp of fundamentals is still quite rare. Grover Whitehurst's impressive résumé proves the Clint Eastwood line (as 1970s cop Dirty Harry) that "a man has got to know his limitations," and that virtually everyone has strengths *and* weaknesses. Dr. Whitehurst headed a university psychology department and served as a Bush 43 Assistant Secretary of Education, among other impressive job titles. Co-author Klein has a rhetoric BA, plus a 2014 MPA degree.

They have impressive strengths, but among the key factors they don't understand is that ***the*** number 1 key element of genuine competition is ease of market entry/exit. Low entry barriers should be essential for a high competition score. Yet their index assigns A grades to places that retain the public schools' public finance monopoly that makes it very difficult to launch a private school. And their scoring rubric doesn't recognize that the competition process, including market entry/exit choices, is typically driven by price change and opportunity for profit. Genuinely competitive settings can include nonprofits but cannot exclude for-profit service providers. The New Orleans system does not allow for-profit providers or market-driven price formation but still got the highest possible Whitehurst-Klein Competition Index score in 2014, still second highest in the most recent index! The discussion of the index and the scoring rubrics makes no mention of entry/exit potential (presence/absence of barriers) or other essential elements such as price change or pursuit of profit. That's also true of an article about the index written by Aaron Churchill of the pro-reform Thomas Fordham Institute. Like many others with expertise in K-12 policymaking, the Fordham Institute folks usually mistake the ***potential*** for some rivalry for genuine competition.

An example of ***potential*** for rivalry, without genuine competition and likely without even any actual noteworthy rivalry, are the magnet schools that Whitehurst-Klein include in some scoring rubrics. The district people directly involved with magnet schools—specialized schools run by public school districts—have nothing tangible directly at stake in the enrollment level of the magnet schools or the schools' effectiveness at executing their specialized missions. They won't be forced to exit the district if the magnet schools don't meet expectations, and they won't share profits if they create a popular, cost-effective school. Likewise, the district people that authorize such schools will not suffer for picking specialty areas that are less popular or more costly than the other specialty areas they might have chosen. Those are things the price system would reward or punish.

Another noteworthy Whitehurst-Klein blind spot is their definition of availability, and their assumption that presence of other schools necessarily yields competition. To them, presence = available, which is, sadly, not nearly true of magnet schools, for choice among TPS or for CPS. Public school choice can exist officially but usually with little choice existing in practice. Schools that must aim to serve all children cannot differ greatly, and school leaders typically have little or no reason to behave competitively. With just choice from the district's uniformly comprehensive TPS, nearly all families agree on which schools are the best choices, and so the probability of gaining an open seat in a preferred school is very low, i.e., little availability. In contrast, with the menu of specialized schooling options that would very likely result from nondiscrimination in public funding, the diversity of children would cause families to disagree on which schools are the best choices for their children; they'd prefer different specialized schools of choice.

There are complete (≠perfect) measures of education markets and education freedom. We should rely on those for assessments of competition in action. The Whitehurst-Klein Index is an oversold, splendid public school choice index. Research can help us improve the existing measures of freedom or market presence and establish the significance of differences, if any, between different forms and levels of rivalry and potential rivalry.

Lousy Experiment Examples

Successive, debilitating disputes arise from the widespread failure to recognize lousy experiments. Jason Riley's February 5, 2014, *Wall Street Journal* op-ed, "Obama's Education Fibs," is a great example. It is about the restriction-laden, price-less Milwaukee low-income voucher program. Riley's article was a reaction to part of President Obama's brief pre-Super Bowl chat with Fox News' Bill O'Reilly. Asked why he opposed school vouchers that "level the playing field" and "give poor people a chance to go to better schools," President Obama replied, "Actually, every study that's been done on school vouchers says that it has very limited impact, if any." Though it is true that achieving terrible academic outcomes for less money is not a worthwhile objective, greater efficiency is still a noteworthy outcome of escape-hatch, non-transformational school choice expansions.

President Obama's accurate statement of the findings of US tuition voucher studies did not address Mr. O'Reilly's question about vouchers that level the playing field. The only publicly funded US tuition voucher programs that level the playing field limit eligibility to special needs children. No existing or former publicly funded US tuition voucher programs level the playing field, even for targeted low-income students or failed-school students. Even the best example, the privately funded, temporary Edgewood Program, did not nearly level the playing field. Sadly, many people see citing evidence from tiny restriction-laden programs as an acceptable answer to a question about a very different policy (nondiscrimination), one that would level the playing field and hopefully lack other common restrictions including price control—that would hardly resemble existing restriction-laden programs. And contrary to Bill O'Reilly's implicit assumption that a level playing field only impacts poor people, a level playing field would improve the menu of schooling options for all but the wealthiest Americans.

Jason Riley cited some noteworthy Milwaukee program participant effects to dispute the president's small-effects claim, but the fact remains that at the school system level, school choice program impacts have been imperceptible, probably because the programs have been very limited. Market conditions are absent. Pricelessness has probably been an especially significant factor. Milwaukee private schools must achieve better results, after their students struggle—fall behind—in their assigned TPS and then undergo a disruptive school change, with about 60 percent of the Milwaukee public schools' per-pupil funding. Despite mountains of theoretical evidence and indirect evidence (track record of markets vs. the central planning alternative) to support my explanation, I said "probably" for lack of direct, contemporary US evidence to substantiate my causal claim.

Lousy experiments are taking a toll on support for expanded private school choice as a school system transformation catalyst. Supporters of school system reform, including advocates of increased school choice such as Charles Glenn, Sol Stern, and Michael Petrilli probably acquired a distorted view of markets in action from lousy experiments such as Milwaukee's price-controlled, low-income-targeted tuition voucher program. Mike Petrilli heads the influential Thomas Fordham Foundation think tank (edexcellence.net). Glenn says we need government oversight for quality assurance and to prevent chaos. Having asked Stern personally, I know he was influenced by the Milwaukee disappointment.[6] Petrilli's colleague Kathleen Porter-Magee probably reflects the Fordham Foundation perspective:

> Take, for instance, the experience in Milwaukee, where the nation's first voucher program demonstrated that market forces alone weren't enough to drive quality, particularly in urban areas that serve predominantly poor and minority students.

What market forces? Milwaukee's schooling markets are severely distorted by the absence of nearly all of the key characteristics of high-performing markets: no scarcity-driven price change, no profit potential, and there are entry barriers. Only low-income families are voucher eligible—for a long time, only enough vouchers for a small fraction of them. If we keep giving school system reform opponents statements from school system reform supporters that markets have disappointed, we will make a promising reform strategy, true market accountability, politically infeasible.

The failure to meet the hyped expectations took the choice proponent spotlight off of Milwaukee. Even though the replacement poster child—CPS-dominated New Orleans—is another lousy market experiment, the hype continues, including reckless, groundless use of the term *competition. Potential for rivalry* is the correct term for what is actually happening there. The New Orleans school system is price-less. Profit-seeking entrepreneurs cannot apply for charters, and other normal components of genuine competition are absent. Until the authorities centralized charter enrollment (competition for the authorities to assign children to your school?), nearly half of New Orleans schoolchildren were on wait lists, which in the new OneApp system means that many don't get their first choice. But Jeff Murray's "How Do School Leaders Respond to Competition? Evidence from New Orleans" insists it is a "highly competitive marketplace."

Before I go on, I want to clearly establish the basis for my criticism. I do not object to the Milwaukee or New Orleans school choice expansions. They are improvements, and they have helped thousands of families. They may have been the maximum expansions possible politically and may still be. I object to characterizing them as insightful experiments in market conditions.

The Murray article is bizarre. He notes that there is little actual competitive behavior, mostly more aggressive marketing, and then asserts "that low level of response in this hypercompetitive market should be worrying." Hmm! Maybe it's because it's not hypercompetitive? Does "nearly all of the surveyed school leaders reported having at least one competitor for students" mean hypercompetitive to you (some lack even one credible competitor), even without taking into account schools with no incentive to compete for students (long wait lists), and missing prices and profits, the key drivers of market-driven outcomes?

Another tell-tale sign that some potential for rivalry did not create genuine competition is that "non-academic considerations (bus transportation, sports, after-school care) are often bigger factors than [general] academic quality when parents choose schools." It means that the potential for rivalry hasn't yet driven the specialization that typically results from competitive market behavior. Many of New Orleans' CPS are former comprehensively uniform TPS that don't differ much academically. And some of the new schools have chosen not to specialize. So, lacking major academic differences between many schools, the parents must base their school choices on the differences that do exist. That's why they often choose from those nearby based on non-academic considerations (bus transportation, sports, after-school care).

Conclusion

The most important point to be made about competition in school systems, and reinforced with research wherever possible, is that there is no genuine evidentiary basis to believe that market forces—even well short of a truly free market—cannot provide the best possible resolution of what to teach, where, how, and for whom. Let's actually test market forces in K-12 education before we pass judgment on their potential to be transformation catalysts. For now, the best evidence is indirect. The overwhelming indirect evidence and undocumented direct evidence from K-12 schooling is that central planning, which creates pricelessness, always yields terrible outcomes, and decentralized planning guided by a price system produces the best results. We need to apply research to identify the most efficient and most acceptable ways to harness decentralized planning.

The next chapter describes the sometimes rough road between our current system and one with the essential elements for high performance and relentless improvement.

---

[1] The Milwaukee program isn't terrible. It is just a lousy test of competitive effects.

[2] Over 500,000 unique names are on CPS wait lists. Summing the wait lists yields a larger number yields a larger number since many schoolchildren are on more than one list. However, but for the chance introduced by lottery-based admission, more schoolchildren would enroll in CPS. https://www.edreform.com/wp-content/uploads/2018/03/CER_National-Charter-School-Law-Rankings-and-Scorecard-2018_screen_3-21-18.pdf

[3] For example, harassing information requests, and failure to comply with choosers' new school record requests.

[4] The Edgewood district competed for residents without any action by district officials. The incentive to relocate to the Edgewood district arose from the private philanthropic choice to limit voucher eligibility to Edgewood residents.

[5] Danielsen (2017).

[6] Confirmed here: http://reason.com/archives/2008/02/06/not-hot-for-teachers

CHAPTER FOURTEEN

Winning Desirable Reforms—Transformation Transition Issues

There are two parts to a successful transition: (a) achieving enactment of the desired policy, and (b) preventing its abandonment because of unpopular, temporary effects. So, what is proposed for enactment must anticipate grounds for opposition, including, especially, factors that are part of the process of establishing the long-term conditions of the new school system.

The contents of this chapter will rely heavily upon Myron Lieberman's (1994) brilliant "The School Choice Fiasco." Twenty-five years later, it is still a solid starting point for efforts to maximize the political feasibility of transformational (= very controversial) school system reform. Lieberman's article was a response to the rejection of California's Prop. 174 (1993). He explained the many correctable political failures that caused Prop. 174 to lose by a wide margin.

Push for Change Where the Opposition Is Weakest

One of Lieberman's (1994) many key points was that California was a terrible choice for a political battlefield. So, if proponents of transformational reform were to attempt formulation of a national strategy, where to initially focus political effort is a non-trivial issue. Success is contagious, even before reform results can be known. So is political failure.

Where to Find a Real Win

Currently, the probability of success with a productively transformational school system reform is probably highest in (a) one of the ten solidly Republican states (AL, ID, KS, MT, ND, NE, SD, TN, UT, and WY)[1] or (b) one of the strong charter law states, states with low barriers to charter start-up and diversity. Of the ten states that got a grade of A or B on the Center for Education Reform strong charter law scorecard, Arizona, Colorado, Florida, Indiana, Michigan, and South Carolina are the most predisposed politically (perhaps still not much) to price decontrol, which would entail allowing CPS to ask applicants to top off the per-pupil state funding with a co-payment. I judge the other four strong charter law states (CA, MA, MN, and NY) to be utterly unlikely to further strengthen their charter laws with the price decontrol that would make their laws transformational. It's either amazing or shameful that the top ten Republican and the strong charter lists do not overlap at all. Utah had a B charter law, but increased regulation dropped Utah to a C. Five of the six strong charter law states are among the other fifteen with full Republican control.

Regarding the significance of the Republican top ten, it's not because Republican leaders have distinguished themselves as school system reformers. Indeed, none of those states has significantly changed the funding or governance of their school systems. The public school system monopoly on public funding is intact in all fifty states. But in those ten states, at least the electorate is open to school system reforms that face knee-jerk, tooth-and-nail opposition from the solidly Democrat educator groups, including, especially, the teacher unions that are more dominant in other states. All fifty states contain the grounds for opposition that has kept the Republican top ten from fostering decentralized planning. Lieberman (1994) also urged school choice proponents to wage political warfare in smaller political jurisdictions. None of the Republican top ten states are nearly as large as California, where Prop. 174 failed, allowing for a credible campaign at a much lower cost. Among the least Democrat states, the ideal political battlegrounds are the growing states with some metro areas large enough to support a diverse menu of schooling options, and with the potential for substantial in-migration to drive economic development effects.

The Growth Factor

Economic and population growth eliminates some potential fiscal conflict and some possible adjustment costs. The fixed cost argument (see below) against parental choice expansion proposals is least plausible in growing states. In growing states, the increased opting out of the assigned public school that will result from (probably gradually) ending discrimination against private school users will mostly slow the growth of public school enrollments, which saves a lot of money, while probably increasing the per-pupil funding of public school students, especially initially. Only in declining or very slow growth states are there plausible scenarios in which enrollment gains by private schools that increase per-pupil funding of the public schools still create budget stress for the public school system because of fixed costs.

For those not familiar with the fixed-cost basis for opposition to parental choice proposals, the opposition claim is that departures from a public school do not create many savings—that it costs almost as much to provide services (such as buses), pay for utilities, and staff schools with, say, 10 percent fewer students. That is briefly true in very limited circumstances, or by choice. Districts can choose not to adjust to decreased enrollment. TPS enrollment losses in non-growing areas can create temporary budget stress when the losses are too small or too widely dispersed within the district to close schools or reduce teacher hiring for the following year. But with any population growth, small losses do not create fixed-cost problems. Instead, the enrollment shifts we've seen for the largest school choice expansions postpone costly new TPS construction, and they reduce the need to recruit and hire new teachers. Without the shifts to private schools, population growth forces especially high recruiting effort.

Enrollment losses too large to be offset by growth are big enough to allow for savings from reduced staffing (which can be large because of high turnover and high recruiting costs). However, districts may choose to not reduce the number of teachers even when district-wide enrollment losses justify it. A key reason for that choice might be that saving other folks' money might not be as important to the authorities as avoiding unpopular redrawing of attendance area boundaries that could be needed to maximize staff reduction savings. The fixed-costs argument against school choice expansion also assumes a plausible but nearly nonexistent direct connection between school system budgets and school system performance. The roots of the low-performance problem discussed in chapter 3 explain the absence of the plausible connection between total spending or per-pupil spending and school system performance.

Anticipate or Address Relevant Scandals

It is rare when an insider confesses some serious flaws in their system. In *Reinventing Government*, Vice President Al Gore (1993) noted that scandal has much more political significance than routine failure. So, to achieve a major policy change, be sure to avoid scandals and make sure to inoculate your cause against past scandals. Shortages of space in chartered public schools (CPS) eliminate accountability to customers, which creates room to cut corners, which can yield scandalous behavior. We need to clearly and credibly explain the root causes of scandalous behavior that may appear to result from a proposed policy regime. In the case of the CPS scandals, we need to thoroughly document that the shortages created by price control are the root cause of scandalous behavior and other forms of charter malaise.

Potential to Maximize School System Improvement

Proponents of a decentralized planning basis for school system reform must establish that the potential for diverse menus of schooling options—the benefits of school systems that use the price system to determine which privately produced instructional approaches are available, where, and to whom—is not equal everywhere. Metro area total population and population density are key determinants of the potential to develop and sustain a diverse menu of specialized, relentlessly improving schooling options. Sparsely populated places may only be able to sustain the assigned public school and online options. This is a reason that recent policy improvements such as the West Virginia Hope Scholarship law may not fully demonstrate the potential for choice expansion-driven school system improvement. The modest size of West Virginia's largest metro areas may yield menu diversity way below what larger/denser metro areas would support. The same problem may exist in Arizona, the other state that enacted a universal-eligibility-for-ESA law.

The likely continued, significant improvement of online options is a key reason to eliminate the public funding monopoly of the public school system everywhere, even where there are only enough families to sustain one or a few brick-and-mortar options.

The Likely Significance of Economic Growth Effects of School System Reform

Noting the potential for substantial in-migration is important because school system reform will demonstrate on a large scale what we've already seen on a small scale in San Antonio's Edgewood district and other places highlighted by Bart Danielsen's real estate research.[2] School system reform that substantially levels the playing field between public and private schooling options yields economic growth before there is any school system change. The combination of job opportunities available in larger metro areas and the improved affordability of private schooling that results from ending discrimination against private school users yields in-migration. That is much more likely to be seen in states with significant adjacent population concentrations. So, sparsely populated states in sparsely populated regions are not good places to demonstrate the benefits of transformational school system reform. Because economic growth effects will be evident much more quickly than school system improvement, growth effects are much more likely to spread school system transformation that includes ending public funding discrimination against private school users.

From just that cursory assessment, from among the Republican top ten, Alabama and Tennessee seem ideal. A needed, much more rigorous assessment may say otherwise. Both states have multiple large urban areas and millions of people in neighboring states, including many near their state lines. The urban areas of Alabama and Tennessee also include many ready-for-last-resort inner cities that can serve as demonstration sites and are more likely to do so, for best or second-best approaches to school system reform.

A Second-Best Approach

When statewide school system reform (best) is not politically feasible, it may be possible to still realize and demonstrate major academic gains and economic development benefits while also conducting a true experiment. The second-best approach is to end discrimination against private school users in just the urban zones suffering devastating middle/upper-income flight from seemingly especially bad inner-city public schools. Inner-city eagerness, indeed a virtual need, to retain and attract middle-class families with school-age children may be sufficient for adoption of universal nondiscrimination in public funding of students near the worst public schools and poorest families. The often horrific circumstances of those places may be enough to convert the relative political correctness of means-tested *household* eligibility for greater access to private schools into average low-income *place resident* eligibility for greater access to private schools. A key political advantage of the second-best approach of *place*-targeted school choice expansion is that it curbs an opposition talking point that the proposed reform will cause an "underclass" invasion that would destroy great suburban public schools. Eliminating that talking point may be important even though it has a weak factual basis. The typically better suburban public schools are mostly "Not as Good as You Think," because affluence does not make the heroic key assumptions of the public school system business plan less heroic. School system reform is needed everywhere.

Weakening Likely and Potential Opposition

Lieberman recognized the key underlying truths created by our massively overextended electorate. One of them is that the people that derive income from the status quo can usually be a decisive swing vote against implementation of transformational reform. Another one is, eliminate distractions such as fiscal cost. The policy specifics and tactics underlying the preferred strategy can matter a lot. And finally, do what you can to disunite the opposition,[3] including especially expose hypocrisy within key elements of the opposition.[4]

Be Nice to Educators

Given the uncertainties created by major changes, and the Stockholm syndrome, it might be too much to expect teachers, administrators, and vendors to enthusiastically support transformational change. But a serious reduction in their effectiveness as opponents is achievable through provisions such as golden handshakes (severance pay, early retirement), pension portability, and retraining for jobs within the new system, or outside schooling.

A proposed transformational reform could assure, or create uncertainty about, a decline in the total number of traditional teaching jobs in the new system, and the degree of reduction in the share of those jobs in the public school system. Retraining assistance and pension portability from the public system to a private school job assures a soft landing for the people that want to remain educators. That, in turn, reduces opposition to the proposed transformation. It will likely even flip some votes, for example, entrepreneurial educators and those most frustrated with the uncompetitive teacher labor markets and unprofessional circumstances of the current system.

The nondiscrimination against private school users I have advocated would yield business opportunities for education entrepreneurs. So, it would be politically astute and economically efficient to provide programs that provide education-related business skills and then provide school system employees discounted access to those programs.

Avoid Fiscal Cost

Given the added difficulty of trying to win support for something no one else has tried (so a lack of direct empirical support), it is important that there be no fiscal basis for opposition, which has been a frequent refuge for fence-sitting legislators not eager to take on an entrenched system. The frequent occurrence of such behavior caused two prominent school choice proponents to support my proposal to create a school choice fiscal notes calculator so that we'd have a firm basis to avoid proposals with a noteworthy fiscal cost and to refute the fiscal cost claims that are baseless. Fiscal cost has been especially important to the households without school-age children (the majority), including especially seniors, who have well-above-average propensities to vote.

Avoiding fiscal cost may require a phase-in of full-blown nondiscrimination. So, for example, limiting access to private school subsidy to students not already enrolled in a private school creates a thirteen-year phase-in period for universal nondiscrimination. I don't have a preference for a thirteen-year phase-in. It's just an example of a way to slowly get to a desired end state. A phase-in of public school user eligibility reduces the credibility of opposition claims of not enough private school capacity, something that no one should believe, because of the potential to quickly enlarge schools or to create new ones through construction or by repurposing existing buildings. But static-world fallacies underlie many mistaken judgments, especially by an overextended electorate. Transformation advocates must be careful to not confuse legislating a phase-in with the failed incrementalism strategy that argued that small-scale system upgrades would pave the way for later passage of increasingly significant, new school system reform measures.

Optional Policy Specifics and Tactics Can Matter a Lot

Likewise, reform process differences that divide proponents are to be avoided if at all possible. As a general principle, that is obvious, but early discovery of avoidable points that could divide allies is not easy. Identifying low-cost ways to avoid them can require considerable effort. For example, some initial supporters of Prop. 174 balked when the final form of the proposition allowed voucher recipients to supplement the voucher funds with private funds or third-party subsidy payments. Potential for such public-private co-payment is critical because the potential for shared financing of tuition is what avoids price control and causes tuition levels to be market-determined. And that allows the price system to orchestrate which instructional approaches will be available, how they'll be produced, where, and made available to whom. As I've argued frequently in this book, market-determined prices are essential to avoid debilitating price control, and thus reliance on central planning. As I noted in chapter 8 (on subsidy issues), intense opposition to shared financing (demanding that schools accepting vouchers accept them as full payment of tuition) is widespread on equity/fairness grounds (disputed in chapter 9) and seems to even survive, to some extent, my personal delivery of detailed arguments to avoid the devastating price control that results from banning shared financing.

So, to avoid dividing folks that agree on the importance of nondiscrimination as a key element of transformational reform, pursuit of nondiscrimination must occur in a way that minimizes the potential to ban shared financing. That points to pursuit of nondiscrimination through tuition tax credits or education savings accounts and to avoidance of tuition vouchers. Forgive me for making this critical point at least twice in this book. Just once in this book might not have been enough to make up for having it appear nowhere else.

The potential for nondiscrimination, or a more limited basis for school choice expansion, to prompt increased regulation of private schools is another factor that could divide people that agree on the importance of transformational change that relies on nondiscrimination. That concern favors having nonrefundable education tax credits as the school choice driver of transformational change. Because courts rule that nonrefundable credits do not constitute government spending, such credits are seen to be the school choice expansion mechanism that is least likely to prompt more regulation of private schools. To keep nonrefundable credits from being too small to be transformational, the credit amount must be made bankable so that households can earn credits over the same timeline that they pay schooling-earmarked taxes, namely over their entire adult lives. Then small multiyear tax credits can finance repayment of a loan taken out to fund opting out of the assigned TPS.

Weaken the Opposition

The same point, in reverse, applies to the opposition. Find every basis for weakening the opposition and use as many as cost and morality allow. For example, Lieberman pointed out that teacher unions often fail to practice what they preach: for example, treatment of teacher union staff and widespread use of private schooling for children of TPS teachers. Widespread deep dissatisfaction with the public system, especially inner-city schools, by key traditional supporters of Democrat party candidates, and opposition to school system reform by leaders of those traditional supporters creates some underexploited opportunities to weaken reform opposition. Likewise, a document that makes it difficult to recycle superficially plausible but repeatedly failed approaches to school reform or school system reform would prevent that basis for opposition. Prevent more of the same—harder (MOTS-H) and the same things over and over. A significant part of that would be a well-articulated argument that there are no best pedagogical practices. The public school system is not going to be made high-performing by the discovery of the magic curriculum or a mode of instruction delivery that really does fit all.

Keep Unpopular Temporary Effects
from Causing Abandonment

Identify and anticipate unpopular temporary effects and credibly argue that they are temporary. For example, ending TPS monopoly on public funding will definitely increase the demand for private schooling. Even if market entry occurs in anticipation of the demand increase, it is quite possible (perhaps likely since the existing private schooling sector is quite small) that some private schools will raise their tuition prices. Higher prices are a textbook **short-run result** of increased demand. Much less well-known is that an immediate price increase will trigger market entry that will drive prices down, sometimes below where they were before the demand increase. That market entry effect must be made much better known.

Especially relevant to efforts to foster a substantial role for decentralized planning are past episodes of price decontrol. For example, you can cite the 1981 decontrol of gasoline prices, which caused an immediate, very unpopular price spike, but then prices fell to below the pre-decontrol level. That may happen with schooling. The additional competition from new schools may offset the cost of expanding existing private schools. But, I believe that the most likely long-run outcome is slightly higher tuition levels for existing private schools, even after market entry has driven profitability down to normal for the profit-seeking education entrepreneurs. Most existing private schools are church-run and church-subsidized. So, to expand their offerings, churches may have to charge a full-cost (not a church-subsidy discounted) tuition rate. If, as seems likely to avoid a fiscal cost, we phase in nondiscrimination, that tuition hike may hammer pre-reform (self-pay) private school users. Minimize the phase-in time to avoid the political impact of that. Consider providing some tuition-increase assistance to the self-pays.

Combine good forecasts of total system enrollment growth and public-to-private shifts to predict TPS closures, if any, and possible need to redraw attendance areas for the remainder. That will also help private schooling entrepreneurs predict where property might become available to start a new school in an existing school building. To soften the political downside of that, point out the TPS savings from reduced new school construction, reduced teacher replacement, and reduced maintenance spending because the oldest schools are the most likely to be closed.

The upcoming final chapter ties together the book's why and how arguments.

---

[1] There are twenty-five states with Republican governors, and Republican majorities in both houses of legislature (Nebraska is unicameral). I'm focusing on the top ten to avoid dealing with nuances such as Texas' House Speaker being elected by a coalition of all Democrats and a few centrist Republicans. The result: in 2015 and 2017, the TX House refused to consider Senate-passed private school choice expansions. Among the twenty-five, only Arizona, Florida, and Indiana are notable exceptions to the failure to achieve noteworthy school choice expansion, and they stopped far short of nondiscrimination in student funding.

[2] http://aresjournals.org/doi/abs/10.5555/1052-7001.24.1.1?code=ares-site
https://papers.ssrn.com/sol3/papers.cfm?abstract_id=2539242

[3] For example: Glass, Stephen. 1995. "A Pension Deficit Disorder: Teacher Unions Betray Their Members." *Policy Review*, n71 p71–74 Win 1995; https://eric.ed.gov/?id=EJ500645

[4] See Myron Liberman's (1997) *Teacher Unions.*

Chapter Fifteen

Putting the Pieces Together

We need better central plans until we can escape that mindset. A shift to transformational decentralized planning is urgent everywhere, so we need to quickly demonstrate its effectiveness in at least some of the fifty-one school systems in our nation at ever greater risk. That Nation at Risk status has been repeatedly reaffirmed by groups of nonpartisan and bipartisan experts. To quickly spread the better versions of the needed decentralized planning through free enterprise orchestrated by market-determined prices from the early adopters to everyone else, we need to anticipate and accept transitional challenges, generate some benefits, and quickly document some of those. The first places to adopt near nondiscrimination in public funding of K-12 education will quickly attract families unhappy with assigned traditional public schools' (TPS) futile attempts at one size fits all. Therefore, in-migration-driven, economic development effects are likely to be seen first. That will be especially evident, and important, where the economic development need is greatest: in our inner cities, which is where TPS usually seem to be at their worst.

The essential academic performance gains are very likely to be the last to be formally documented by research. And for several reasons, there will always be motive and room to muddy the waters. The appropriate performance issues and research designs are typically controversial. The status quo always has friends, and reform proponents never agree on which reform design features are best. So, there will be disagreement on what the gains, if any, have been and whether different groups have gotten a fair share of the gains. For example, broad-based gains could widen the achievement gap. Would there be noteworthy objections to school system reform that yielded significant gains to the least advantaged, but even larger gains to the advantaged? Probably.

Surviving the Political Gauntlet

The specific proposed transformational alternatives to the price-less central planning that will always yield massive disappointment—because central planning always disappoints—have to be made politically feasible and sustainable. Possible uneven sharing of gains, and transitional hardships, are among the possible threats to feasibility and sustainability. I argued that calling for nondiscrimination in public funding of schooling represents the best opportunity to achieve and sustain productive transformational change, but still, by no means will it be anything short of extremely difficult, and painfully slow. Doing nondiscrimination right means finding the policy design intersection of political feasibility and sustainability and maximum effectiveness.

Equity Factors

A key objection to the co-payment potential needed to avoid price control is inequitable access to the choices. But access is more than out-of-pocket cost. With price decontrol, the resulting much larger, dynamic menu of schooling options more than makes up for unavoidable, uneven access to that menu. In the equity chapter (9), I argued that access to the new schools made possible by nondiscrimination and ending pricelessness (ending price control) will be much more even—not as family income dependent—than probably the vast majority now believe. Poorly informed assumptions and inertia are often much greater barriers to productive change than actual well-grounded concerns.

Nondiscrimination will not eliminate unhindered access to the existing menu of mostly traditional public schools (TPS) or all chartered public schools (CPS) wait lists. And even without positive competitive effects on TPS, which are dubious, students remaining in TPS are likely to benefit from the exit of outliers. Exit of students for whom the mainstream pedagogy is not a good fit will make TPS classrooms more teachable through reduced need for differentiated instruction.

Key Political Strategies and Tactics

To advance a transformational policy that has not yet been tried in modern times, and only in the past in the no-public-subsidy version of nondiscrimination, will take extraordinary political will and wisdom. Extraordinary wisdom must drive strategy and tactics. Opposition insistence on data-driven and supportive empirical evidence must be met with one or all of the following: (1) Have as much direct evidence as possible. (2) Assert that relevant data and experience includes the experience from industries other than modern schooling for children. For example, the early US and early UK no-public-subsidy versions of nondiscrimination produced good results, and many industries have benefited from deregulation and price decontrol. Price control has always yielded disaster, schooling applications included (Nation at Risk = disaster). (3) Given positive feedback from available vetting methods (simulation, indirect evidence, theoretical analysis), we can't afford a delay of at least twenty years until someone else overcomes those challenges, tries it first, and data are generated and analyzed. In case those arguments are not sufficient, we should initiate some real experiments, where that is possible, and reject the alleged evidence of lousy experiments.

Build a New System Based on Non-Heroic Assumptions

Breathtakingly heroic assumptions underlie the current system. Enumerating them quickly explains why the current system suffers from persistent low performance. The factors that I've said are the classroom-level roots of the low-performance problem' are symptoms of even deeper causal agents. That's why we need to create school systems that effectively and efficiently eliminate reliance on heroic assumptions such as (to name two discussed earlier): (1) incentives don't matter, and (2) politically correct schooling practices by schools with a monopoly on public funding will discover and implement the best ways to engage diverse children in a coproduction process that does not work without their enthusiastic cooperation.

Appropriately Anticipate the Opposition's Standard Operating Procedure (SOP)

Reactions to the Merrifield-Ortiz chapter in *Improving Lives in Alabama: A Vision for Economic Freedom and Prosperity* illustrate what to anticipate. Through school system facts such as persistent low performance in Alabama and nationwide, noncontroversial core principles such as the diversity of children and educators, we argued for a system that would have a dynamic menu of specialized schools of choice. We cited evidence of widespread disengagement in the current system's implicit efforts to make comprehensive uniformity fit all.

Because we dared to rigorously, systematically question the public school system's central tenets and the public finance monopoly that finances them, we drew fire from local and national defenders of current governance and funding processes; the standard operating procedure (SOP) for such denunciations. (1) The status quo defenders will allege lack of due diligence regarding reform plans by pointing to the need to consider the most recent "more of the same—harder" (MOTS-H), sure-to-fail efforts to elicit acceptable outcomes from the structures already in place. For example, a former director of the Center for Rural Alabama and a longtime public school advocate, cited (without any specifics) the new State Schools Superintendent Tommy Bice's Plan 2020, alluded to in chapter 10. (2) They make vague references to unspecified alleged evidence that almost always turns out "wrong, misleading, and irrelevant," a phrase that literally describes the central motivation of my critically acclaimed 2001 book, *The School Choice Wars*.

The most amazing denunciation came from the Diane Ravitch blog. Dr. Ravitch is an outstanding education historian. But her exceptional ability to ferret out important facts often does not extend to comprehension of what they mean. Both Dr. Ravitch and Dr. Helen Ladd (cited in the article) said the "school choice evidence" does not support the Merrifield-Ortiz assertion that school choice expansion will yield improved student outcomes. That shameful overgeneralization of studies of small, restriction-laden school choice expansions is quite common. As I've often pointed out (my 2008 *Journal of School Choice* article) and everyone agrees when pressed, the evidence that has been generated by the recent minor expansions of school choice in the US and abroad do not provide guidance on the likely outcomes of the large, low-restriction versions recommended by Merrifield-Ortiz. And charter school experience only minimally qualifies as any kind of school choice evidence. The nearly ubiquitous charter wait lists (shortages) that result from pricelessness make it school **chance**, not school choice.

Ravitch and Ladd are often self-refuting. They often provide evidence that refutes what they assert other evidence means. For example, early in Dr. Ladd's widely cited book about the New Zealand public school choice policy reform of the 1990s, she describes it as an example of large, unrestricted school choice. Near the end of the book, she provides a detailed refutation of that assertion. The New Zealand policy excludes private schools and places significant restrictions on transfers among public schools. Extensive rules that apply to all subsidized schools allow for very little difference between schools. In another words, the ostensible school choices differ very little. New Zealand is yet another lousy, alleged school choice experiment, and like the largest, oldest US school choice expansion (Milwaukee's CPS, and vouchers for a fraction of students from low-income families), the New Zealand experience is widely cited as a failure of school choice and market accountability, generally. But the New Zealand experience only informs thinking about limited public school choice. For assessments of anything that might be truly transformational, the New Zealand and Milwaukee experiences are very misleading and mostly irrelevant.

Dr. Ravitch's transformation from brilliant education historian to blogger and paid political hack is even more incredible than Ladd's failure to fully absorb the contents of her own findings. Ravitch makes the same shameful generalization of the evidence derived from small, restriction-laden, lousy experiments to school choice, generally. And she vaguely alludes (political hack SOP) to an alleged relevant body of evidence that Merrifield-Ortiz failed to consider. If it exists, she also failed to consider it or condemned it already in, for example, her books *The Language Police*, *Left Back*, and *Death and Life of the Great American School System* (2010). All but the 2010 book predate her embrace, despite the earlier work, of the key existing funding and governance processes. I often cite her studies of education system history, her article ("Adventures in Wonderland") that describes her service in the "bowels of the beast," and the 2010 book that signaled her re-embrace of a system whose persistent, massive failings she has documented better than anyone.

From time as George H. W. Bush's (the elder) Assistant Secretary of Education, Dr. Ravitch concluded that "federal K-12 policy was a special interest candy factory driven by congressional committee staff." Ravitch's "Adventures in Wonderland" experience occurred towards the end of Jack Jennings' 1967–1994 tenure as general counsel of the House of Representatives Education and Labor Committee. Jennings' book *Presidents, Congress, and the Public Schools* (2015) makes no mention of the Ravitch-asserted special interest candy factory element behind policy formulation.

Jennings' hindsight yielded implicit agreement—with me, Ravitch, Vicki Alger (2016), and many others—on the ineffectiveness of the federal policies: "Externally imposed reforms (including many Jennings said he supported) have seldom, if ever, had the success promised."[1] So, what should we conclude from the ineffectiveness of externally imposed central plan optimization, evidence that self-reform almost never occurs, and scholarly assessments of the workings of the central planning process? From Ravitch and Jennings, from the planners in the bowels of the beast, we verify that central planning, with or without that label, whether staffed by tyrants or well-meaning people like Ravitch and Jennings, doesn't work, except, at times, to enrich those in power.

Jennings' observations, Ravitch's stunning "Adventures in Wonderland" and her conclusion in *Left Back* that "there never was a Golden Age" is enough (there's much more, such as all of her *Language Police*) to make you wonder how she could later (Ravitch 2010) assert that the current US school systems are great. Since the golden-age-less system is declining (falling output per dollar: see Hoxby 2005) from whatever its low high point was and the roots of the problem remain intact, she is likely, at best, guilty of hope triumphing over experience, including, especially, her own. I suppose we can appreciate her optimism that it will not take a transformation of officials' incentives to act differently for the system to suddenly make the changes that would actually yield the improved outcomes we all know must be forthcoming to keep our country from further economic and political stagnation. But past behavior is the best predictor of future behavior.

Eva Moskowitz's description of the persistently terrible outcomes of the New York City system is another interesting sidebar to the Ravitch re-embrace of the current K-12 systems. Dr. Ravitch lives in New York City and has studied that system extensively. In a *New York Post* article, schooling entrepreneur and city councilwoman Eva Moskowitz (2014) notes, "It's easy to harbor romantic ideas about public education," as Ravitch does, if it worked at least acceptably well for you. But "acceptably well" is not nearly a universal outcome (as the two most recent federal law names attest—NCLB and ESSA), despite high and longtime rising levels of per-pupil spending in New York, in Alabama (where the Merrifield-Ortiz recommendations received their initial airing), or anywhere. The defenders of the existing K-12 governance and funding processes don't say what factors will cause price-less political control (central planning) outcomes to differ in a way that will begin to yield dramatically improved schooling outcomes. Despite a decades-long frenzied search and numerous past and ongoing central plan optimization efforts, the behavior and outcomes are essentially unchanged, except for higher per-pupil costs, from what Ravitch and others have extensively documented.

Status-quo-plus-money defenders equate the well-being of schoolchildren with the fate of the public school system—that choice expansion would, in effect, amount to a raid on the system. So, they believe that the public school system, not schoolchildren, own school taxes. And they believe that, voluminous evidence to the contrary, fewer total dollars in that system, even with increased per-pupil funding, would diminish the public school system's effectiveness. Also consistent with that belief but contrary to the evidence from past per-pupil funding growth, the system's defenders insist that additional funding is the answer and that low socioeconomic status as a learning disability, not poor public school system performance, is the reason for persistently disappointing school system outcomes. Thomas Sowell's (2020) *Charter Schools and Their Enemies*, and Pondiscio's (2019) study of Eva Moskowitz's highly acclaimed network of New York CPS, refute the low income = learning disability assertion of school system reform opponents.

Key Impediments to School System Transformation

Blaine Amendments

Many state constitutions have Blaine Amendments that, depending upon exact wording and precedent created by court interpretations, block public subsidy of non-public schooling. Until the US Supreme Court sweeps away James Blaine's codification of nineteenth-century anti-Catholic bigotry, which is a real possibility,[2] it may take success in a non-Blaine or weak Blaine state to sufficiently motivate other states to change their constitutions.

The Usual Suspects

Teacher unions and the rest of the Stockholm syndrome line-up of employees and leaders of existing school systems, are not the only key impediments to transformational school system change. In some states, they are not even the most important impediments. But they are reliable opponents, everywhere on earth, who must be skillfully weakened and confronted.

Suburban Bliss Myth

The myth of high-performing suburban public schools is probably a bigger barrier—certainly more consistent between states—to productive school system transformation than teacher union opposition. Teacher unions are weak in many states. That suburban bliss myth undermines school system reform everywhere. There are two choices for coping with that sad fact: (1) Duck that opposition by means-testing nondiscrimination *by place*.[3] That is, initiate transformational school system reform where average income levels are low. Nondiscrimination applies to every resident of qualifying low-income communities.[4] That would create a lot of entrepreneurship-and-price-decontrol-driven, genuine experiments in school system reform; or (2) Confront the suburban bliss myth with already abundant evidence. Despite the high quality of that evidence, it will be a hard sell. Acceptance of that evidence may force widespread family recognition of neglect of their own children. Yes, it was unwitting neglect, but still, parents that believed they did right by their children would have to face that they did not. But it may be a steep mountain that must be climbed.

Rural Part-Time RINO Gridlock

Rural areas typically elect Republicans, but many are part-time Republicans in name only (RINO). Look at the national map for the past several presidential elections. The blue is not easily seen on any map even though 2004 is the only recent popular-vote Republican victory. But on the school choice issue, avoidance is the watchword for a lot of rural Republican legislators crossing the aisle—to vote with the "usual suspect" reform opponents at times. They don't want to go on record opposing school choice expansion. It's bad for political career advancement, but when push comes to shove, factors such as the significance of school district employment in rural areas and other undocumented motivators that arise in discussion of this part-time RINO phenomenon can yield rural rep no votes on school choice expansion. Until we can gain a much better understanding of the part-time RINO motivation, we may have to initiate nondiscrimination only in urban areas.

Find Slippery Slopes

Recognize and create good ones. Avoid the bad ones. A slippery slope is an informal phase-in process. An example of a good or bad slippery slope, depending upon your perspective, is the tendency of private money to gradually dominate co-payment. For the people that favor the phasing in of separation of schooling and state, an informal phase-in process by fostering co-payment is their best bet.

The key slippery slope is the spread of school system reform that produces immediate economic development effects and high-performing school systems. Make sure to point that slope in the right direction. Make sure that replication doesn't miss a key ingredient or add a poison pill.

What *Should* Be Done?

The administrators and educators won't change their behavior until the key incentives and constraints of their circumstances change. Because special interests dominate the low turnout of school district elections, local school system policymakers probably cannot change their behavior. But with thousands of districts nationwide, there have already been some exceptions. A few have taken noteworthy steps. Some districts have already attempted small steps in central plan optimization and harnessing of market forces, at least limited specialization.

It is up to state and national policymakers, especially state policymakers, to recognize, with assistance from scholars, the severe limitations of the political process for deciding which kinds of instructional approaches to deploy, how, where, and for whom, and thus supplement attempts at central plan optimization, with its low upside, with TPS alternatives created by decentralized planning through the price system. Allocated to schools through their customers, nondiscrimination-based public funding and governance will yield relentlessly improving diverse schooling options for diverse schoolchildren. The revival of the United States as a nation wisely governed by the people depends on it.

---

[1] Jennings, Jack. 2015. "Shifting School Reform from the Negative to the Positive." *Education Week*, February 25, 2015, 36, 30.

[2] https://ij.org/issues/school-choice/blaine-amendments/

[3] Plan B described in chapter 2 (p 51).

[4] For example, for the New Markets Tax Credit, a community qualifies if the family median income is below 80 percent of the state or metro area family median income, or has a poverty rate above 20 percent.

REFERENCE LIST

Aarons, Kadarai I. 2009. "Moving On." *Education Week*, April 24, 2009.

AEI Book Forum. 2013. *Balance: The Economics of Great Powers from Ancient Rome to Modern America.* American Enterprise Institute.

Ahlstrom, T. Robinson. 2016. "Education Is Absent From the 2016 Presidential Race." *Education Week*, March 8, 2016.

Ahn, Byong-man. 2012. "Education in the Republic of Korea: National treasure or national headache?" *Education Week*, January 9, 2012.

Alger, Vicki E., 2016. "Failure: The Federal Misedukation of America's Children." Independent Institute.

Allen, Jeanne, Cara Candal, and Max Eden. 2017. "Chartering a New Course: The Case for Freedom, Flexibility and Opportunity Through Charter Schools." Center for Education Reform.

Anderson, Cami. 2016. "Resolving the Charter School Debate." *Education Week*, January 26, 2016.

Arons, Stephen. 1997. *Short Route To Chaos: Conscience, Community, and the Re-constitution of American Schooling.* Amherst: University of Massachusetts Press.

Artz, Kenneth. 2018. "Merit-based Teacher Pay Leads to Higher Student Achievement, DOE Study Finds." The Heartland Institute.

Austin, Ben. 2013. "Empowered Families Can Transform the System: Forum: Pulling the Parent Trigger." *Education Next* Vol. 13 No. 3.

Bartley, W. W. III 1988. *The Fatal Conceit: The Errors of Socialism.* University of Chicago Press.

Batdorff, Meagan, Larry Maloney, Jay F. May, Sheree T. Speakman, Patrick J. Wolf, and Albert Cheng. 2014. "Charter School

Funding: Inequity Expands." University of Arkansas Department of Education Reform.

Baumol, William J., Robert E. Litan, and Carl J. Schramm. 2009. *Good Capitalism, Bad Capitalism, and the Economics of Growth and Prosperity*. Yale University Press.

Bednar, Christian M. 2009. "Education as Ritual: Uncovering Standardization's Depths." *Education Week*, April 8, 2009; p 24.

Berner, Ashley. 2017. *Pluralism and American Public Education: No One Way to School*. NY: Palgrave MacMillan.

Bernstein, Marc F. 2016. "Who's Responsible for Student Learning?" *Education Week*, August 23, 2016.

Blumenfeld, Sam. 2011. "Why Johnny STILL Can't Read." *The New American*.

Bovard, James. 2000. "Freedom in Chains: The Rise of the State and the Demise of the Citizen." St. Martin's Press.

Brenneman, Ross. 2016. "Gallup Student Poll Finds Engagement in School Dropping by Grade Level." *Education Week*, March 22, 2016.

Brickman, Michael. 2014. "Expanding the Education Universe: A Fifty-State Strategy for Course Choice." Thomas B. Fordham Institute.

Burnette, Daarel II. 2016. "Teachers' Unions Spend Big, Reap Little in Elections." *Education Week*, November 15, 2016.

Candal, Cara Stillings. 2018. "The Case for Education Transformation: Part II. Opportunity." The Center for Education Reform.

Carnevale, Anthony P. 2005. "Education and the Economy: If We're So Dumb, Why Are We So Rich?" *Education Week*, February 1, 2005.

Carnoy, Martin, Emma Garcia, and Tatiana Khavenson. 2016. "What PISA Can't Teach Us." *Education Week*, February 9, 2016.

Cason, Mike. 2016. "Alabama school superintendent Tommy Bice retiring." Advance Local Media.

Chingos, Matthew M. and Grover J. "Russ" Whitehurst. 2011. "Class Size: What Research Says and What it Means for State Policy." Washington, DC: Brookings Institute.

Chokshi, Niraj. 2015. "Map: The most Democratic and Republican states." *Washington Post*.

Christensen, Clayton M., Michael B. Horn, and Curtis W. Johnson. 2008. *Disrupting Class: How Disruptive Innovation Will Change the Way the World Learns*. New York: McGraw-Hill.

Churchill, A. 2012. "Blended learning: innovating the teaching process." Thomas B. Fordham Institute.

Churchill, Aaron. 2015. "The 2014 Education Choice and Competition Index." Thomas B. Fordham Institute.

Ciotti, Paul. 1998. "Money and School Performance: Lessons from the Kansas City Desegregation Experiment." Cato Institute No. 298.

Coleman, James S., and others. 1966. "Equality Of Education Opportunity." National Center for Educational Statistics.

Coulson, Andrew J. 2006. "The Cato Education Market Index." Washington D.C.: Cato Institute.

Coulson, Andrew J. 2006. "Why Federal School Vouchers Are a Bad Idea." Cato Institute.

Coulson, Andrew. 2009. "Comparing Public, Private, and Market Schools: The International Evidence," *Journal of School Choice* 3 (1): 31–54.

Cuban, Larry. 2004. "The Open Classroom." *Education Next* Vol. 4, No. 2.

Cuban, Larry. 2009. "Hugging the Middle: Why Good Teaching Ignores Ideology." *Education Week* 4/27/2009.

Curwin, Richard. "How to Beat 'Teacher Proof' Programs." George Lucas Educational Foundation.

Danielsen, Bartley R. and Fairbanks, Joshua and Zhao, Jing. 2014. "School Choice Programs: The Impacts on Housing Values." *Journal of Real Estate Literature*.

Danielsen, Bartley. 2017. "CPR Scholarships: Using Private School Choice to Attack Concentrated Poverty, Crime and Unemployment." American Enterprise Institute.

De La Rosa, Michelle. 2009. "Consolidation Not all Bad: Bigger School can add Electives," *San Antonio Express-News*, June 10, 2009; p 1B, 5B.

DeAngelis, Corey A. 2018. "Is Public Schooling a Public Good? An Analysis of Schooling Externalities." Cato Institute.

Demille, Oliver. 2009. *A Thomas Jefferson Education: Teaching a Generation of Leaders for the Twenty-first Century*. George Wythe College Press.

DiLorenzo, Thomas J. 2005. "The Price Control Calamity." *The Free Market* 23:12, p 1–3.

Duncan, Arne. 2012. "Remarks of U.S. Secretary of Education Arne Duncan to the Inter-American Development Bank." US Department of Education.

Dworkin, Anthony G., Lawrence J. Saha, and Antwanette N. Hill. 2003. "Teacher Burnout and Perceptions of a Democratic School Environment." *International Education Journal* 4:2, p 108–120.

Epple, Dennis, Richard E. Romano, and Miguel Urguiola. 2017. "School Vouchers: A Survey of the Economics Literature." *Journal of Economic Literature*, Vol. 44, No. 2.

Epstein, Richard A. 2014. "Civil Rights Enforcement Gone Haywire." *Education Next*, Vol. 14, No. 4.

Evans, Dennis L. 2006. "A Second Look at Compulsory Education." *Education Week*, April 11, 2016.

Evans, Robert. 2016. "K-12 Principals, Get Your Irish On." *Education Week*, March 29, 2016.

Fairchild, Daniela. 2011. "The Rise of K-12 Blended Learning." Thomas B. Fordham Institute.

Field, Brian. 2016. "Do We Give Students Too Much Choice?" *Education Week*, August 23, 2016.

Finn, Chester E. Jr. and Brandon L. Wright. 2015. "The bright children left behind." Thomas B. Fordham Institute.

Finn, Chester E. Jr., Bruno V. Manno, and Brandon L. Wright. 2016. "We Must Diversify Charter School Options." *Education Week*, August 23, 2016.

Finn, Chester E., Jr. 1991. Quoted in Barbara Kantrowitz and Pat Wingert. 1991. "A Dismal Report Card," *Newsweek*, June 17, 1991 65.

Finn, Chester E., Jr. and Diane Ravitch. 2004. "The Mad, Mad World of Textbook Adoption." Thomas B. Fordham Institute.

Finn, Chester E., Jr. and Jay P. Greene. 2012. "Should All US Students Meet a Single Set of National Proficiency Standards?" *Wall Street Journal.*

Fiske, Edward B. and Helen F. Ladd. 2000. "When Schools Compete: A Cautionary Tale." Brookings Institution Press.

Flanders, Will and Natalie Goodnow. 2018. "Collateral Damage: The Impact of Department of Education Policies on Wisconsin Schools." Wisconsin Institute for Law and Liberty.

Fraser Institute. 2017. "Economic Freedom of the World: 2017 Annual Report." Cato.

Free to Choose Media. 2017. "School Inc.: A Personal Journey with Andrew Coulson." Public Broadcasting Service.

Friedman, Milton and Rose Friedman. 1980. "Free to Choose: A Personal Statement." Harcourt.

Friedman, Milton. 1962. *Capitalism and Freedom.* Chicago: University of Chicago Press.

Fryshman, Bernard. 2008. "Curriculum Is Not Dogma: A Call for Re-Examining Secondary Education in America." *Education Week*, August 22, 2008.

Fryshman, Bernard. 2014. "Let's Be Honest: We Don't Know How to Make Great Teachers." *Education Week*, Teacher August 11, 2014.

Galbraith, John K. 1952. "A Theory of Price Control." Harvard University Press.

Gauri, Varun. 1998. "School Choice in Chile: Two Decades of Educational Reform." Pittsburgh: University of Pittsburgh Press.

Gillespie, Nick. 2005. "The Father of Modern School Reform." Reason: Free Minds and Free Markets.

Gillon, Steven M. 2000. "That's Not What We Meant to Do: Reform and Its Unintended Consequences in the Twentieth Century." Independent Institute.

Glass, Stephen. 1995. "A Pension Deficit Disorder: Teacher Unions Betray Their Members." *Policy Review* 71 (Winter): 71–74. https://eric.ed.gov/?id=EJ500645

Gordon, Nora. 2017. "Race, poverty, and interpreting overrepresentation in special education." Washington, DC: Brookings Institution.

Green, Erica L. 2017. "De Vos's Hard Line on New Education Law Surprises States." *New York Times.*

Greene, Jay P. and Josh B. McGee. 2012. "When the Best Is Mediocre." *Education Next* 12, no. 1.

Greene, Jay P., 2012. "Best Practices Are the Worst: Picking the anecdotes you want to believe." *Education Next* 12, no. 3.

Griffith, David and Amber M. Northern. 2017. "Discipline mandates are unlikely to fix tough schools' underlying issues." Thomas B. Fordham Institute.

Griffith, David, and Victoria McDougald. 2016. "Undue Process: Why Bad Teachers in Twenty-Five Diverse Districts Rarely Get Fired." Thomas B. Fordham Institute.

Hall, Joshua C. 2006. "Positive Externalities and Government Involvement in Education." *Journal of Private Enterprise* 21 (2): 165–175.

Hanushek, Eric A. 2012. "Misplaced Optimism and Weighted Funding." *Education Week*, March 26, 2012.

Hanushek, Eric A. 2010. "The Economic Value of Higher Teacher Quality." http://www.nber.org/papers/w16606.pdf

Hanushek, Eric and Alfred Lindseth. 2009. *Schoolhouses, Courthouses, and Statehouses.* Princeton, NJ: Princeton University Press.

Hanushek, Eric A. and Ludger Woessman. 2008. "The Role of Cognitive Skills in Economic Development." *Journal of Economic Literature* 46 (3): 607–668.

Hanushek, Eric A. 2008. "What Do Test Scores Really Mean for the Economy?" *Education Week*, June 4, 2008.

Hanushek, Eric. 2004. "What If There Are No 'Best Practices'?" *Scottish Journal of Political Economy* 51 (2): 156–172. https://doi.org/10.1111/j.0036-9292.2004.00300.x

Hayek, Friedrich August von. 1974. "Prize Lecture: The Pretence of Knowledge." Nobel Prize.

Hendrie, Caroline. 2005. "Researchers Ask Tough Questions of K-12 Charities." *Education Week*, April 26, 2005.

Henig, Jeffrey R., Katrina E. Bulkley, and Henry M. Levin. 2010. "Can 'Portfolio Management' Save Urban Schools?" *Education Week*, October 4, 2010.

Hersh, Richard H. 2009. "Our 21st Century Risk," *Education Week*, April 22, 2009, 28–29

Hess, Frederick M. 2010b. *Education Unbound: The Promise and Practice of Greenfield Schooling*. Alexandria, VA: Association for Christians in Student Development (ACSD).

Hess, Frederick. 2006. *Tough Love for Schools*. DC: American Enterprise Institute.

Hill, Paul T. and Ashley Jochim. 2015. "A Democratic Constitution for Public Education." *Education Next*.

Hill, Paul T. and Ashley Jochim. 2015. "Seeking Clarity in Charter School Governance." *Education Week*, March 3, 2015.

Hirsch, E. D. Jr. 2008. "An Epoch-Making Report, But What About the Early Grades?" *Education Week*, April 22, 2008.

Hirsch, Julius. 1943. *Price Control in the War Economy*. (New York: Harper).

Hole, Jackson. 2008. "Confronting Challenges, Creating Opportunities." Alliance for School Choice.

Holley, Marc and Marc Sternberg. 2015. "Three School Reform Lessons." Skoll Foundation.

Howard, Philip K. 2005. "Class War." *Wall Street Journal*, May 24, 2005, page A12.

Hoxby, Caroline M. and Andrew Leigh. 2004. "Pulled Away or Pushed Out: Explaining the Decline of Teacher Aptitude in the United States." *AEA Papers and Proceedings* 94 (2): 236–240.

Hoxby, Caroline. 2004. "Productivity in Education: The Quintessential Upstream Industry." *Southern Economic Journal* 7 (2): 209–231. http://www.texaspolicy.com/pdf/2001-veritas-2-3-school.pdf

Hubbard, Glenn and Tim Kane. 2013. *Balance: The Economics of Great Powers from Ancient Rome to Modern America*. Simon and Schuster.

Izumi, Lance T. Vicki E. Murray, and Rachel S. Chaney, with Ruben Peterson and Rosemarie Fusano. 2007. "Not as Good as You Think: Why the Middle Class Needs School Choice." Pacific Research Institute. http://www.pacificresearch.org/docLib/20070924_Middleclass.pdf

Jabbar, Huriya. 2015. "How Do School Leaders Respond to Competition? Evidence From New Orleans." Education Research Alliance for New Orleans.

Jacobs, Jonathan. 2013. "As Education Declines, So Does Civic Culture." *Wall Street Journal.*

Jefferson, Thomas. "Nothing is more unequal… (Spurious Quotation)." The Jefferson Monticello.

Jennings, Jack. 2015. "Presidents, Congress, and the Public Schools: The Politics of Education Reform." Harvard Education Press.

Jennings, Jack. 2015. "Shifting School Reform from the Negative to the Positive." *Education Week*, February 25, 2015, 36, 30.

Johnson, Jean. 2008. "'Copers' and 'Transformers': Which kind of principal do we want for our struggling schools?" *Education Week*, August 11, 2008.

Johnson, Lyndon B. 1965. "Elementary and Secondary Education Act of 1965." United States Congress.

Kern, Nora and Wentana Gebru. 2014. "Waiting Lists to Attend Charter Schools Top 1 Million Names." National Alliance for Public Charter Schools.

Kihn, Paul. "A Vision for the K-12 Urban School District." *Education Week*, April 12, 2016.

Kimball, Roger. 2018. "When Reagan Met Lenin." The Wall Street Journal.

Kimmelman, Paul. 2013. "Three Ed. Leadership Lessons From Donald Rumsfeld." *Education Week*, February 19, 2013.

Kirby, Brendan. 2014. "Supporters, critics weigh in on Troy University studies on school choice, privatization." Advance Local Media.

Kirkpatrick, David W. 2006. "School Criticism: Older than the System." *School Report*, March 9, 2006, 695.

Kirkpatrick, David W. "Violence in Our Schools." *School Report*, 9/20/2007.

Klein, Alyson. 2018. "State Restrictions on School Choice Earn Betsy DeVos' Ire." *Education Week*, May 29, 2015.

Kline, Malcolm A. 2018. "Graduation Rates Are Deceptive." Accuracy in Academia.

Knowledge is Power Program Foundation. KIPP Foundation.

Koch, Charles. 2007. *The Science of Success*. Hoboken, NJ: John Wiley and Sons.

Kolderie, Ted. 2014. *The Split-Screen Strategy: Innovation and Improvement*. Edina, MN: Beaver's Pond Press.

Kronholz, June. 2014. "California's Districts of Choice." *Education Next* 14, no. 3.

Levinson, Eliot. 1976. "The Alum Rock Voucher Demonstration: Three Years of Implementation." Santa Monica, CA: RAND Corporation. https://www.rand.org/pubs/papers/P5631.html.

Lhamon, Catherine E. 2014. "Dear Colleague Letter from The Assistant Secretary." U.S. Department of Education.

Lhamon, Catherine E. and Jocelyn Samuels. 2014. "Joint 'Dear Colleague' Letter." U.S. Department of Education.

Lieberman, Myron. 1993. *Public Education: An Autopsy*. Cambridge, MA: Harvard University Press.

Lieberman, Myron. 1997. *The Teacher Unions*. New York: The Free Press.

Lieberman, Myron. 1993. "Public Education: An Autopsy." Cambridge, MA: Harvard University Press.

Lieberman, Myron. 1994. "The school choice fiasco." National Affairs.

Loveless, Tom. 1998. "The Tracking and Ability Grouping Debate." Thomas B. Fordham Institute.

Lybbert, Blair E. 2016. "Why 10th Grade Should Be the New Senior Year." Education Week, May 17, 2016.

Maxwell, Lesli A. 2013. "Poll Finds School Chiefs Lukewarm on School Boards." *Education Week*, October 1, 2013.

McAllister, Peter. 2018. "A Teacher's Perspective on What's Wrong with Our Schools." Cato Institute.

McCluskey, Neal P. 2007a. *Feds in the Classroom: How Big Government Corrupts, Cripples, and Compromises American Education*. Lanham, MD: Rowman and Littlefield.

McCluskey, Neal P. 2007b. "Why We Fight: How Public Schools Cause Social Conflict." Cato Institute Policy Analysis #587. http://www.cato.org/pubs/pas/pa587.pdf

McCluskey, Neal. 2016. "Ding, Dong, No Child Left Behind Is Dead…Or Is It?" Cato Institute.

McCluskey, Neal. 2016. "ESSA Seems Ripe for Federal Control." Cato Institute.

McDougald, Victoria. 2016. "How teacher specialization affects student achievement." Thomas B. Fordham Institute.

McFarland, J., B. Hussar, X. Wang, J. Zhang, K. Wang, A. Rathbun, A. Barmer, E. Forrest Cataldi, and F. Bullock Mann. 2018. "The Condition of Education: Characteristics of Children's Families." National Center for Education Statistics.

McFarland, J., B. Hussar, X. Wang, J. Zhang, K. Wang, A. Rathbun, A. Barmer, E. Forrest Cataldi, and F. Bullock Mann. 2018. "The Condition of Education: Elementary and Secondary Enrollment." National Center for Education Statistics.

Merrifield, John and Jesse A. Ortiz Jr. 2015. "Reinventing the Alabama K-12 System to Engage More Children in Productive Learning." Troy University.

Merrifield, John and Michael Ford. 2013. "School Choice Fiscal Notes Calculator."

Merrifield, John and Nathan Gray. 2009. "An Evaluation of the CEO Horizon, 1998-2008, Edgewood Tuition Voucher Program." UTSA College of Business.

Merrifield, John D. 2002. "School Choices: True and False." The Independent Institute.

Merrifield, John. 2001. *The School Choice Wars*. Lanham, MD: Rowman and Littlefield.

Merrifield, John. 2009c. "The Potential for System-Friendly K-12 Reform," *Cato Journal* 29 (2): 319–335. http://www.cato.org/pubs/journal/cj29n2/cj29n2-6.pdf

Merrifield, John. 2012. "Instructional Comparative Advantages Exist Despite the 'Comprehensive Uniformity' of Traditional Public Schools," *Journal of School Choice* 6 (1): 128–140.

Merrifield, John. 2009. "The Potential for System-Friendly K-12 Reform." *Cato Journal.* 20, no. 2, 326.

Merrifield, John. 2013. "Customization Through Free Enterprise." SchoolSystemReformStudies.net

Merrifield, John. 2013. "Strategies to Pursue Improved Teaching." SchoolSystemReformStudies.net

Merrifield, John. 2014. "Charter Law-Driven School System Reform: Politically Correct in Both Parties." SchoolSystemReformStudies.net

Merrifield, John. 2014. "Classroom-Level Root Causes of Our School System's Ineffectiveness." http://nebula.wsimg.com/de7a505e69a5da1955afc3fa273fe806?AccessKeyId=DA21F-C8554A675E9CF7B&disposition=0&alloworigin=1

Merrifield, John. 2014. "The 1979 UK Experience: School Choice Plan Abandoned for Lack of Evidence." SchoolSystemReformStudies.net

Merrifield, John. 2015. "Ability Grouping By Subject, Re-Visited." SchoolSystemReformStudies.net

Merrifield, John. 2015. "Differentiation Delusion: More Exposure Needed." SchoolSystemReformStudies.net

Merrifield, John. 2015. "Washington State's Big Spenders are Slow Learners." SchoolSystemReformStudies.net

Merrifield, John. 2016. "Nation at Risk Declarations." School System Reform Studies.

Merrifield, John. 2016. "The Right and Wrong Ways to Improve School System Performance." SchoolSystemReformStudies.net

Merrow, John. 2017. "Addicted to Reform: A Twelve-Step Program to Rescue Public Education." The New Press, p. xiv.

Mincberg, Cathy. 2016. "School Boards Must Narrow Their Focus." *Education Week*, June 7, 2016.

Mises, Ludwig von. 1951. "Socialism: An Economic and Sociological Analysis." New Haven: Yale University Press.

Mitgang, Herbert. 1992. "Republicans in Houston: For the Record, Reagan Put Words in Lincoln's Mouth." *New York Times*.

Moe, Terry M. 2009. "Yes, He Can—but Will He?" *Hoover Digest* No. 2.

Moskowitz, Eva. 2014. "Stop stealing New York kids' future." *New York Post*.

Murphy, Michael M. 1980. "Price Controls and the Behavior of the Firm." *International Economic Review* 21 (2): 285–291

National Academy of Sciences, National Academy of Engineering, and Institute of Medicine. 2007. *Is America Falling Off the Flat*

Earth?. Washington, DC: National Academies Press. https://doi.org/10.17226/12021.

Nguyen, Anthony. 2018. "The debate on school discipline reform." Thomas B. Fordham Institute.

Obama, Barack. 2014. "Transcript: Full interview between President Obama and Bill O'Reilly." Fox News Politics.

Osborne, David. 2017. *Reinventing America's Schools: Creating a 21st Century Education System*. New York: Bloomsbury.

Ouchi, William with Lydia Segal. 2003. *Making Schools Work*. New York: Simon and Schuster.

Ouchi, William G. 2009. "Accept No Substitutes for Real Decentralization." *Education Week*, October 30, 2009.

Paige, Rod. 2015. "Why has education policy produced such little improvement?." Thomas B. Fordham Institute.

Peterson, Paul E. 2010. *Saving Schools*. Cambridge, MA: Harvard University Press; 18; 89; 93; 160; 178.

Petrilli, Michael J. 2011. "All Together Now?: Educating high and low achievers in the same classroom." *Education Next* 11 (1).

Petrilli, Michael J. 2014. "Arne Duncan's Office of Civil Rights: Six years of meddling." Thomas B. Fordham Institute.

Petrilli, Michael J. 2017. "One reason why affluent, liberal parents often choose segregated schools, even when that may not be their intention." Thomas B. Fordham Institute.

Petrilli, Michael J. 2018. "7 Suggestions for Better School Discipline: If the Trump administration rescinds Obama-era discipline guidance, what's next?" *Education Week* May 29, 2018.

Phillips, Matt. 2013. "Korea is the world's top producer of unhappy school children." Quartz.

Plank, David N. and Gary Sykes, eds. 2003. *Choosing Choice: School Choice in International Perspective*. New York: Teachers College Press.

Pondiscio, Robert. 2015. "New Orleans: A success story? Yes. A national model? Maybe not." Thomas B. Fordham Institute.

Pondiscio, Robert. 2019. *How The Other Half Learns: Equality, Excellence, and the Battle Over School Choice*. NY: Avery.

Porter-Magee, Kathleen, James Leming, and Lucien Ellington. "Where Did Social Studies Go Wrong." Thomas B. Fordham Institute.

Porter-Magee, Kathleen. 2014. "A Tale of Two Movements Why Standards and Choice need each other." Thomas B. Fordham Institute.

Powell, A.G.; E. Farrar, and D. Cohen. 1985. *The Shopping Mall High School.* Boston: Houghton-Mifflin.

Program for International Student Assessment. 2012. PISA 2012 Results. National Center for Education Statistics.

Program for International Student Assessment. 2015. PISA 2015 Results. National Center for Education Statistics.

Public Agenda. 2004. "Teaching Interrupted: Do Discipline Policies in Today's Public Schools Foster the Common Good?" Public Agenda Foundation.

Rand, Ayn. 1957. *Atlas Shrugged.* Random House.

Ravitch, Diane. 2010. *The Death and Life of the Great American School System.* New York: Basic Books.

Rebell, Michael A., Jessica R. Wolff. 2012. "We Can Overcome Poverty's Impact on School Success." *Education Week,* January 17, 2012.

Reisman, George. 1998. *Capitalism.* Ottawa, IL: Jameson Books; 221, 239.

Reville, Paul. 2016. "An Urgent Call to Action for Education Leaders: Fixing the 'disillusionment' in education reform." *Education Week,* October 11, 2016.

Rickover, Hyman G. 1959. *Education and Freedom.* New York: E. P. Dutton.

Flesch, Rudolf. 1955. *Why Johnny Can't Read.* NY. Harper-Collins.

Riley, Jason L. 2018. "No Racial Quotas in Special Education: Betsy DeVos is preparing to undo another pernicious Obama school policy." *Wall Street Journal.*

Riley, Jason. 2014. "Obama's Education Fibs." *Wall Street Journal.*

Robbins, Jane. 2015. "Alexander, Murray Bill Tightens the Screws of Mandated Assessments." Townhall.

Robinson, Eugene. 2012. "Teachers not Responsible for Education Crisis," *San Antonio Express-News,* September 19, 2012, A13.

Robinson, Gerard, David Cleary, Lindsey Burke, Neal McCluskey, and Michael Hansen. 2016. "From 'No Child' to 'Every Student': How Big a Change." Cato Institute.

Robinson, Martin. 2018. "The narrowing curriculum." Thomas B. Fordham Institute.

Rogers, Will. BrainyQuote.

Rose, Todd. 2016. *The End of Average.* NY: Harper-Collins.

Roselli, Anthony. 2005. *Dos and Don'ts of Education Reform.* New York: Peter Lang.

Ross, Ernest G. 1983. "The Price of Education." *The Freeman* 33 (2).

Roza, Marguerite and Katherine Hagan. 2017. "ESSA's Financial Transparency Reporting Requirement." Building State Capacity and Productivity Center.

Sarason, Seymour. *The Predictable Failure of Educational Reform.* San Francisco: Jossey-Bass Publishers, 1990; p 25–26.

Sargrad, Scott. 2017. "What Matters for Charter Performance: Policymakers should heed 3 key findings in a recent charter school study." *U.S. News & World Report.*

Schmoker, Mike. 2014. "Why Make Reform So Complicated?." *Education Week*, January 14, 2014.

Shuettinger, Robert L. and Eamonn F. Butler. 1979. *Forty Centuries of Wage and Price Controls: How Not to Fight Inflation.* Thornwood, NY: Caroline House Publishers, Inc.

Silberman, Charles. 1971. "Crisis in the Classroom: The Remaking of American Education." New York: Random House.

Simon, Stephanie. 2009. "Texas School Board Set to Vote on Challenge to Evolution." *Wall Street Journal.*

Smarick, Andy. 2010. *The turnaround fallacy: Stop trying to fix failing schools. Close them and start fresh. Education Next.*

Snell, Lisa. 2008. "Not hot for teachers: Why an 'instructionalist' approach to school reform won't help poor kids." Reason Foundation.

Sowell, Thomas. 2004. *Basic Economics: A Citizen's Guide to the Economy.* New York: Basic Books.

Sowell, Thomas. 2007. *Economic Facts and Fallacies*, 2nd Edition. New York: Basic Books.

Sowell, Thomas. 2018. *Discrimination and Disparities*. New York: Basic Books.

Sowell, Thomas. 2020. *Charter Schools and Their Enemies*. NY: Basic Books.

Standard & Poor's. 2005. Standard & Poor's Separates Fact from Fiction in Analysis of Urban School Districts. SchoolsMatter.com; May 26, 2005.

Steinberg, Matthew P., and Johanna Lacoe. 2017. "What Do We Know About School Discipline Reform?" *Education Next* 17 (1).

Stern, Sol. 2008. "School Choice Isn't Enough: Instructional reform is the key to better schools." New York: City Journal.

Sternberg, Marc and Marc Holley. 2016. "Walton Family Foundation: We Must Rethink Online Learning." *Education Week*, January 26, 2016.

Stitzlein, Sarah M. 2018. "Does School Choice Put Freedom Before Equity?" *Education Week*, May 8, 2018.

Stuit, David A. and Sy Doan. 2013. "School Choice Regulations: Red Tape or Red Herring?" Thomas B. Fordham Institute.

Superville, Denisa R. 2018. "How Long Do Big-City Superintendents Actually Last?" *Education Week*, May 15, 2018.

Susanne E. Cannon, Bartley R. Danielsen, and David M. Harrison. 2015. "School Vouchers and Home Prices: Premiums in School Districts Lacking Public Schools." *Journal of Housing Research* 24, no. 1: 1–20.

Szafir, CJ, and Martin Lueken. 2015. "More Spending Doesn't Lead To Improved Student Learning." *Forbes*.

The Center for Education Reform. 2012. "What is the BLOB?" The Center for Education Reform.

The Center for Education Reform. 2017. "Beyond the First 100 Days: Transforming government's role in education." The Center for Education Reform.

The National Commission on Excellence in Education. 1983. "A Nation At Risk: The Imperative for Educational Reform."

Toch, Thomas. 2018. "35 years after a groundbreaking Reagan-era report, how far have we come?" *Education Week*, April 20, 2018.

Tooley, James. 2003. *Government Failure: E. G. West on Education*. London: Institute of Economic Affairs.

Truman, Harry S. BrainyQuote.

Tully, Sarah. 2016. "First Parent-Trigger School Leaves District Oversight." *Education Week*, March 15, 2016.

Tyack, David. 1974. *The One Best System: A History of American Urban Education*. Cambridge, MA: Harvard University Press.

Vanderkam, Laura and Richard Whitmire. 2009. "What Ever Happened to Grade Skipping?: Accelerating the Gifted in a Time of Tight Budgets." *Education Week*, August 11, 2009.

VERITAS—A Quarterly Journal of Public Policy in Texas

Vigdor, Jacob. 2008. "Scrap the Sacrosanct Salary Schedule." *Education Next* 8 (4).

Walberg, Herbert J. 2012. "School Reform, the Texas Way." Stanford University: Hoover Institution.

West, E. G. 1994. *Education and the State: A Study in Political Economy*. Liberty Fund.

Wikipedia. "Bismark, Otto von."

Wikipedia. "Goals 2000."

Wikipedia. "Individuals with Disabilities Education Act."

Wikipedia. "Kidnapping."

Wikipedia. "Pete du Pont."

Wikipedia. "Sausage Factory."

Wikipedia. "Stockholm syndrome."

Will, George. 2010. "Doubling Down on Education," *San Antonio Express-News* March 18, 2010, 7B.

Wilson, Woodrow. BrainyQuote.

Winters, Marcus A., Jay P. Greene, and Greg Forster. 2003. "Apples to Apples: An Evaluation of Charter Schools Serving General Student Populations." Manhattan Institute.

Woessmann, Ludger. 2016. "The Importance of School Systems: Evidence from International Differences in Student Achievement." *Journal of Economic Perspectives* 30 (3): 3–32.

Wolk, Ronald A. 2004. "Perspective: Still Tinkering." *Education Week*, November 11, 2004.

Wolk, Ronald A. 2012. "Common Core vs. Common Sense." *Education Week*, December 3, 2012.

Wolk, Ronald A. 2016. "To Change Education, Change the Message." *Education Week*, January 5, 2016.

Woodworth, James L., Margaret E. Raymond, Chunping Han, Yohannes Negassi, W. Payton Richardson, and Will Snow. 2017. "Charter Management Organizations." Stanford University: Center for Research on Education Outcomes.

Wright, Brandon L. 2018. "America's graduation rate malfeasance is a symptom of a broken system." Thomas B. Fordham Institute.

Zeehandelaar, Dara, David Griffith, Joanna Smith, Michael Their, Ross Anderson, Christine Pitts, and Hovanes Gasparian. 2015. "Schools of Thought: A Taxonomy of American Education Governance." Thomas B. Fordham Institute.

INDEX

About the Author

Dr. John Merrifield is a cheerful purveyor of the dismal science. An immigrant from Germany that arrived in the USA on the SS *United States* in 1960, he was born a Hamburger and raised a Frankfurter (tall—John 6:6). He has been a @Bigpicturedoc economics professor for thirty-five years, serious academics with a sense of humor.

9 781645 599616